Martin Versfeld

A SOUTH AFRICAN PHILOSOPHER IN DARK TIMES

Martin Versfeld

A SOUTH AFRICAN PHILOSOPHER IN DARK TIMES

Ernst Wolff

with contributions by
Ruth Versfeld
Paul van Tongeren
Kobus Krüger
Marlene van Niekerk
Antjie Krog

Leuven University Press

Published with the support of the
KU Leuven Fund for Fair Open Access

Published in 2021 by Leuven University Press / Presses Universitaires de Louvain / Universitaire Pers Leuven. Minderbroedersstraat 4, B3000- Leuven (Belgium).
Selection © Ernst Wolff, 2021.
Individual chapters © the respective authors, 2021.
Poems by Antjie Krog, © 2014 by AE Samuel, all rights reserved. Permission for re-use should be sought from the rights-holder.
Poem by Marlene van Niekerk, © 2021 by Marlene van Niekerk, all rights reserved. Permission for re-use should be sought from the rights-holder.

This book is published under a Creative Commons Attribution Non-Commercial Non-Derivative 4.0 International Licence.

The license allows you to share, copy, distribute, and transmit the work for personal and non-commercial use providing author and publisher attribution is clearly stated. Attribution should include the following information:
Ernst Wolff. *Martin Versfeld: A South African philosopher in dark times*. Leuven, Leuven University Press. (CC BY-NC-ND 4.0)
Further details about Creative Commons licenses are available at http://creativecommons.org/licenses/

ISBN 978 94 6270 297 4 (Paperback)
ISBN 978 94 6166 414 3 (ePDF)
ISBN 978 94 6166 415 0 (ePUB)
https://doi.org/10.11116/9789461664143
D/2021/1869/35
NUR: 730

Layout: Friedemann Vervoort
Cover design: Daniel Benneworth-Gray
Cover illustration: Martin Versfeld, photo by Tom Burgers
(Private collection Family Versfeld).
p. 2: Martin Versfeld, photo by Cloete Breytenbach
(Private collection Family Versfeld).

Vir Wilhelm, Heinrich, Bernard en Friedel Wolff

CONTENTS

PREFACE – Between joy and disquiet: Philosophising in dark times — 11

Major publications by Marthinus Versfeld — 17

INTRODUCTIONS — 19

1. "Fertilizer to the last" – Biographical snips
   (by Ruth Versfeld) — 21
2. What was Versfeld doing when he was doing philosophy? — 37
   1. On the warts — 37
   2. From autobiography to enigma — 41
   3. Genre – Or, how to do things with words — 46
   4. Theology: A portrait of the philosopher as an odd fish — 48
   5. Polyphony of philosophy: Introductions, liberal translations, historical work — 52
   6. Apartheid and other empiresque behaviour — 55
   7. A note on celebration — 58
   8. On its most intimate lesson — 58
   9. Conclusion — 60

STUDIES 61

3. Self-knowledge and practical reason in a time of political madness 63
1. Introduction: Self-knowledge in a period of political madness 64
2. "Gods" and "idols" 66
3. War, exploitation, racism. Critique of social and political violence 68
4. Urgency, time and incarnation 71
5. Unity and decay 74
6. The concept of unity – Or, a philosophy of incarnation 77
7. Reception and continuation 84

4. Versfeld and Nietzsche: Strange bedfellows
(by Paul van Tongeren) 93
1. Introduction 93
2. Sounding out idols 94
3. Man, morality and metaphysics 96
4. Nihilism 101
5. Conclusion 104

5. Grasping the truth from where we are 105
1. Introduction: Flux, stability and where we are 105
2. Anthropology as first philosophy 108
3. Traditions and cultural criticism 111
4. Using a thorn to take out a thorn, and throwing both away 113
5. Questioning from where we are 120

6. Versfeld's dialogue with Eastern thought
(By J. S. Krüger) 125
1. Introduction 125
2. Groundbreaking early works 127
3. Midcareer 130
4. Mature thought 138
5. Conclusion 146

7.	*Poiesis* – On the voice of poets, philosophers and other potters	149
	1. On writing	150
	2. Connectedness	152
	3. Creativity, love, generosity	156
	4. *Poiesis*	158
	5. Silence	161
8.	Reverberations (poems by Marlene van Niekerk and Antjie Krog)	166

CONCLUSIONS   173

9.	Sanctus Marthinus laudator philosophicus – Or, sitting at the guru's feet	175
10.	What is living and what is dead of the philosophy of Martin Versfeld? – Or, the philosopher read by a vultur	191
	1. Augustine: Ventriloquism or interpretation as independent thought?	192
	2. Plurality	195
	3. Something or nothing?	196
	4. Close to the earth?	197
	5. Land in *Klip en klei* – You said, "the obvious"?	205
	6. Ecology: The logos on our common home	209
	7. On subtle critique	212
	8. Ambiguities of anthropology	215
	9. The end	217

Bibliography   219

PREFACE

BETWEEN JOY AND DISQUIET: PHILOSOPHISING IN DARK TIMES

Martin Versfeld (11 August 1909–18 April 1995) is generally recognised as one of South Africa's greatest philosophers. Professor of Philosophy at the University of Cape Town from 1937 to 1972, he was an inspiring lecturer and a stimulating author. Among his students, who became well-known themselves, are Athol Fugard, Richard Turner, Breyten Breytenbach, Adam Small, Jane Carruthers, Jeremy Cronin and Augustine Shutte. His influence stretched beyond the sphere of students and professional philosophers to activists, authors of literature and a broader public readership. A critic of apartheid from the first hour, he was also the first to introduce the study of oriental wisdom to South African academia, and among the first philosophers of ecology. One simply cannot bypass this figure of South African intellectual life. His writing career (1935–1990) coincided with one of the darkest times[1] of twentieth-century world history, and because he came through this era with his moral and intellectual integrity intact, the contemporary reader would want to explore the stakes that he had to deal with as a philosopher. How did he, as a professor of philosophical ethics and political philosophy, cope with the demands of this situation? Which strategies of reflection were available to him? How did he understand the strategic options of reflection open to him? How did he identify the difficulties of his task and how did he negotiate his way through them?

---

[1] I allude to the title of Hannah Arendt, *Men in dark times* (San Diego, CA: Harcourt Brace Jovanovich, 1968).

Two major concerns justify studying Versfeld today. In recent years, events at universities have again demonstrated that in South Africa, as much as elsewhere,[2] our history is a domain of stakes and struggles, not a reliquary of ideas. Intellectual life is undergoing rapid change, as is indeed the society on which people try to reflect. We need to work constantly through our history and submit our diverse heritage to critical assessment. By doing so, we orientate ourselves in the present, albeit by destabilising our views. Hence the importance of intellectual history. Correspondingly, the first justification for this book is to do justice to this important figure and his thought by submitting his work to careful, scholarly analysis. This study is part of a broader research interest in South African intellectual life,[3] and I hope that it will make a modest contribution to alleviating the relative paucity of studies on intellectual history in South Africa. In metamorphosed ways, the questions that preoccupied Versfeld are still with us.

That is already the second motive for writing this book. It is about Versfeld's philosophical concerns – many of which are still ours today. What is a human person? How is one to understand the relation between generality and particularity? How does one deal with the failures of one's own cultural traditions? Is it possible to make oneself at home in the modern world without destruction of human lives and the environment? The chapters are designed not only to present Versfeld's views (on modernity, literature, social diversity, injustice, the relation between intellectual traditions, etc.) but to engage critically with his ideas from today's sociopolitical and scholarly perspective. Only through proper critique can Versfeld remain our contemporary.

---

[2] Cf. Mahmood Mamdani, "Between the public intellectual and the scholar: Decolonization and some post-independence initiatives in African higher education," *Inter-Asia Cultural Studies* 17, no. 1 (2016): 68–83; Ernst Wolff, "Decolonizing Philosophy. On the protests in South African universities," *Books and Ideas*, published 15 May 2017 (original French version published 28 October 2016), http://www.booksandideas.net/Decolonizing-Philosophy.html.; Harriet Swain, "Students want their curriculums decolonised. Are universities listening?", *The Guardian*, 30 January 2019, https://www.theguardian.com/education/2019/jan/30/students-want-their-curriculums-decolonised-are-universities-listening [last access: 6 February 2020].

[3] Cf. Ernst Wolff, *Mongameli Mabona. His life and work*. Leuven: Leuven University Press, 2020; E. Wolff, "Adam Small's shade of Black Consciousness," in *Philosophy on the border. Decoloniality and the shudder of the origin*, ed. Leonhard Praeg (Pietermaritzburg: University of Kwa-Zulu Natal Press, 2019), 112–147; E. Wolff, "Four questions on curriculum development in contemporary South Africa," *South African Journal of Philosophy* 35, no. 4 (2016): 444–459; E. Wolff, "Anatomie van 'n teologiese ideologie. Die Hervormde Kerk se steun aan die Apartheid ideologie" [Anatomy of a theological ideology. The Reformed Church's support of the apartheid ideology], *Historia* 51, no. 1 (May 2006): 141–162.

A number of traits of Versfeld's thought make it particularly apt to stimulate reflection on these contemporary questions. He was a severe critic of modernity, without being a conservative traditionalist. A scholar of ancient Greek philosophy, mediaeval philosophy and modern European philosophy, he had a strong command of the Western philosophical heritage and could engage creatively and critically with it. Yet, he gradually became aware of the narrowness of this form of open-mindedness and consciously strove to adopt elements from Indian and Chinese philosophy. The fruit of this endeavour is a philosophical anthropology that is enriched by a kaleidoscope of influences. The suggestive force of this work is of acute relevance to contemporary debates in the academic politics of intellectual traditions. Furthermore, Versfeld's thought remains poised between the critique of political atrocities and celebration of the natural environment for which we have to care. Finally, his persistent experimentation with discursive forms stimulates reflection on how ideas are or should be conveyed, about the grounds of validity for any truth claim.

Versfeld's name is synonymous with a philosophical celebration of life, coupled with a critique of political injustice, exploitation of nature, and consumerism. This tension between joy and disquiet is arguably the most salient trait of his work. This difficult marriage is also a primary reason why his work is – despite its masterful prose – more difficult to interpret than a superficial reading would lead one to believe. This book aims to advance the interpretation of Versfeld's work. It is not intended as a substitute for it, but to invite those who have not yet read Versfeld to take up his books, and for those who have, to reread and restudy them attentively.

For this purpose, I have brought together a number of studies that clarify different aspects of Versfeld's work. Some chapters are devoted to themes in his work, and others to specific books of his, or to his work as a whole. Without claiming that the book covers it all, the chapters are certainly representative of the largest part of Versfeld's work. This is the first monograph on Martin Versfeld.[4] There is a host of important things that one may want to do in such a

---

[4] Helpful texts for situating Versfeld intellectually are Jonathan Allen, "A Competing Discourse on Empire," in *South Africa, Greece and Rome: Classical Confrontations*, ed. Grant Parker (Cambridge: Cambridge University Press, 2017), 235–261; Andrew Nash, "Marxism and dialectic, from Sharpeville to the negotiated settlement," in *The dialectical tradition in South Africa* (London and New York: Routledge, 2009), 159–184, here 159–164; Hennie Rossouw, "Die kuns van die lewe is om tuis te kom. Gedagtes oor die filosofie van Martin Versfeld," *Tydskrif vir Geesteswetenskappe* 36, no. 1 (1996): 11–20; W.A. de Klerk, "Marthinus Versfeld: mens en denker," *Tydskrif vir Geesteswetenskappe* 23, no. 3 (1983): 178–186; W.A. de Klerk, "Marthinus Versfeld: die man en sy denke," *Tydskrif vir Letterkunde* 4 (1966): 62–72.

volume. Besides, the material is extremely rich. Still, Rome was not built in a day. For this book, I have decided to focus mostly on Versfeld's work – a substantial part of the book consists of an immanent reading. Certainly, this includes some historical and intellectual contextualisation, but this is not the main thrust of these chapters.

The major part of the book was written by myself and consists either of essays published elsewhere[5] (translated and improved where needed) or written for this volume. In addition, three co-authors have filled in important gaps in my competence. To Ruth Versfeld, Paul van Tongeren and Kobus Krüger, my sincerest gratitude. Antjie Krog and Marlene van Niekerk gave their support to this project in poetic form. Why this is so fitting for this book I discuss later, but I would already like to thank these writers here.

The chapters have been arranged in three parts: introductions, studies and conclusions.

Together, the first two chapters serve as a presentation of Martin Versfeld. They help to orientate the reader to Versfeld's life (Chapter 1 is written by one of his daughters, Ruth Versfeld) and to his writing (Chapter 2).

The second part traces the development of Versfeld's thought, by zooming in on a number of his books, selected from the early, middle and late periods: *Oor gode en afgode* (Chapter 3), *Our Selves* (Chapter 5) and *Pots and Poetry* (Chapter 7). The other contributions to this part of the book each develop a specific issue that came up in these three studies. Thus, the exploration of Versfeld's earliest work reveals an unexpectedly positive appraisal of Nietzsche – his relation to Nietzsche is examined by Paul van Tongeren in Chapter 4. The presence of insights from Eastern thought, clearly foregrounded in *Our Selves*, raises the

---

[5] Where I reproduce older texts I have not thought it necessary to erase my traces. I decided to maintain the original form of the texts, rather than to iron out the history of their composition, which would have required completely rewriting them. However, I have made small improvements where needed and I have added cross-references where applicable. With thanks to the relevant publishers, I used the following texts: "*Poiesis*. Oor maaksels en hul wêreld na aanleiding van Versfeld se *Pots and Poetry*," *Tydskrif vir Letterkunde* 48, no. 1 (2011): 206–215 [Chapter 7]; "Grasping the truth from where we are," introduction to the re-edition of Martin Versfeld, *Our Selves* (Pretoria: Protea, 2010), 7–39 [Chapter 5]; "Selfkennis, verstandigheid en inkarnasie. 'n Interpretasie van Versfeld se *Oor gode en afgode*," *LitNet* 7, no. 2 (2010): 257–279 / "Selfkennis en verstandigheid in 'n tyd van politieke raserny," introduction to the re-edition of Martin Versfeld, *Oor gode en afgode* (Pretoria: Protea, 2010), 7–40 [Chapter 3]; "Die neukery met verval en herstel in Versfeld se storie van die appelboom," *Koers* 74, no. 3 (2009): 539–542 [inserted into Chapter 7] and "Sanctus Marthinus laudator philosophicus," *Fragmente* 4 (1999): 87–101 [Chapter 9].

question of the profile of Versfeld's reception and use of Eastern wisdom in general. Kobus Krüger deals with this question in Chapter 6. The poems of Marlene van Niekerk and Antjie Krog[6] – Chapter 8 – complete the meditation on *poiesis* in the preceding chapter.

In conclusion, I offer two readings of Versfeld's work as a whole, two views written twenty years apart. While not uncritical, the first reading is more appreciative, written as it were at the guru's feet. Still appreciative, the second is more critical, written in the spirit of the "philosopher as vulture" (an image that Versfeld advanced).

There are some minor overlaps between chapters. I have decided to retain these to maintain each chapter's autonomy. The reader may indeed read any chapter on its own.

I thank Rika Opper for draft translations of Chapters 3, 7 and 9, and Christiaan Naudé for copy-editing the manuscript. To Mirjam Truwant, Annemie Vandezande, Beatrice van Eeghem and their colleagues at Leuven University Press, again my deep-felt recognition.

Christof Heyns – specialist of human rights law, United Nations Special Rapporteur, member of the United Nations Human Rights Committee and a very amiable colleague – was acquainted with Versfeld in his youth. I discussed this book project with him some years ago already and, when the manuscript was accepted for publication in March 2021, asked him to write an endorsement for the cover. He readily accepted, but unexpectedly passed away a few days later on 28 March. I would like to pay tribute to him here.

I have characterised Versfeld's work as situated in the tension between joy and disquiet. This book will be a success if it could facilitate its readers' participation in this joyous celebration of life and ignite in them the disquieting concern for the atrocities of our own time.

Ernst Wolff
Leuven, June 2020

---

[6] The four poems of Antjie Krog, "Sunday lunch", "the founding principle of generosity", "to feed someone" and "convivium", come from her volume *Synapse*, translation by Karen Press (Cape Town: Human & Rousseau, 2014), 26, 43, 44, 80–82. I thank the publisher for permission to use them here.

MAJOR PUBLICATIONS BY MARTHINUS VERSFELD

          Martin Versfeld, *An Essay on the Metaphysics of Descartes* (London: Methuen & Co, 1940).

          Martin Versfeld, *An Essay on the Metaphysics of Descartes* (2nd edition) (London: Routledge, 2016).

          Martin Versfeld and W.A. de Klerk, *Die berge van die Boland* [The mountains of the Western Cape] (Stellenbosch: Kosmo, [1947] 1965).

GA   Martin Versfeld, *Oor gode en afgode* [On gods and idols] (Cape Town: Nasionale Pers, 1948).

GA 2nd ed.   Martin Versfeld, with an introduction by Ernst Wolff, *Oor gode en afgode* [On gods and idols] (2nd edition) (Pretoria: Protea, 2010).

PO   Martin Versfeld, *The Perennial Order* (Dublin: Brown & Nolan, 1954).

GCG   Martin Versfeld, *A Guide to The City of God* (London: Sheed and Ward, 1958).

MP   Martin Versfeld, *The Mirror of Philosophers* (London: Sheed and Ward, 1960).

RM   Martin Versfeld, *Rondom die Middeleeue* [On the Middle Ages] (Cape Town: Nasionale Boekhandel, 1962).

"Talking"   Martin Versfeld, "Talking Metaphysics", in M. Versfeld and R. Meyer, *On Metaphysics* (Pretoria: Unisa, 1966).

          Martin Versfeld, *Wat is kontemporêr? Vier opstelle oor ons tyd* [What is contemporary. Four essays on our time] (Johannesburg: Afrikaanse Pers-Boekhandel, 1966).

KK   Martin Versfeld, *Klip en klei* [Stone and Clay] (Pretoria: Human en Rousseau, 1968).

          Martin Versfeld, *Klip en klei* [Stone and Clay] (2nd edition) (Pretoria: Protea, 2008).

BU	Martin Versfeld, W.A. de Klerk and J.J. Degenaar, *Beweging uitwaarts* [Movement outwards] (Cape Town: John Malherbe, 1969).
	Martin Versfeld, *Plato. Die simposium of die drinkparty* [Plato. The Symposium or the Drinking Party] (Cape Town: Buren, 1970).
	Martin Versfeld, *Die buitelewe* [Life outdoors] (Cape Town: Buren, 1970).
SS	Martin Versfeld, *The Socratic Spirit*. University of Cape Town. Inaugural Lecture Series, no. 7, 1971 [also published in *Persons*, chapter 1].
Persons	Martin Versfeld, *Persons* (Cape Town: Buren, 1972).
	Martin Versfeld, *'n Handleiding tot die Republiek van Plato* [A Guide to Plato's Republic] (Cape Town: Buren, 1974).
	Martin Versfeld, M. Scholtz and I.L. de Villiers, *Wyn en wysheid. Vier sienings met foto's deur Chris Jansen* [Wine and Wisdom. Four views with photo's by Chris Jansen] (Cape Town: Tafelberg, 1978).
OS	Martin Versfeld, *Our Selves* (Cape Town: David Philip, 1979).
OS 2nd ed.	Martin Versfeld, with an introduction Ernst Wolff, *Our Selves* (2nd edition) (Pretoria: Protea, 2010).
TD	Martin Versfeld, *Tyd en dae* [Time and days] (Cape Town: Tafelberg, 1982).
FT	Martin Versfeld, *Food for Thought. A Philosopher's Cookbook* (Cape Town: Carrefour, [1983] 1991).
NA	Martin Versfeld, *Die neukery met die appelboom* [The trouble with the apple tree] (Cape Town: Tafelberg, 1985).
NA 2nd ed.	Martin Versfeld, with an introduction by André Brink, *Die neukery met die appelboom en ander essays* [The trouble with the appletree] (2nd edition) (Pretoria: Protea, 2009).
PP	Martin Versfeld, *Pots and Poetry* (Cape Town: Tafelberg, 1985).
PP 2nd ed.	Martin Versfeld, with an introduction by André Brink, *Pots and Poetry and other essays* (2nd edition) (Pretoria: Protea, 2009).
	Martin Versfeld, *Die lewensweg van Lao-Tse* (Cape Town: Perskor, 1988).
ACCG	Martin Versfeld, *St Augustine's Confessions and City of God* (Cape Town: Carrefour, 1990).
Sum	Martin Versfeld, *Sum. Selected Works / 'n Keur uit sy werke* (Cape Town: Carrefour, 1991).

INTRODUCTIONS

CHAPTER 1

"FERTILIZER TO THE LAST" – BIOGRAPHICAL SNIPS

By Ruth Versfeld
– with thanks for contributions from other family members

"A loafer all my life", is how Martin Versfeld, my father, described himself in his honorary graduation ceremony speech at the University of Cape Town in 1987. He did indeed spend many hours in the armchair he had made for himself – a simple, wooden structure with curved arms and a chequerboard of broad leather straps across the seat and back. It sat in his study at Blyde Huis, a double-storeyed Victorian house built in 1840 in Rosebank, Cape Town. This was to be the house where he and his wife, Barbara, lived from 1945 until his death in 1995. Their nine children grew up here, and Martin would often rattle off the list until he reached the name of the one he was looking for … "Joan, Adie, Cathy, Ursie, Dirk, Ruth, Molly, Tinie … no, no I mean Balie."

It was from his armchair that Martin did all his writing and much of his conversing. He had no typewriter and a hatred for ball-point pens. Instead he had a writing board and a pencil, kept sharpened with his ever-present pocket knife. Nothing was ever erased, though he did cross out or add the occasional word.

Many visitors came to Blyde Huis, passing through the squeaky wrought-iron gate, up the rough path under a huge magnolia tree to the wide front steps and the never-locked front door. The study was the first room on the left, a large room lined with books with the limerick volumes on a top shelf, ostensibly out of the reach of children. On the mantelpiece above the fireplace stood a crucifix along with, in later years, a statue of Buddha. If Martin was not here, he could usually be found cooking in the kitchen or wandering the rambling garden, often with company.

Martin had many friends: neighbourhood children, poets and academics; Scrabble companions, mountaineers and farmers; local beggars, teachers and former students; priests, infidels, along with, heaven forbid, judges and lawyers. For the sit-in-the-study visitors, Barbara seldom had time nor the inclination to be the tea-making wife. We children watched and commented, often irreverently, as "fans of the guru" traipsed from the study through to the kettle in the kitchen. Having said that, my brother, Dirk, recalls that

> sitting in the study when Dad was with his friends was incredibly important to me. It was about friendship, and this must have been deeply comforting to me. This has guided my life and my way of being with my own friends and their children – I hope [to give] some of that same sense of pleasure and security.

Sunday evening was the time for student visitations with Martin, who from his armchair read extracts from books and his latest pencilled writings. But much of his teaching came through aphorisms and casual remarks such as, "I hope he doesn't end up a mere academic," or "So damnably the suffering elect. Virtue – Bah", or "Potatoes are pure poetry ... so is good prose" and "People who think Western thought and art superior to that of the East are only half educated." He loved these sessions and his students clearly did too. They kept coming back.

Denis Cowen, a frequent visitor to his study and friend from 1935 until the time Martin died, notes that

> although I know Martin better than I know Barbara, I actually know more about Barbara's antecedents than Martin's – a subject on which he was always surprisingly reticent, however hard or subtly one might try to draw him. Perhaps he set little store by such things. Perhaps he did not consider it worth the time and effort to find out ... but speculation on the subject is, so it seems to me, unnourishing.

I too, recall him saying that one learns more about a person by watching how he peels an orange than by studying his family tree.

Marthinus Versfeld was one of two children. His younger sister was Alma. Their parents were Anna Gertruida (born Le Roux) and John Henry Versfeld. "Ouma" Anna was a warm and welcoming woman with a brightness in her eyes. She was of French Huguenot descent. Her ancestors fled from France in 1685, at the time of the Revocation of the Edict of Nantes when Calvinist Protestants were no longer allowed to practise their religion in the predominantly Catholic state. (This adds interest to Martin's conversion from Calvinism to Catholicism some 260 years later).

"Ouma" Anna's family belonged to a Dutch Reformed Church congregation in Tulbagh, a small town in a mountainous part of the Western Cape. Her father farmed in the area. Anna herself was a staunch member of the Dutch Reformed Church all her life, ensuring her children attended church services as well as Sunday school and spent what was left of their Sundays "bettering" themselves and reading books with a "good moral tone" rather than having fun. Both Marthinus and Alma resented this, and my father would tell us of a sentimentally illustrated book he won at Sunday school and stuffed down a drain en route home.

Anna's mother was known in Tulbagh for her nursing skills and had a formidable knowledge of indigenous plants and herbal medicines which she passed on to her daughter. Ouma in turn imparted both the knowledge and values of the goodness and power of nature to her children. Marthinus likewise was quick to apply pads of linen soaked in *blousalie* (blue sage) over a wound or to make a brew of *wildeals* (wormwood) if any of his children admitted to a stomach ache. He also had a reputation for feeding his family "weeds" from the garden. Some saw this as deprivation but we thrived.

One of ten children, Anna Le Roux trained as a primary school teacher and got a post some distance away in the Little Karoo town of Barrydale. Here she lodged at "Rose Cottage", the home of the Versfeld family. John Henry Versfeld, whom she later married, had an only sister, Hilda, who taught at the same school.

John Henry was the middle son and his mother, we were told, favoured his older and younger brothers. He probably suffered from depression most of his life. At the time Anna was lodging with his family he was a law student and doing brilliantly. However, he then became deaf after a bout of illness, possibly meningitis or simply a severe cold. This, in those days, ruled out his wish to become a lawyer and restricted him to the deathly boring job of "Registrar of Deeds".

John Henry Versfeld married Anna le Roux in 1908. His was the Dutch side of the family originating from the Netherlands in the early 1700s and with relatives in the Cape west coast upcountry regions of Darling, Malmesbury and Piketberg. There were also familial connections with branches of the Smuts, Gie and Duckitt families. The Versfeld web spread from the farm Groote Post west of the Cedarberg Mountains to the farm of Klaassenbosch in the Constantia valley, across to Caledon in the Overberg district, through Swellendam and Riversdale and on east to Knysna.

Marthinus Versfeld was born on 11 August 1909. Christened "Marthinus" in the Dutch Reformed Church, he kept this name but used "Martin" more and more as time went by. He and Alma grew up with their parents at 12 Camp Street, a double-storeyed, semi-detached house in Gardens, Cape Town. Marthinus had an upstairs room that led onto a balcony that commanded a fine view of the face of Table Mountain, a place he roamed from boyhood to old age. His father had a love of the outdoor life, often taking his family for walks along the "Firepath" (now Tafelberg Road) and the "Pipe Track" which contours the skirt of Table Mountain.

The family later moved to a larger house with a bigger garden in Hofmeyr Street, also in Gardens. This house they named "Tradouw" after the route through the Langeberg Mountains linking Barrydale to Suurbraak in the Overberg. Anna and John Henry would have enjoyed outings in this area when Anna lodged with the Versfelds in Barrydale.

Martin's love of carpentry no doubt also stemmed from his father. The two shared a cramped workshop in the basement of their Hofmeyr Street home. Here they made *bankies* of black stinkwood and *witels* (white alder) along with bigger yellow wood tables, bookshelves and other useful pieces for the house. This fine feel for wood has been passed on to my generation and particularly to my brother Tinie (Martin), who started working wood with his father in the workshop at Blyde Huis and is now a craftsman himself.

It seems that John Henry became increasingly frustrated and gloomy with age. Denis Cowen recalls Martin telling him that his father "yearned to spread his wings in the competitive world of affairs, but was prevented by his deafness from getting out of the civil service rut". Martin, as a schoolboy, had to deal with his father's breakdowns and suicidal threats. He also successfully nursed both his parents when they contracted the Spanish Flu of 1918.

Martin matriculated from South African College Schools (SACS) and went on to study at the University of Cape Town. One could have expected him to study entomology as he was keen on the natural sciences and had already developed a deep interest and knowledge of *goggas*. However, he initially selected law, as his father had done, but then discovered that philosophy was a lot more fun.

For postgraduate study, Martin went to Glasgow University in Scotland where he garnered his PhD in 1933. A major revelation during his PhD studies was his discovery, under the guidance of A.A. Bowman, of mediaeval philosophy, particularly the writings of Augustine and Thomas Aquinas. He was dismayed that the narrow Protestantism of his University of Cape Town education had omitted this period of Western thought. He dutifully completed his PhD on Descartes, but no longer admired the thinking of that style of philosophy.

In 1942 Martin met and married Barbara Barry. He was a junior lecturer in ethics at the University of Cape Town while she was an undergraduate student. Barbara also had ancestral roots in the Overberg that ran through Swellendam to the south coast. Hers was an English-speaking, Church of England family while Martin's was Afrikaans-speaking and Dutch Reformed. Their families generally supported opposite sides in the Second Anglo-Boer, or South African, War at the start of the twentieth century. Martin's father and a friend, for example, climbed Lion's Head one night during this war and erected a "Vierkleur" – the Transvaal/Boer flag. It has to be said that Barbara's great-uncle John X. Merriman, then Treasurer General of the Cape in the ministry of J.P. Schreiner, was accused of being "Pro-Boer" in the British House of Commons as he appealed for the prevention of the Second Boer War. Merriman even lost his seat in Parliament for a period because of his anti-war sentiments. Both families had a rebellious element, which Martin and Barbara each took on in their pacifist ways.

Within a couple of years of their marriage, Martin and Barbara together converted to Catholicism, a move of which neither the Dutch Reformed Church nor Barbara's family approved. However, this was an exciting and uplifting time for them both as reflected in a letter from Martin to Simon Bisheuwel, a psychologist friend who had challenged him on the need for organised religion: "the function of the church is to present to us the Divine Values in the form in which they are visible to merely human eyes". The writings of Catholic philosophers including Jacques Maritain and Étienne Gilson (both of the Thomas Aquinas tradition), Cardinal John Henry Newman and South Africa's Monsignor F.C. Kolbe clearly aided them in looking upon the Divine. G.K. Chesterton was another oft-quoted influence. I'm interested to discover that of all these professed Catholics, only Gilson was born into a Catholic family.

Later, and while essentially staying in that faith, Martin broadened his interests to include Eastern thought, especially Zen Buddhism. So, for example, in 1979 his essay "The Yin and the Yang in Christian Culture" was published in his collection *Our Selves. Pots and Poetry*, a 1985 collection of essays which includes "Plato and Confucius" where once again he draws parallels between Western and Eastern thought. I'm sure these ideas were brewing all along and remember, from the time I learnt to read in the early 1960s, trying to decipher the word "Upanishads" on the spine of one of the many books on his shelves. In 1988 Martin took enormous satisfaction in the publication of his *Die Lewensweg van Lao-Tse*, a translation into Afrikaans of the *Tao Te Ching*, authored by the ancient Chinese philosopher and poet Lao Tzu. He always said that philosophers peak at eighty. He was seventy-nine at the time!

This was also about the time when my brother Tinie had a discussion with his father about atheism. The old man explained that he was not brave enough to have no faith. Christianity as illuminated by the great Catholic thinkers, he said, appealed to him because it offered redemption from the terror of history. History did indeed plague him.

As a child I had little comprehension of what it was my parents did. When asked, my father's response would go something like, "Well, it's something like a blind man in a dark room looking for a black cat that isn't there ... and finding it!" I remember my Sub-B (grade two) teacher going around the class asking our parents' occupations for a list she was compiling. I was seven years old. When it was my turn, I proudly announced that my father was a carpenter, and my mother a secretary. (At the time, my mother was going to "the office" to do paralegal advisory work for transgressors of the pass and other apartheid laws.) My sister Ursie once explained what her father did with the words, "Sometimes he sits and thinks, and sometimes he just sits." I'm sure my parents would have approved of both accounts!

Although he never served on any of their "stodgy" committees, Martin was an active and respected member the Mountain Club of South Africa (MCSA). He was first introduced to MCSA activities as a schoolboy at SACS, then situated on Government Avenue in a building now used by University of Cape Town's Michaelis Art School. SACS had its own mountain club through which Martin and his friends opened many climbs on both the front and back of Table Mountain. They also joined countless MCSA meets. From the age of thirteen Martin kept careful record of these expeditions with descriptions:

> One has to go up perpendicularly doing back and foot work for perhaps 30 feet. One must now walk astride of the crack for some distance. My hobnails, having worn down and being therefore very slippery, afforded no grip. There being a big drop below, the situation was, to say the least, uncomfortable. Climbing up a few feet we hit off to the left and, passing through a passage under the rock, we came out a few feet below the summit of the mountain at 1.20pm. [...] We had grub at the top of Porcupine Ravine. Flegg made a villainous stew, and while he was eating it we told him horrible stories to make him feel sick. (Blinkwater Needle, Table Mountain – 1924)

From this time on, Martin and friends made numerous excursions to the Boland and Cederberg mountains. He recorded these trips in a series of diaries, startling in their purely factual nature with names, times, routes and cuisine carefully recorded. However, these trips inspired other writing, such as *Die berge van die Boland*, which he and "Oom Bill" (W.A. De Klerk), a close climbing friend and intellectual soulmate, penned together for publication in 1947.

Martin remained a traditional rock climber, saying that the new generation, including his own son Tinie, had "more gym chalk than ink on their fingers". In 1991 he was asked to deliver a speech at MCSA Centennial Memorial Service held at Maclear's Beacon on the summit of Table Mountain. He started:

> I am amazed at being here. The honour is almost too much for me, especially when I remember that I am standing where my fellow member, and fellow philosopher, Oubaas Smuts, once stood. In 1923 at the unveiling of this memorial I was present as a schoolboy – the reward of our class for carrying up cement – listening to Smuts' speech of dedication.

Martin was also a keen fisherman, mostly on the Cape Peninsula and mostly in the company of another soulmate, Leon "Bubi" Meyer. As with his mountain trips, Martin kept diaries with mostly dry and detailed records of fishing spots, weather conditions and catches. His greatest joy was hooking a *galjoen*, but these catches became further and further apart as *galjoen* were an increasingly scarce resource. People often asked him whether he contemplated philosophical ideas as he gazed for hours into the unrewarding sea, to which he would respond, "Bah, I was fishing!" He liked simply to be in the present.

Another passion was his garden at Blyde Huis in Rosebank. Many an hour was spent standing gazing at this and that, often – until he dropped the habit – with pipe in hand. I was away from South Africa during the 1980s, and my father was a regular correspondent, often sending descriptions of the garden:

> As you stand in the front door you will see in the middle of the fairway a globular bush of brilliant purple shimmering with bees. Behind it a patch of lettuce, and to the left verdant beds of carrots, turnips, broad beans and coriander. The arums are coming up in the usual spot, and below are improved rockeries.

The garden was also a source of nourishment for yet another of Martin's loves, cooking. This is best explained using his words: "When you take the lid off the tureen, you should in fact be opening a window onto a garden." Martin took great pride in producing pots of food for his family along with guests, lodgers and those who happened to pass by at meal times. We had a large dining table, which he made, but this was for many years made even larger when a ping-pong table board was placed on top. Barbara would stand forbearingly over the big, black pot serving rounds to hungry mouths while Martin lapped up the praise.

A favourite family memory is of the time Martin served one of his rare baked *galjoen*, stuffed and garnished with pickings from the garden. With his usual flourish, he opened the cover of the baking pan only to reveal his mislaid pipe lying on top of the fish. Guests that night were none other than Lady Luyt and her husband, Sir Richard, the University of Cape Town vice chancellor at the time.

In 1947 Martin purchased a property, then a poor and run-down farm, called *Diepte van Ellende* ("Depths of Despair"). The property was essentially a wild piece of mountainous land in the Kouga Mountains of the Langkloof. He renamed it *Lentelus* ("Spring Joy"). Barbara recalls this time:

> Over the next few years Martin travelled up every winter and summer vacation to get our two-roomed cottage built – always with the help of a student friend ... and some local labour – first the foundations had to be laid, trenches were dug and many rocks laboriously rolled down the hillside ... Then the bricks had to be made in a mould, mud and cement ... Once the foundations were laid, the bricks were cast, another major operation, and the walls started to rise ... at last the roof beams were in place ... Three big steps led up to the front door and the floor was stamped earth ... Now came the furnishing – a long pine table with a long bench for each side, still extant, a set of four metal bunks we were given ... salvaged from the wreck of a Union Castle steamer in Table Bay, around 1920. These bunks had metal railings to prevent passengers from rolling out in rough weather, very suitable for young children.

And young children there were in increasing numbers. Following Joan, Adie and Cathy there was now toddler Ursie who

> arrived with delight and ran round and round the long table shouting "Oh Daddy it's loverly" over and over. Year after year we came from mid-December to mid-January and again most years in July – although I missed out at the end of '52 as Dirk was about to arrive ... Ruth joined

the mob 15 months later and there were still three to come (Molly, Tinie and Balie). The saga continued and we all loved it, only missing 1965–1966 when we were in the USA.

Lentelus was to remain an anchor for the family and a huge number of friends. As the long summer holidays approached we would start preparing with Martin packing his suitcase weeks in advance. He often pointed out that although we never had a car, we at least had a place to go to. (Martin never learnt to drive and we would never have fitted into one vehicle anyway.) We travelled to "The Farm" by overnight steam train, usually booking two compartments, which bedded six each, and a coupe for another three. Friends came along too. Tin trunks of supplies such as bully beef, spaghetti and tinned peaches were loaded into the guard van at the back, while bedding rolls and baskets of padkos came to our compartments of green leather. The dining car was out of the question for meals, although I recall the rare ice-cream treat in that teak-clad coach. "Coke" was never on the menu, with Martin spitting out the words, "I've drunk Coca-Cola on two occasions in my life – and I remember them both".

The train went through Mossel Bay and George before climbing so slowly over the Montagu Pass that passengers could run alongside the train, helping themselves to the watsonia flowers that grew in profusion alongside the tracks. We disembarked at Camfer station on the other side of the pass and then took an old railway bus as far as Avontuur, where a local farmer would collect us in his bakkie. Martin would worry about the logistics and costs of all this but it was our mother, Barbara, who really did the work.

Ann Harries, one of our friends on such a trip, recalls how tough these rough and otherworldly holidays sans taps, electricity or washing facilities could be on Barbara:

> As the holiday continued, I began to observe vulnerabilities in the Versfeld parents. I once saw Barbara display her true feelings when she thought no one was looking. It happened when I was curled up in my top bunk (grudgingly given to me as a guest by the children) enthralled by the recently published *The Lion, The Witch and The Wardrobe* which I'd found in a pile of random literature. Barbara had cleared the table, done the washing-up and was now sweeping the dusty floor (the children usually helped to an extent with these tasks but had all gone out with Martin on a bug-catching expedition which I'd declined to join). Suddenly she threw down her broom and shouted: Bugger housework! Bugger babies! Bugger Martin! and collapsed sobbing on a

chair. I climbed down from my bunk, picked up the cast-down broom, and began sweeping.

Martin's *Klip en klei* (*Stone and Clay*) essays (1968) are inspired by Lentelus, which was unbelievably formative for us all. He and Barbara both enjoyed people and especially young people. "The Farm" became a place where they could enjoy friends and their families together and, in time, make an essential contribution to the raising of their grandchildren. We would have river expeditions, fishing, swimming and camping under the stars. We collected mushrooms and explored Bushman caves. Martin and his sons hunted for the pot, often subjecting Barbara to cleaning a gamey dassie or rock rabbit.

Our father had a deep love for the land and instilled this love in all of us. My brother Dirk recalls Martin's descriptions of the cultivated Italian terraces he had admired when taking a break from his Glasgow studies. Together they attempted to create a similar citrus terrace on the stony hillside alongside the little Lentelus cottage. I could not agree more with Dirk when he says, "The farm remains our parent and our single touch point. I feel that as long as we have the farm we are not orphans".

1966 was the year that we missed out on the farm as Martin and Barbara took their six youngest children on sabbatical leave to South Bend, Indiana, in the United States. It was an unforgettable journey: we took a Union Castle liner from Cape Town to Southampton in England and then the SS United States, a huge ship that had been used for troops in World War Two, across a very bumpy Atlantic Ocean to New York. From here we took a flight to Chicago and another to South Bend, home to Notre Dame, a Catholic university that admitted only men and nuns as students. It seemed nuns were counted as gender-free! Notre Dame was also known for its mighty American football team. It did, however, have an interesting philosophy department – to my father only attraction.

Our year in the United States may have been fun for us children, but it was not for our parents. Martin battled and so, as a consequence, did Barbara. He found the food synthetic and missed bread with texture and wine with flavour. Summers were hot and humid, winters icy and the Indiana landscape was entirely flat. I recall my father's return from a fishing expedition along the river that ran through the town. He disdainfully tipped a sack full of small, bony fish into the basin. We did our best to clean and eat some but they tasted of mud. He told us how he had seen a hand moving with the flow above the surface of the water. Convinced it was a corpse, he had tried to hook it. It flopped over – a plastic glove in a polluted river.

When he returned to the University of Cape Town, Martin had to submit his sabbatical report for the year. He simply wrote, "Went fishing". This was typical of his attitude to the formalities of academia. Never in all his time at University of Cape Town did he attend a faculty meeting. His colleagues in the philosophy department had to pick up the pieces. One such colleague was Professor Andrew Murray. Prof. Murray also served the South African government as an adviser and expert on communism. He was never a family friend. He did, however, get Martin out of a couple of tight spots: first being when he posted himself some "Communist literature" from the United States and second when he ordered himself a "wok from Sui Hing Hong". Murray explained to the authorities that the literature was for academic research and that the wok was not a weapon of mass destruction but a cooking utensil.

Reading and music were of paramount importance to Martin. He would say that he read *Robinson Crusoe* at the age of four. His sister, Alma, in her memoirs, recalls what a library their house was:

> Marthinus and I were given the Arthur Mee *My Magazine*, and the *Children's Newspaper* to build up our general knowledge. We had just about all the Rider Haggard books ... Then Conan Doyle's Sherlock Holmes Books, the Boy's Own Annual given to Marthinus ... also Harmsworth's *Wonders of the Past* and his series on Natural History – all about goggas and animals. ... The Oubaas would also read to us from *Jock of the Bushveld*, one of his favourite books, and from *Outa Karel's Stories*, by Sanni Metelerkamp. The Ounooi would read the Beatrix Potter stories to us.

The list goes on, with the books named written mostly in English. There would not have been many books in Afrikaans available when Martin and Alma were children. Afrikaans only became an official language in 1925, until which time Dutch was taught, but not spoken, in schools. English reigned in the classroom and on the playground. During the childhood of John Henry and Anna Gertruida, Afrikaans-speaking children caught speaking Afrikaans at school were forced to wear placards reading "I must not speak Dutch at school". (There was no word for "Afrikaans" at that time.) Their generation was never comfortable with reading Afrikaans, having been brought up on the Dutch Bible. When Martin was studying in Scotland he and his father had a great correspondence – all in English.

As children we were read to extensively. I particularly remember our father's delight in Rudyard Kipling's *Just So Stories* and Arthur Ransom's *Swallows and Amazons* series, now in the possession of his great-grandchildren. Homer's

Odyssey flew over most of our heads, but he took great pleasure in the reading. We were also raised on the Bible, with selected blood-thirsty readings from the Old Testament, including the tale of Judith seducing Holofernes and then cutting off his head.

Martin was no great connoisseur of the modern novel and seldom acquired new books for general reading. He preferred to read and reread those he had on his shelves. Rudyard Kipling and Thor Heyerdahl were favourite authors. Charles Darwin's *Voyage of the Beagle* was much loved. *King Lear* was an almost annual event, with Shakespeare play-readings as a variant on his Sunday evening discussions.

Martin would often quote long passages of poetry – Tennyson, Coleridge, Wordsworth and others. Many of the Afrikaans poets were close to his heart. To quote from a letter he wrote to me in 1986:

> End of a quiet day, a good deal of which I spent reading Leipoldt, with whom I have so much affinity. You don't know a people until you know their poetry. I'm sick of people who know all about "the Afrikaner" and can't quote a line. Poets are the only begetters and preservers of their people.

Old friends of Martin recall how he would whistle Bach on mountain walks. On his death one of his granddaughters, Shirley Apthorp, published a newspaper article entitled, "Oupa tapped life's memory". She describes the gramophone which, like his armchair, had its place in his study:

> a prized possession, dark wood carved in ornate Gothic arches and polished to a high sheen. [...] My grandfather's hands shake as he tries to fit the needle into its socket. It's an old cane needle, which he has just laboriously trimmed with special scissors [...] He keeps an open box of 78 records, each in its yellowing sleeve, catalogued in neat blue fountain pen lists. Bach, Mozart, Sibelius, Elgar; more Bach. [...] "This is an excellent machine, when it's working properly." He is scrutinising the dusty interior of his gramophone again. "And," turning to his collection, "there are some magnificent things in there. But it doesn't matter. I've got them all inside me, here." He taps his head. "Every note of every one of them." And he shuffles out of the room, oblivious to Elgar's melancholy chords, humming a Bach violin concerto.

Martin often said that for every organiser one needed two disorganisers. A favourite fable was about a crocodile who lies in bed hypnotised by the orderly pattern of flowers on the wallpaper. He is persuaded to go out and see the wild profusion and confusion of his wife's flower garden and, shocked by this lawlessness, returns to his bed and wallpaper, where he smugly becomes paler and paler and sicker and sicker.

As Martin grew older he stopped seeking out that invisible black cat. A great fan of Friedrich Nietzsche, he marvelled more at the insoluble and disliked the compartmentalising of ideas. He couldn't stomach sermons, woolly thinking or dogmatism. To those calling themselves feminist, fundamentalist, imperialist, socialist, capitalist or whatever, he would simply say "Bah". He would no doubt have said "Bah" to anyone calling him a existentialist although this is what I say he essentially was. However, labelling was not beyond him: "Voter" was his ultimate insult to Nationalists of the time. Until the first democratic elections of 1994 neither of our parents had ever voted. A "whites only" ballot box was not for them. Come 1994, Martin put his mark next to the Green Party.

No one could have called Martin a "political activist" in the sense that this term was used in the apartheid years. He certainly did not march the streets or speak the language of anti-apartheid activists. Barbara, his wife, did this and more. She was a member of the Black Sash and Dependents Conference, an organisation that ensured the families of political prisoners were provided for and afforded opportunities to visit incarcerated family members. Our house was both a "railway station" of people passing through and a "safe house", where activists on the run could hide from the security branch and enjoy anonymity. (We only learnt their real names later.) Martin was clearly quite proud of all this, keeping a running commentary and writing letters to me such as this extract from 28 August 1985:

> This has been our sort of Day of the Barricades. We don't really know yet what has occurred or is occurring, but the govt. and police are in a sort of fury of fear. Well, I've seen this coming for a great many years. Ego-phenomenon! [...] I am very seriously convinced that Original Sin is the lust for power.

Martin, like his father, suffered from depression, although less so, to my memory, in his later years than when I was a child. He had a major depressive episode in early 1959, resulting in months of hospitalisation in the psychiatric ward at Groote Schuur. During this time Barbara gave birth to their eighth child. Martin later saw this illness as a turning point in his philosophical thinking.

I recall how unsettled he could be, suffering terrible nightmares, and strutting back and forth, unable to communicate with any of us. This depressive gene was passed down to some of his children, notably Cathy, who committed suicide at the age of twenty-three. This brought deep sadness to the whole family, my parents only reaching a level of peace within themselves some twenty years later. This was when their eldest son, Adrian, became ill with cancer. During his illness, Adie spoke and wrote about what it was to face death in a way that somehow brought resolution to our loss of Cathy. Adie died in 1992.

In early April 1995 our paterfamilias had a stroke that left him partially paralysed, without speech and bedridden. It was clear that his life was drawing to a close and the best we could do was to care for him as he lay in his study at home. He was surrounded by family, including three-year-old twin grandchildren Adrian and Xavier, discussing the hole they were going to dig to put him into. (A twinkle in his eye told us that he enjoyed this exchange!) From here Martin could enjoy the magnolia tree casting shadows across the window and a garden posy of pink nerines on the sill. This was butterfly season, with a profusion of his favourite autumnal black butterfly outside. He watched a pupa on a twig placed at his bedside, and particularly enjoyed being shown a picture book of butterflies.

Martin would often look towards a piece of calligraphy that had always hung on the wall next to this bed. It had been beautifully executed by Joan Tebbutt, a Scottish artist with whom he had a close friendship through much of the 1930s and into the early 1940s. The inscription, from St Thomas Aquinas, reads:

Ex
divina pulchritudine
esse omnium
derivatur

Translated by Joan – my eldest sister and Joan Tebbutt's namesake – the text reads:

From
the divine beauty
is all being
derived

Anyone who has read Martin Versfeld's work will recognise his fascination with the concept of beauty, as opposed to reason, goodness or truth, and most particularly with the beauty of the divine.

For me, it is significant that these are the words he watched to his last. Martin, despite his protestations that people are essentially good, had always recognised the barriers of the ego and obstinacy to humility in himself and in humanity at large. He had, through the sacred and profane, reached long and hard towards beauty as that which is proportioned, harmonious and complete.

In a typical swipe of humour, he suggested his gravestone be inscribed with the words:

Here lies Martin Versfeld
Safe in the bosom of Mother Earth
Fertilizer to the last.

CHAPTER 2

WHAT WAS VERSFELD DOING WHEN HE WAS DOING PHILOSOPHY?

Having provided a character sketch of the man in the previous chapter, the present chapter similarly aims to characterise Versfeld's writings. Everything will be done to escape two kinds of reading for which he himself repeatedly expressed his allergy: generally, simplifying the complexity of the author and, particularly, exaggerating the author's beauty – in other words, writing a hagiography. To demonstrate my commitment to this cause, I will give a few reasons for *not* reading Versfeld today. Thereafter a number of salient traits of his writing will be examined. Each dimension of his work suggests a possible response. One quickly realises that there is not just one Versfeld and that the attempt to find the one, simple and obvious way of receiving his work will necessarily end in frustration.

1. On the warts

> I admit that there is a pressure cooker in our kitchen and that I often use it. There! I have made my confession, I am purged of my guilt, I can see both sides of the question. (*FT* 94)
>
> We have to love Augustine, tares and all. (*ACCG* 103)
>
> The biographer must sketch the warts. (*ACCG* 35)

The Roman rhetoricians recommended that one start a plea with a *captatio benevolentiae* – an introduction to capture the goodwill of the audience. I shall do so here, but in a somewhat circuitous way – namely, by evoking what seems to me dispersed blots of irredeemable ideas in Versfeld's work. Admittedly, this strategy runs the risk of chilling the enthusiasm of the eager reader. However, I reckon that my wager will pay off: rather start with "a little candid explanation" (*MP* 3), than face the accusation of hiding the blemishes. Presented here, then, are a number of concessions to the philosopher's critics, not an encompassing philosophical assessment of his entire work – this will come out in the subsequent chapters of the book. I will, as it were, speak about the warts, before I examine the whole warthog.

I have another reason for proceeding in this way. A great number of people have grown to love the work of Versfeld; fewer have really read him. By confronting them straightaway with unfortunate and often unknown blots on his work, I hope to offer them a shock by which to discover and learn to appreciate Versfeld a second time.

These blemishes are diverse. A few reflect social prejudices, others are gargoyles of Versfeld's own making.

1.1. Spots of prejudice

There is no obstinate exercise of prejudice in Versfeld, but it seems fair to report on those rare or isolated instances I know of. Likewise, it would be unfair not to contrast these lapses with his explicit ideas.

The gender-sensitive present-day reader will find some regretful turns of phrase. Apart from the formerly accepted use of "man" for "humanity", there are some places where Versfeld demands too much of readers' generosity. I think of the way he translates *virtu* (virtue) into manliness (*manlikheid*, e.g., *GA* 56). True enough, this is a historical equivalent for *virtus* and the etymology of the word is "vir" (man), but if the argumentative context doesn't require this translation, why not simply use "virtue"? Let it be said that I cannot remember having seen a recurrence of this practice beyond the 1948 book. A long decade later came the following passage in a commentary on Thomas Aquinas's theory of knowledge: "Contemplation is the most masculine of activities, and there is something not feminine but effeminate in a theory of knowledge and of language that makes philosophy the housemaid of the special sciences." (*MP* 143) Versfeld, or Versfeld rendering Aquinas? Not clear. But even then, such a passage calls out for relativising commentary. And I'm not sure that the manoeuvre by which the philosopher dresses himself up in the mediaeval feminine imagery of a housemaid suffices to redeem him. At the same time, his work is not devoid of true gender reversal, for instance when, in *Pots and Poetry*, he happily replaces the Pauline theological pair of Adam and Christ with Eve and Mary (*PP* 2).[1] This reversal has an anthropological flip side, which consists of problematising the essentialist gender duality (cf. *PO* 212–213). We are thus far from justified to generalise this point about gendered expression, as if we were dealing with a crude paternalistic writer.

I recall one occurrence of a homophobic slur. Describing a public celebration by followers of the goddess Cybele in Carthage in the time of Augustine, Versfeld summarised this as a "faggot parade" ("moffie-optog", *RM* 13). One does not oblige Versfeld to sympathise with this historical practice; one does expect of him to mind his tongue. Or to be consistent with his better self: a slightly different version of the same discussion simply does not contain this slur (cf. *GCG* 9–10).

But one has to be careful with this author. I am thinking of the exceptional and curious case of "Nordwand of the Vierge Maigre. Report on the international Alpine expedition", written for *The Journal of the Mountain Club of South Africa*. Exceptional, because it is intended as a humoristic sketch and has no direct relation to his philosophical work; curious, because I do not know how to take it. In this sketch is a fictive character, who may be a black South African farm worker and who is given the name Adoons (a name formerly frequently given to baboons). It starts off badly! However, some doubt is left as to whether it is not perhaps a real baboon.[2] Furthermore, the other characters of this fictive expedition are portrayed in the most stereotypical ways (an Algerian, a Frenchman, a German and a Brit). Burlesque humour? Finally, the Adoons figure turns out to be the hero of the story. Reversal of stereotypes or a humoristic confirmation? Difficult to assess. It is surely ill advised to write a piece today that remains so ambiguous. However, whatever we make of this, we will see later how opposition to all sorts of racial discrimination was a central tenet of his developed sociopolitical critique.

Without claiming to have presented an exhaustive catalogue, I have made the case against the infallibility of the philosopher. At the same time, we have seen in each case that the cited points are in contradiction with the intellectual stance defended explicitly in his work.

---

[1] Or his ideas about gender "balance" in mediaeval thought, cf. *PO* 212–213.
[2] The issue is even more complex, if we consider a later remark that evidently also applies to himself: "Personally I believe in a God who is the Origin of everything. It requires great originality to make a baboon into a man of the church" (*NA* 2nd ed. 78).

1.2. Gargoyles

Surely, I have to acknowledge that in labelling some of the author's ideas as monstrosities, I give only my own view. However, I expect that not many contemporaries will contradict me on the following.

As will be discussed in Chapter 3, Versfeld early on advocated a Christian science; his ideas are formulated in *GA* (ch. V) and even extended into *PO* (chapters 10 and 11). Yet, one has the impression that Versfeld himself came to new insights: in *Rondom die Middeleeue* (*On the Middle Ages*) he claims that the "mediaeval spirit" made modern science possible, without itself being that science (*RM* ch. VII). Furthermore, in *The Perennial Order* and *Rondom die Middeleeue* he works out a vision of the unity of faith and science – a unity he sees figured in the work of Mgr Kolbe (*MP* ch. 5). However, the idea of Christian science fades in his thought. That is, except in the sense of claiming at the end of his life that science has to be rooted in wisdom, where wisdom is equivalent to theology. However, in the same breath, he rejects the "dreadful efforts to theologise the sciences, so that we have a 'Christian mathematics', 'Christian biology' and so forth" (*ACCG* 55).

This point can help us identify and understand a number of Versfeld's monstrosities, which, like gargoyles, are planted in the sacred world of the church, yet extend into the secular world. One finds him writing without a wink about angels[3] (*RM* ch. II; *GCG* ch. II and III and in *ACCG* ch. IX on Augustine's doctrine of the angels), yet it is not clear if he expects his readers to subscribe to their real existence.[4] He can seemingly celebrate pope, emperor and divine social order (*PO* 223, 225[5] – less clearly in *RM* 121–122), yet politically he nurtured not the least desire to restore theocracy. With a sharp, ironising tongue, Versfeld could critique contraception (*MP* 204–205), yet later, with equally acute wit, he struck out at opponents of contraception: "I have heard some Catholic objections to birth control which would make you picture God as someone sitting with a paper bag filled with little prefab souls, complaining about the shortage of

---

[3] Cf. Michel Serres, *La légende des anges* (Paris: Flammarion, 1993). On other secularising receptions of "angelology", see Sybille Krämer, *Medium, Messenger, Transmission. An Approach to Media Philosophy* (Amsterdam: Amsterdam University Press, 2015), 87–96.

[4] E.g., in *Persons* 71 angels are only "functions", namely of transmitting messages; see his quite demythologising way of dealing with "daemons" in *GCG* 23ff; *ACCG* ch. X.

[5] However, that pope and emperor stood under the law, according to mediaeval legal doctrine, is recalled in *PO* 220.

apartments for them" (*NA* 2nd ed. 78[6]). On occasion, he vehemently critiqued travelling (*PP* 41; *NA* 2nd ed. 36–38), and still, his own first experience of foreign countries was an inexhaustible intellectual and personal resource.[7]

This list can be extended, but it is not my intention to draw up a comprehensive compendium of strange ideas in Versfeld's work. Even this short excursion suffices to confirm that there are reasons why some readers may, at some places, be repelled by his work. However, more importantly, the cited points give us a starting point from which to appreciate an author who continued to pursue the improvement of his own thought. As little as one should transfigure this author into an infallible version of himself, so little may one reduce the hog to his warts.

There! I have recognised the blemishes, I'm above suspicion, I can see both sides of the question.

2. From autobiography to enigma

> *factus eram ipse mihi magna questio*, I became a great puzzle to myself.
> (Augustine, cited in *Sum* 16)

The reader who has survived the paragraph above can now take pleasure in meeting the man himself. For reasons that I will explain below, Versfeld frequently found it fit to introduce himself to his readers. This never amounted to a full autobiography (hence the value of the contribution of Ruth Versfeld in Chapter 1). The closest he got to this was a presentation he gave on "Why I Became a Catholic"[8] and an essay of intellectual autobiography, published in *Sum* under the title "Descartes and me. Truth and Things" (*Sum* 13–24). But the most enjoyable way to make the acquaintance of Martin Versfeld is to listen to his own voice.

---

[6] "Ek het al Katolieke besware teen geboortebeperking gehoor wat jou God laat voorstel as iemand wat met 'n kardoes vol *prefab* sieltjies sit en oor die tekort aan woonstelle vir hulle kla."

[7] See references in next footnote.

[8] The original title is "Waarom ek Katoliek geword het". A copy is held in the Versfeld Archive at UCT, file 59, and lengthy citations thereof are available in W.A. de Klerk's article "Marthinus Versfeld: die man en sy denke," *Tydskrif vir Letterkunde* 4, (1966): 62–72.

The opening paragraphs of his 1985 book *Pots and Poetry* read as follows:

> Allow me to introduce myself. I am a professor of philosophy who, I am pleased to say, would be disowned by most schools of philosophy in the English-speaking world. I believe a young man once said of me that I wrote good essays but was no philosopher. I suppose what he meant was that I wrote intelligibly. I have always felt a certain affinity with Socrates, who was my superior also in this, that he never wrote at all. And one of the things I have learnt from him is that it is the ordinary which is extra-ordinary, that philosophy is a descent to the earth, and that "this is a good stew" may be a statement carrying more weight than some of the sentences in Hegel which I have not breath enough to quote. That is why Callicles could object: "You keep talking about food and drink and doctors and nonsense: I am not speaking of these things." Or again: "By heaven, you literally never stop talking about cobblers and fullers and cooks and doctors, as if we were discussing them."
>
> I must admit that to earn my living as an academic I often battened on the higher unintelligibilities, but I have since endeavoured to amend my ways by speaking of such things as food and houses and cooks and builders. I am still fascinated by the problem of what I mean when I say: this cabbage is green; but I cannot dissociate it from the question: how shall I cook this cabbage?, nor from the statement: this is a good cabbage bredie. The eidolon of an Epicurean Socrates appears to me and says: Friend, what do you mean by a good stew, or, for that matter, a good cook? I grow more and more interested in the higher obviousnesses, and aspire to understand a remark of A.N. Whitehead's, that it requires a great mind to take an interest in the obvious. (*PP* 1)

Marvellous. Perhaps, but one should not be fooled by the playful prose. Later in this book, we will see how Versfeld situated himself as a kind of neo-Thomist with a particular affection for Augustine. Although he always wrote well, one should not underestimate how severely he was sometimes afflicted by the philosophical malady of unintelligibility. And it is simple retrospective fantasy to claim that he contracted that illness as though in a workplace accident – he wrestled with hardcore philosophy with all his guts! Yet, as a description of what Versfeld aspired to increasingly from his midlife, this claim is not inaccurate, and one has to concede that he succeeded quite well in his pursuit of the virtue of clarity.

At the centre of his self-presentation is the profession of the philosopher. Let us zoom in on this dimension of his self-understanding by listening to what he had to say about philosophy in his 1971 inaugural lecture "The Socratic Spirit":

> I suppose that in an inaugural lecture a man should declare himself, and tell his colleagues and the public how he stands towards the subject which he has been called upon to profess. For better or worse they should be given a chance of sampling their acquisition. Not that I can tell you anything new. I have been here a long time, and a prophet is honoured indeed when he is honoured in his own country. For this I thank you.
>
> I must confess at once that I do not know what philosophy is. This sometimes embarrasses me before the innocence of students, but not before those who have come to realise that the things by which we live are the things about which we know least. We do not know what life is, or what knowing is, or what truth and goodness are. Or if we do know we can't say, like St Augustine who confessed that he knew what time was until he began to think about it. Philosophy seems to be one of those primordial things by which we are all tinctured, of which we cannot get rid however hard philosophers themselves have tried, and of which the most varied, and at times, the most fantastic ideas have been entertained.
>
> Perhaps the reason for this is that philosophy is so eminently concerned with itself. Physics is not primarily concerned with itself but with bodies, mathematics with the abstract properties of figures and numbers, rather than with themselves. When they got worried about themselves they share the embarrassment and become philosophical. Philosophical thought must ask itself what philosophical thought is. Thought about thought becomes philosophical thought. And the fact that the nature of thought is itself a problem suggests that the problem is insoluble. (*Persons* 1)

This view of his discipline could rightfully be claimed to reflect the outcome of a career in teaching and research in philosophy (he gave the inaugural address after more than three decades at the University of Cape Town, shortly before his retirement). But we have to recognise it for what it is. First, these words are not a rejection of philosophy, but a philosophical position – the remainder of his inaugural address shows this clearly. It is the fruit of many years of hard work. Second, this position requires continued exploration and examination, as is unambiguously witnessed by the fact that he kept writing until very late in life. Versfeld is, as he later claims of the mystics, "talkative" (*ACCG* 25), because he wants to acquire and share wisdom.

Understanding this position requires inspection of his books. Or at least of Versfeld as their author. And hence we take another step back to the first chapter of the 1960 volume *The Mirror of Philosophers*, entitled, "Wherein this book looks at itself":

> I happen to be a South African of bourgeois and peasant origins, with a fair education, a bald head, and the usual crop of financial worries, family felicities, political headaches, and duties obstructive to writing with which the human race is pretty generally acquainted. I have no interest in writing a book to prove that I haven't a body, or that marriage is miserable, or that philosophy has nothing to do with the emotions. I want to present a book which is philosophical precisely in being somewhat autobiographical, and somewhat disjointed because I am a human being, interested in being, and somewhat involved in my own. Only thus can I hope to achieve an objective unity of presentation. I shall then be in the illustrious company of Plato and Kierkegaard, who didn't pretend to finish what they hadn't, and of St Thomas, who had the grace to say at the end of his life that the *Summa* looked like rubbish to him. Further, I can but I won't write in the language of those who would like to pretend that they have never read a modern detective novel. After all, philosophy is partly an attempt to tear the mask from the criminal at our own hearts. We have to do with an inside job, a being indoors. Life and writing is clues and vestiges.
>
> I am therefore going to tell you how I came to hold certain things, and when I said them, and this in the contingent form in which I said them. I shall do this by sometimes prefacing a section with an account of its *raison d'être*, not with any hope of achieving the unity of a system, but rather with the intention of confessing the imperfect unity of a life. I have something to say not because I am a noumenal ego or the spokesman of the Idea, but because I am a man with a name and a telephone number. I want to speak as a South African, because only thus have I anything to say of any general interest. (*MP* 2–3)

We learn something quite essential from this: the autobiographical dimension of his work[9] – the extension of which is his very recognisable style – is not a redundant addition or stroke of self-indulgence. It is the mark of an author who knows himself to be situated and knows that he has something to contribute to the treasure of human wisdom only insofar as he is willing to think through his own particularity. That this is stated upfront, in a book in which Versfeld confronts his own reception of the "perennial order"[10] with the most important philosophers of his day, says a lot. It is not a celebration (or a denigration) of his own person, it is simply his primary orientation in the domain of speculative thought. Or as I will explain below, he attempted to write about the truth from where he was (see Chapter 5).

Now, it is essential to understand that this point of orientation is not at all an unmovable basis of certainty. On the contrary, in "Descartes and Me. Truth and Things" (*Sum* 13–24), the essay of intellectual autobiography of the same year as *The Mirror of Philosophers* (1960), Versfeld describes his own development as a departure from the Cartesian certainty of a thinking ego – his doctorate and first book having been *An Essay on the Metaphysics of Descartes*[11] – and a turn to the bewildering question that he is to himself. Augustine's words, repeatedly cited by Versfeld, "I became a great puzzle to myself" (*Sum* 16, similarly *Sum* 221), captures this central point of orientation to an uncertainty or a not-knowing. By placing his own thought in this Augustinian spirit after a tradition that remains true to the foundational metaphysics of Descartes and his successors, Versfeld became a "post-modern" philosopher (*Sum* 20) in a sense quite different from Lyotard.[12] As he says elsewhere: "One can't be modern unless one isn't" (*MP* 5).

In this line of inquiry, starting in the mystery that one is to oneself, we have to understand Versfeld's interest in philosophical anthropology "as first

---

[9] I say "dimension" because, apart from evidently autobiographical passages like those cited, he relates his own experiences and activities on many pages. *Klip en klei* and *Food for Thought* abound in examples.
[10] The metaphysical order – mysteries and all – of human, cosmic and divine existence.
[11] On this subject of a critique of the Cartesian ego, see especially *An Essay on the Metaphysics of Descartes*, 165–170.
[12] See also *PO* 205 where, speaking in 1954, Versfeld considers it "clear that the 'modern period' is drawing to a close". (Besides, I am not sure that this typological simplification would convince a good scholar of Descartes.)

philosophy".¹³ This primacy of reflecting the human is echoed in a number of the titles of his books, notably *Our Selves, Persons* or *Sum* (*I am*). Connecting a certain kind of philosophy with the peculiarities of his own existence paved the way to an examination of the conflicting forces at work in each person and likewise in each kind of "person writ large", such as societies and civilisations (*PP* 70): the real, mysterious, vulnerable, generous self versus its dominating, subjugating and grabbing deformations. But the relation between these two possibilities remain a puzzle, the "clues and vestiges" (as in the citation above) of which require painstaking examination. The self-assured claim to know the first self may already be a first act of collaboration with the second.

3. Genre – Or, how to do things with words

As is evident from Versfeld's self-presentations, he considered himself a philosopher. Factually, he was obviously a university professor of that discipline. Yet, we would do well not to hastily conclude that his writings form a uniform block of philosophical reflection. This has to be questioned in different ways over the course of this section of the chapter. I start with the question of genre and discursive strategy.

Two of Versfeld's books can safely be classified as non-philosophical. *Die berge van die Boland* (*The Mountains of the Boland*) (1947), a book on mountaineering in the Western Cape region, written with W.A. de Klerk, and *Die buitelewe* (*Life Outdoors*) (1970), which, like the first, is a practical guide on how to make the best of expeditions in nature. They may be non-philosophical, but they provide some background of Versfeld's concern for nature, or "creation" as he would often prefer to say, and ecology.

Forming a bridge to his philosophical writings is *Klip en klei* (*Stone and Clay*) (1968) – one of his most popular books. As the table of contents reveals, this book contains descriptions and ruminations on house building, angling, carpentry and hunting – scenes from country or holiday life. But the book ends with a critical essay on patriotism in which many central themes of his philosophy

---

[13] "Philosophy ought to start with anthropology in the Continental use of the term. What comes first is not theory of knowledge, but the problem of the being of man [*sic*]" (*OS* 2nd ed. 74.). This idea has been advanced more recently by Ernst Tugendhat, "Anthropologie als 'erste Philosophie,'" in *Anthropologie statt Metaphysik*. (Munich: Beck, 2007), 34–54.

and religious convictions are mobilised. This book also makes apparent Versfeld's predilection for the form of the essay.

In fact, a close inspection of his major publications quickly reveals this. Versfeld's only monograph in the strict sense is his published doctoral dissertation, *An Essay on the Metaphysics of Descartes* (published in 1940). He made some effort to consolidate the unity of his 1954 *The Perennial Order*. However, as one advances through this book the difference in argumentative approach (either philosophical or theological) becomes striking, and each chapter could well be read on its own. This is even more the case in *The Mirror of Philosophers* (1960), and thereafter Versfeld simply embraced the genre of the essay.

As we saw above, Versfeld argued in 1960 for an explicit correspondence of thought and form: if his thought emanates from his "disjointed" (*MP* 2) life, then his thought naturally will take on a somewhat disjointed form. But this self-stylisation of his reflective work, as announced in *The Mirror of Philosophers*, does not even determine the form of that same book until the last chapters, and in the later books even this urge to provide an apology, "in which the book looks at itself", is abandoned. In short, in the bulk of his work, Versfeld presents as an essayist.

Even so, one has to distinguish between different genres of his work. On the basis of different epistemic orientations, one can identify reflections of theological nature next to, and sometimes intertwined with, his philosophical work (more will be said about this below, §4). His philosophical work consists of introductions, translations, historical work (more on these later, §5) and independent reflections – of which some are more technical and others more playful.

One should not be fooled into taking instances of apparently light-hearted prose as merely directing his thought to a broader readership. The celebration of beauty in descriptive passages or in poetic exclamations, the condensation of connections in the form of aphoristic-like claims, his surprising connection of apparently disparate things, and recourse to humour comprise the fibre of his textual practices, of his persuasive strategies, without being reducible to either philosophical or theological reasoning. Thus, before writing off these texts as essays for mere amusement, one first has to ponder. How many ways are there of convincing people? Whom did he want to convince of what? And why would a philosopher of his erudition, as demonstrated in his more voluminous works, bother to write in these other ways?[14]

---

[14] Cf. *KK* 42: "Perhaps there is some similarity between poets and philosophers, or rather, some

My hunch is that this writing practice was informed by a lot of hard thinking about the meaning of his own practice and context. This resulted in a host of finer persuasive strategies, which requires the critical sceptic not to read such texts only through the logician's lens, but also with the analytical tools and sensitivity of scholars of literature. And then, on another level, many of these later essays may simply be read for the fun.

With this first glimpse of the textual kaleidoscope of Versfeld's writing behind us, let us turn to another aspect thereof, the theological.

4. Theology: A portrait of the philosopher as an odd fish

> That men ignorant in all arts, without rhetoric, logic, or grammar, plain fishers, should be sent by Christ into the sea of this world, only with the nets of faith, and draw such an innumerable multitude of fishes of all sorts, so much the stranger, in that they took many rare philosophers!
> (Augustine, cited in *GCG* 126 and *KK* 79)

Although the pervasiveness of Christian ideas in Versfeld's thought would not appeal to all readers, one should not precipitately reach the verdict that this preoccupation is philosophically untoward.[15] The first reason to reserve judgement is because a part of the society for which he wrote has been, and even today remains, attached to the Christian faith. Given the fact that Versfeld, insofar as he spoke as a Christian to that society, strove for both an informed articulation and a critical view of that faith, I am not sure from which position one could require

---

philosophers, since some of them just want to obscure [*vertroebel*] language, while others want to make their language so clear and unambiguous that they have nothing to say, because the things that are worthwhile to speak about are obscure [*duister*]."

[15] One should recall here Alain de Libera's insight that the "Christian" Middle Ages may have tolled the bell for the ancient philosophical schools, but did not do so before they stuck the epithet "philosophy", inherited from those schools, to Christ and to the love of God and by so doing paved the way for a thousand years of transmission and appropriation of ancient philosophy by Christian theologians. See De Libera's inaugural address at the Collège de France, "Où va la philosophie médiévale? *Leçon inaugurale prononcée le jeudi 13 février 2014*" (Paris: Collège de France, 2014), https://books.openedition.org/cdf/3634, § 18 [last access 20 May 2020]. This is not to underplay the importance of the Islamic transmission, the influence of which on later mediaeval Europe is consistent with both De Libera's claim and Versfeld's own religious openness.

his rigorous abstinence from speaking his believer's mind in philosophical texts. (Neither would I, contrariwise, know on which basis one could compel people of religious persuasion to do their coming-out in philosophical writing. But that is another question.) This leads directly to a second – in my view, decisive – reason, which is that it would be an act of violent ingratitude to discard summarily a form of thought that provided the light in which the author made accurate judgements in dark times (see the section on apartheid below, §6, and Chapter 3, §3 on forms of sociopolitical violence more generally).

It seems to me much more judicious to distinguish from the outset two possible *readings* of Versfeld's work – namely, one with theological intent (which would include his philosophical argumentation) and one with a narrower, philosophical intent (in which the significance of theological ideas will have to be assessed on a case-by-case basis). Admittedly, this distinction is a creation – a gargoyle? – of my own making, and I am not sure that it would have sat well with Versfeld. But it has the advantage of fending off the incorrect impression that one may enter the land of Versfeld's thought only on a visa of faith. As true as it is that Versfeld (at least in his earlier work) subscribed to the oneness of human intelligence and could thus accommodate a happy cohabitation of philosophy and theology, he made it equally clear that when he philosophised, he made an appeal to public reason (throughout his work from *GA* onwards; this question is explicitly dealt with in *MP* ch. 7). In my reading, I will recognise his theological thought, while aiming to offer a philosophical interpretation. In this way, I leave it to the religiously gifted and the religiously tone-deaf[16] readers to decide for themselves what is to be done with Versfeld's theological voice.

If we now spread open the philosopher's texts in front of us, we can only be struck by the gradual, but persistent, change of attitude with respect to faith reflected in them. To appreciate Versfeld's thought, one has to be sensitive to the variations in his intimate convictions. Let me briefly comment the range of shadings.

We know that he was brought up in a Calvinist home, but that he stopped practising religion during his student years (cf. De Klerk 1983, 178; *Sum* 14; Chapter 1, above). A major event was his encounter with his Glasgow supervisor, Archibald Bowman, whom Versfeld praises as a creative, Christian philosopher. In the dissertation on Descartes's metaphysics, which Versfeld completed at

---

[16] This image is taken from Max Weber (his expression was "religiös unmusikalisch"). Cf. Dirk Kaesler, "Religiös unmusikalisch. Anmerkungen zum Verhältnis von Jürgen Habermas zu Max Weber," *literaturkritik.de* 6 (June 2009), https://literaturkritik.de/id/13142 [last access 20 May 2020].

that time, there is not much about religious conviction – only commentary on Descartes's metaphysical God-talk. Yet, in the critical conclusion of this book, the appearance of names such as Thomas Aquinas and Jacques Maritain hints at the turn that its author was to complete on return to South Africa. Marthinus Versfeld became indeed an odd fish: an Afrikaans[17] Catholic. There are places in the world where being Catholic may be the traditionalist way of least resistance. The least one can say is that South Africa, and in particular the Afrikaans section of it in the 1940s, was not one of them.

Only after *An Essay on the Metaphysics of Descartes* did Versfeld burst forth with the fervour of a neophyte. The result is found in the 1948 book *Oor gode en afgode* (*On Gods and Idols*), which will be examined in detail in Chapter 3. Neither here, nor in the other books into the 1960s, does Versfeld shy away from including apologetics in his philosophy. As far as its theological voice is concerned, the first book emphasises more the sociopolitical significance of the community of believers (e.g., its anti-imperialism, anti-discrimination). On the other hand, *The Perennial Order* (1954) and *The Mirror of Philosophers* (1960) are more bent on clarifying the metaphysical basis and character of theological claims.[18] In this regard, his allies are not Luther, Kierkegaard or Chestov, but Kolbe, Newman, Chesterton and, of course, Augustine and Aquinas.

But from the 1960s, one notices a gradual easing of the tone and a growing porosity to other religious traditions (which, nevertheless, can be found in his very early texts). When, in *Our Selves* (1979), he hits back at "some superficial fools who write books on apologetics" (cf. *OS* 2nd ed. 248), it is not sure that his own earlier self can dodge that blow. And as if to inflict the *coup de grâce*, he later insists that "there are works of Catholic apologetics of the very recent past which claim to provide all the answers, falling very far short of the wisdom of the sage in Chuang-tzu (22.1) who said: 'We come nowhere being near right, since we have the answers'" (*ACCG* 18).

The result is a serious ambiguity that hovers over every joyful statement of faith. And Versfeld fully realised this – for example, when he expressed in frustration that

---

[17] To be sure, the relation between Afrikaans and English in the man himself was more complex than this simple statement. For those readers who don't know, the dominant religious orientation among Versfeld's Afrikaans contemporaries was Calvinism of Dutch stock.

[18] For the relation between faith and reason, see e.g., *MP* 244–247; *GCG* 14, republished in *ACCG* 40.

> [t]o be a Christian cannot possibly mean to conform to a type or to coincide with the paradigm case. And if you are asked by anybody with such an idea in the back of his mind, whether you are a Christian, it is intensely embarrassing. You may say no, not because you are Judas, but because you are trying not to be. (*OS* 2nd ed. 111)

This ambiguity in his mind must have been picked up fairly early by others, because he was invited to address the "Heretics Club" of the University of Cape Town, an event about which he reports in *The Mirror of Philosophers* (*MP* 14 and *MP* chapter 3).[19]

The bridge between the two extremities of his outlook seems to be the changing articulation of the relation between the secular (in the sense of the ordinary or mundane) and the miraculous. Versfeld hints at this when, quite late in his life, he claimed that "[t]he secular is the miraculous" (*FT* 89). The curious path by which he came to this conviction will occupy us later (cf. Chapter 10, §4). Looking from this pinnacle over the changing landscape of his earlier thought, this statement could, earlier in his career, reflect his views on a metaphysical aesthetics of the whole of reality; later on, this opens to an aesthetic view of life with a negative theological twist. The contemporary reader has to remain attentive to this ambiguity stuck, as it were, between secularising the sacred and sacralising the secular.

But even then, the last word has not been spoken, because there remains another climax of his self-reflexive irony: "True religion finds itself comic" (*PP* 91), he claimed with pontifical certainty. And to hammer home the point he confessed:

> I think I can understand why Chesterton could say that the Fall of Man was funny, and why I was once moved to say that the Redemption is excruciatingly funny. What could be more absurd than spiking God to a tree, or God dirtying his nappies? It is a sign of love that we find the loved one absurd. (*PP* 92)

Having given an impression of how Versfeld spoke to the theological ear, let us now turn to the different keys of his philosophical voice.

---

[19] The original is in the UCT Archive, folder 134.

5. Polyphony of philosophy: Introductions, liberal translations, historical work

Reports have it that Versfeld was an excellent and appreciated lecturer.[20] It is true that his published work reflects a continuous pedagogical concern. Nothing is further from his intention than mystification. Most of the time, at least. His writings are alive with the desire to clarify debate, with respect for student and colleague alike, with love for the subject, with desire for truth and insight, with faith in human reason within its limits; all these point to the importance of extending philosophical discussion to new authors and presenting older ones in an accessible way to young philosophers.

This generous spirit animates many of his publications. *Rondom die Middeleeue* (*On the Middle Ages*) is an introduction to themes of mediaeval thought and intellectual and cultural life. Versfeld's lifelong love for Plato is reflected in an introduction and translation of the *Symposium*[21] and an introductory companion to the *Republic*.[22] Later, he tried his hand at a liberal translation of Lao Tzu's *Tao Te Ching*.[23] One can hardly fail to note that the majority of Versfeld's writings that were originally published in Afrikaans are of an introductory nature, and conversely, the majority of his translations and introductions are in Afrikaans.[24] But this is no rule, since one has to add to this list of introductory works *A Guide to the City of God* (1958),[25] *St Augustine's Confessions and City of God* (1990)

---

[20] See for instance Jane Carruthers, "Men in my (historical) life," *Historia* 52, vol. 2 (2007): 269–272, here 270–271.

[21] Marthinus Versfeld, *Plato. Die simposium of die drinkparty* (Cape Town: Buren, 1970).

[22] Marthinus Versfeld, *'n Handleiding tot die Republiek van Plato* (Cape Town: Buren, 1974).

[23] Marthinus Versfeld, *Die lewensweg van Lao-Tse* (Cape Town: Perskor, 1988). This rendering is quite liberal, because knowing no classical Chinese, he had to base this "translation" on other translations.

[24] At this point, I can observe a peculiar fact. In his second overview of Afrikaans philosophy, the disgraced A.H. Murray has a short discussion of Versfeld's work. See "Die Afrikaanse se wysgerige denke," in *Kultuurgeskiedenis van die Afrikaner*, ed. P. de V. Pienaar (Cape Town: Nationale Boekhandel, [1947] 1968) 183–189, here 186. However, in Pieter Duvenage's *Afrikaanse filosofie* (Bloemfontein: SUN Press, 2016), Versfeld is named in the orienting first chapter (and implied to be an Afrikaans philosopher), without substantial attention given to him in the rest of the book. Neither author contemplates the meaning of the use of English in the majority of Versfeld's (academically, at least) most important studies.

[25] This book is still cited as an authoritative reference by Christoph Horn, "Augustinus, De civitate Dei (ca. 413–427)," in *Geschichte des politischen Denkens. Ein Handbuch*, 4th edition, ed. Manfred Brocker (Frankfurt-am-Main: Suhrkamp, [2006] 2012).

(a curious combination of renewal and reprise of the 1958 book, which will be discussed in Chapter 10, §1), as well as the translation of Hulsbosch's *God's Creation*.[26] Furthermore, Versfeld had an explicit objective to introduce Eastern wisdom to South African readers, while appropriating it in his own thought. That is why there will be a chapter devoted to this matter later in this book (cf. Chapter 6). Finally, stretching beyond the more philosophical texts are other works of initiation, namely the guides to the outdoors (mentioned above[27]) and a not-unphilosophical book on cooking, *Food for Thought* (1983).

As one may expect, a lot of Versfeld's historical and introductory work is centred on mediaeval thinkers. He puts this scholarly interest of his into perspective by explaining that studying mediaeval culture in general

> is easier now than it would have been two generations ago. Recent scholarship has shown that the obscurity of the Dark Ages has existed chiefly in the minds of their detractors. It has been the better assured of a hearing now that it is becoming abundantly clear that the "modern period" is drawing to a close, so that we, increasingly detached from its fundamental motives, can more clearly see its nature and origins. (*PO* 205)

Whereas *The Perennial Order* is not presented as a study of mediaeval thought on which Versfeld draws, the book evidently is constructed on it (as is witnessed by the aforementioned *A Guide to the City of God* and *Rondom die Middeleeue*). As prevalent as the desire to introduce and initiate is throughout his work, one should again remain circumspect. Take Versfeld's last book,[28] *St Augustine's Confessions and City of God*, again as an example: it contains as many retractions of the author's previous points of view as it introduces ideas from his own later philosophy, for example, comparisons and borrowings from Eastern wisdom or remouldings of his ideas on science and theology. In short, there is at least as much Versfeld as Augustine in it. And what a reviewer wrote about *A Guide to the City of God* captures quite accurately what Versfeld strove for in his reception of Augustine and *mutatis mutandis* other philosophers too:

---

[26] Ansfried Hulsbosch, *God's Creation: Creation, Sin and Redemption in an Evolving World*, trans. Martin Versfeld (London and Melbourne: Sheed and Ward, [1963] 1965).
[27] Marthinus Versfeld and W.A. de Klerk, *Die berge van die Boland* (Stellenbosch: Kosmo, [1947] 1965) and Marthinus Versfeld, *Die buitelewe* (Cape Town: Buren, 1970).
[28] *Sum* was published a year later, but is a collection of works published earlier.

> One can perhaps best characterize Mr Versfeld's approach by contrasting it with that of a historian. Roughly speaking, the main difference is that Mr Versfeld writes as one who himself knows what Augustine is talking about, while the historian must write as one who knows only what Augustine and his contemporaries say.[29]

In light of his critique of modernity – that will occupy us below (cf. Chapter 3, §§3 and 5, Chapter 5 and Chapter 7, §2) – expositions of modern philosophers were essential to the thesis he was arguing.[30] We have already seen that Versfeld's first book, the published version of his thesis, was a work on the metaphysics of Descartes.[31] Rousseau is taken as a major opponent in *Oor gode en afgode*, Marx[32] in *Beweging uitwaarts* and *Persons* (1972). His most important book in this respect is *The Mirror of Philosophers*, which contains longer expositions on and debates with numerous modern and contemporary authors, including Comte, Darwin, Dostoyevsky, Eddington, Feuerbach, Hegel, Heidegger, Hobbes, Hume, Kant, Kierkegaard, Marx, Nietzsche, Rousseau, Sartre and Spinoza (but also with Socrates, Plato and Aristotle). A surprising companion and opponent is Nietzsche. At least one of Versfeld's earliest lecture series at the University of Cape Town was on Nietzsche,[33] and it is striking how frequently Versfeld sides with him – perhaps contrary to what one would have expected. This is the reason for the chapter devoted specifically to the relation between the two philosophers (cf. Chapter 6).

But his work in the history of philosophy was not motivated only by polemics. There is a form of modernity that Versfeld did not reject; in fact, he learned it from Aquinas and tried to practise that lesson:

---

[29] F. Edward Cranz, "Reviewed Work(s): *A Guide to the City of God* by Marthinus Versfeld," *Speculum* 34, vol. 4 (1959): 696–697, here 697.
[30] This is described in "Descartes & me. Truth and things," *Sum* 13–24.
[31] It is quite remarkable that Routledge republished the book three quarters of a century later: Marthinus Versfeld, *An Essay on the Metaphysics of Descartes* (London: Routledge, [1940] 2016).
[32] On Versfeld's reading of Marx, see Andrew Nash, *The Dialectical Tradition in South Africa* (London: Routledge, 2009), 161–164.
[33] Cf. manuscripts in UCT Archive, file 60. When working on this material, I had the impression that it dated from the late 1930s. Regrettably, it was not possible to pursue an inquiry into this matter. It is certainly from before 1951.

> Philosophy is a way of being in the present, and what impresses one about St Thomas is his modernity. He knew the ancients but he also read and assimilated all the newest stuff. The man who is like St Thomas, analogically speaking, is not the man who, against the saint's own warning, has been bludgeoned by his authority, but your man who is up in Hume, and Kant, and Nietzsche and Heidegger, and who speaks to his contemporaries in a manner relevant to their experience. (*MP* 256–257)

Hence, Versfeld thought it was constructive to debate authors whose approaches or conclusions he did not share. Knowing that he would completely reject the work of Leon Chestov, he still presents the longest chapter of *The Mirror of Philosophers* as "a small service [of] making [Chestov] more available" (*MP* 220). Likewise, he does not hesitate to declare his proximity to phenomenology where relevant. But when he agreed, he also incorporated and this is true for any philosophy he may have studied. He had a critical mind and did not shy away from making fun of what he rejected in philosophy, but overall he was a generous and grateful reader.

6. Apartheid and other empiresque behaviour

As is the case with each of the aforementioned aspects of Versfeld's work, one has to remain cautious in characterising its political side. The reader who searches here for a theory of democracy or of representation, an elaboration on protest and violence in politics, explanations of how people tend to relate to others as friends or foes, or a treatise on the emancipatory virtues of discursive rationality[34] will be disappointed. Versfeld once designed a book that would have been called *Towards an Existential Political Philosophy*,[35] but this project was abandoned. However, one would miss the target by a wide margin if one concludes that we are dealing with a unworldly celebrator of private life.[36] The same turn away from a bodiless *cogito* to a situated human (discussed above) brought Versfeld

---

[34] But see Versfeld's discourse ethics, *MP* ch. 7.
[35] The complete typescript of this book is in the UCT Archive, file 68.
[36] I am formulating just the reverse side of Andrew Nash's legitimate description of the limits of Versfeld as political thinker – cf. Andrew Nash, *The Dialectical Tradition in South Africa*, 163.

thoroughly under the impression of the sociopolitical situatedness of people. The same authors with whose help he started to explore this fundamental fact also helped him to appreciate the stakes of the world in which he lived. The result is a philosophy in which sociopolitical concerns are discussed in numerous chapters and, by the way, all of the chapters of *Towards an Existential Political Philosophy* were published elsewhere.

In the following chapters, a number of elements of his social and political thought will be examined. Allow me to serve them in concentrated form, as an aperitif. Early on already Versfeld recognised the vanity of unqualified praise of Western modernity. His work is marked by a critique of modernity, of modern societies, of modern modes of relation between people and between people and the natural environment. It was not too difficult to find support for this critical view in the monstrous history of the Second World War. However, he considered the imperial desire to endure much longer (throughout modern history) and reach further; in fact, in particular as far as the southernmost tip of Africa.

Correspondingly, his work is permeated with implicit and explicit references to the ambient political system that was contemporaneous with nearly his whole writing life. Apartheid society is unambiguously diagnosed as "a racialist capitalism exacerbated by our industrial and technological revolution, which justifies itself by a scriptural literalism" (*Persons* 11). Yet, Versfeld was not a writer of anti-apartheid tracts, and he never drafted a systematic exploration of the constitutive and factual violence of this system. His critique of the apartheid state is intricately enmeshed with other elements of social critique and his aforementioned broad critical view of Western civilisation. This is the reason why his opposition to apartheid appears in many guises. Often, it is mentioned almost in passing. Elsewhere, as in the early *Oor gode en afgode*, his critique is more to the point (cf. Chapter 3, §3). Sometimes it is the overall "logic" of racial discrimination that is exposed, but sometimes he ironises about the details of apartheid legislation. Let me illustrate this variety of critical approach with two examples.

In an essay on "Our Rapist Society", his irony takes aim at the racial separation of residential areas and forced removals. The trigger is the evacuation of District Six[37] in Cape Town, but we see how it is linked to a broader social critique:

---

[37] A mixed residential area from which inhabitants were forcefully removed during the later 1960s to the early 1980s.

What was Versfeld doing when he was doing philosophy? 57

> Our big-money economy has been a waste economy, resting on the rape of nature. You cannot waste nature without wasting man, and you cannot rape nature without raping man. That should be the basic consideration of the conservationist.
>
> Perhaps this is the point at which I should advert to the rape of District Six, part of which is to be devoted to a technikon,[38] so necessary to the maintenance of the rapist society. District Six is divided from the Foreshore[39] by a road curiously called a freeway. One wonders on which side freedom lies. Like many other lovers of Cape Town I feel strongly about the Foreshore development. In fact it has come to look to me like the creation of the non-city, the scene of our cannibal revels. [...] Well, death is already creeping upon the Foreshore by the shifting of home-life elsewhere. The shops have lost customers because the latter have been apartewoonbuurted[40] elsewhere. The well-padded mausoleum of the Nico Malan[41] has, by the freeway, been separated from one of Cape Town's main centres of humanity, humour and drama: District Six. People were living there, and death couldn't bear the sight of it. (*PP* 34–35)

This text is rather typical of the associative form of thinking found in many of the later texts. But one could find a systematically argued justification of the principles on the basis of which he rejected apartheid, such as in his paper "On Justice and Human Rights" of 1960. His plea concludes as follows:

> If these rights belong to every man whatever his race and colour and by virtue solely of his being made for the truth, their preservation is the due of every man to every man. This prescribes that the means employed may not include trickery, outrage, lies or robbery. Justice is colour-blind, and requires for its realisation that we should see, beyond the contingencies of biology and history the image of truth in every man, which often in spite of himself is striving for expression in a common world. These contingencies are relevant as the material in which justice must be realised. But one could make no greater mistake than to mistake

---

[38] Cape Technikon, later renamed Cape Peninsula University of Technology.
[39] A part of Cape Town developed on land claimed by pushing back the natural shoreline.
[40] A verbal neologism from "aparte woonbuurte" – i.e., racially separated residential areas.
[41] The Nico Malan Theatre Centre (renamed the Artscape Theatre Centre) was opened in the 1970s as the seat of the Cape Performing Arts Board and premier performing arts centre in the region.

the matter for the form, that is, to give justice a racial expression instead of giving race a just expression. This applies impartially to black, white, and yellow since as justice is man's universal due, the doom of injustice done also works impartially upon all. What we have to do with is a law of human nature which extends to its metaphysical roots. It is a prescription to human wills before it is a prescription by them, and as such is as unalterable as the law of gravity.[42]

More about this will be said later in the book (cf. especially Chapter 3, §3 and Chapter 10, §§2, 5 and 7). The same intellectual tools that help him to dissect apartheid also serve to examine other social pathologies: interpersonal violence, exploitation, discrimination and environmental destruction.

7. A note on celebration

Yet, Versfeld's view is limited neither to critique nor to an articulation of despair. We find a major line of his thought that is devoted to celebrating that which is threatened. Hence, the pervasive tension that is characteristic of his work: the tension between joy and disquiet, to which I refer in the Preface. We find a celebration of individual singularity coupled with the critique of political injustice, a lauding of nature as the flip side of his critique of ecological destruction, a call to creative action in the service of others amid a view of social decay (on decay, see Chapter 7, §2; on celebration, see Chapter 10, §§4 and 6).

8. On its most intimate lesson

Provided one takes the term "negative" in the sense it has in "negative theology", it would be accurate to claim that there is a strong current of the negative running through his work. For despite his concerted efforts to obtain insight and despite being quite "talkative" in his writing, there remains something thoroughly true to the Socratic spirit.

---

[42] Cf. Versfeld, "On justice and human rights," *Acta juridica* 1 (1960): 1–10, here 10.

This "something" we may call a negative anthropology, in the sense that the central question of understanding ourselves starts with, and reverts to, an unfathomable mystery.

Likewise, there is something negative in his theological voice, as can be heard in the following train of thought:

> St Thomas could rise to saying that his writings looked to him like stable litter. I know of no Papal pronouncements declaring them to be stable litter. On the contrary, they come to be imposed as the correct word game. Thus we get Thomists and Augustinians and Advaitins, and – God help us! – Christians. (*ACCG* 26)[43]

There is something "negative" about his celebration of life, as one can read in a moving passage of his last years:

> I spent this morning tidying. "Mucking out" would be more appropriate. My old study is just like my head: disordered and too much filled with the past although a stack of present-day paper floods me with the daily mail. [...] New books? They float past like leaves on a dam, pushed by the Northwind in autumn. Accounts and requests – O Lord!
>
> So well, muck out! Pull the wastepaper basket closer and stuff paper recklessly in it and just beware of the devils who stand ready to move into the clean house. A human being's normal conscience is like a river in which all kinds of things wash past: petals, rags, banana peels and the trembling reflections of the birds and the willows. It is one's own fleetingness and one has to learn to distance yourself from it and to deepen yourself in something below it.
>
> It occurs to me that I am moving on in years. The day will come when I will have to leave everything and step out of the room of the world. One has to leave a few things now, just for exercise. To untie yourself from things is a good old advice. Otherwise they depart on their own, and that is what hurts. If you throw away the Bible too in

---

[43] And this is not only a trick of his last days. Elsewhere, he referred to Aquinas, who "said of his greatest work: *Mihi videtur ut palea*. He said this after he was illuminated by mystic insight and it is usually translated as: this looks to me like chaff. What did he mean by chaff? *Palea* would be called *Mist* in German, that means the straw that is placed in a stable to make it easier to remove everything again. There is a German expression: *Du redest Mist*, which refers to this kind of straw and it is this kind of straw that a Mediaeval monk would have had in mind. We have to return to the stable where the Word was born" (*KK* 26).

> the basket, it may be the proof that you have learned its most intimate lesson. If you arrive at the gates of heaven with the Bible clutched in both hands, you may perhaps not be able to ring the bell. One can touch the new life only with open hands. (*NA* 2nd ed. 29–30)

Finally, there is something "negative" in his own writing, of which the increasingly playful prose is no accidental expression. Indeed, he would drive a playful irony against himself in an un-Augustinian kind of confession: "I have fought a long duel with seriousness. That is why there is no need to take me seriously" (*PP* 90).

9. Conclusion

In this chapter, I hope to have illustrated the complexity of the work of Martin Versfeld – diverse in its foundations and discursive practice, driven by an eagerness to learn and advance and by a generous impulse to share. How his difficult combination of joy and disquiet found philosophical expression in the dark times of South African history, will studied in detail in the following chapters.

STUDIES

CHAPTER 3

SELF-KNOWLEDGE AND PRACTICAL REASON IN A TIME OF POLITICAL MADNESS

This chapter is an interpretation of Versfeld's early book, *Oor gode en afgode* (*On Gods and Idols*) (1948). The aim of the chapter is to reconstruct the most important arguments of the five separate essays in the book and to explain the relations between them. The golden thread of philosophy of practice and political philosophy is highlighted and exposed together with the central notion of the "practical reason" (prudence, or *prudentia*). I will explain how the notion of "incarnation" subtends prudence and how the entire complex, through the formation of "self-knowledge", contributes to the orientation of a person in the world. For the young Versfeld, this orientation stands in tension between the decay of Western civilisation and the urgency to respond to it with a radical ethics. The content of *Oor gode en afgode* is further interpreted by situating it within the broader development of Versfeld's work, by clarifying it with the (mostly) unpublished material from the Versfeld archive, and by commenting on some aspects of the existing history of the interpretation and reception of the book. Although the main aim of the chapter is to clarify the content, in conclusion a number of lines of questioning for further critical reading of the book are suggested.

1. Introduction: Self-knowledge in a period of political madness

Oor gode en afgode is a book of dramatic intensity. The entire text is characterised by the tension between the decay of a particular form of cultural and political life and the urgent necessity of taking a decision regarding a new orientation to life:

> The urgency of our times and all-encompassing effect of current events on each one of us forces us to make a personal choice. Which kind of behaviour has more value: to destroy or to be destroyed? To regard your neighbour first and foremost as a fellow human being, or as an enemy? To suppress your intelligence and humaneness for the sake of victory, or not? You cannot avoid the choice. (*GA* 99–100, also 71, 103)

This discussion of destruction, neighbours and enemies, and humaneness in jeopardy must immediately be heard with the morbid resonance given to it by the political catastrophes of the twentieth century. If the author presents these events to encourage intense, renewed reflection on life and a resolute decision to orient one's life in a different direction, it is because he himself had already made this choice.

Versfeld, who had lost his sympathy with the church during his student years, developed a renewed interest in the Christian faith during his doctoral studies in Glasgow (until 1934) and during his first few years as a lecturer in philosophy at the University of Cape Town (from 1935). Anyone who reads *Oor gode en afgode* will be in no doubt that, given the exceptional historical events that humankind experienced during the twentieth century, the appropriate life choice, according to Versfeld, would be in favour of the Christian faith, and more specifically its Catholic variety. However, it should be equally clear to the reader that Versfeld's passionate criticism of culture and politics should not be seen as concerned with simplistic moral lessons; he takes issue with his era on a much more radical level. In a letter addressed to a certain Revd Conradie ten years before the publication of *Oor gode en afgode*, Versfeld wrote:

> It is quite terrifying that so much is said in Synod about mixed bathing, girls who smoke, the virtues and vices of the bioscope, and other more or less unimportant issues; but nothing is said about the fundamental philosophical concepts that are supposed to play a role in the development of our civilisation. The real dangers threatening

the Church go unnoticed. There is a painful lack of theological competence.¹

This fiery statement not only makes it possible for us, with regard to the idols mentioned in the title of the book, to immediately eliminate some of the "usual suspects", but also provides a clear indication of the register that Versfeld hopes to find in his book. The most stubborn problems have to be addressed at the most fundamental level – the level referred to in his letter as "the fundamental philosophical concepts that are supposed to play a role in the development of our civilisation". This concept-directed – or philosophical – approach is important because of a prevailing misplaced belief in a narrow segment of rationality that forms an integral part of the crisis. During a radio discussion on "War against superstition", which was broadcast on 18 March 1945, Versfeld explained:

> Blinded by the conviction that if we are "in favour of science" [*wetenskaplikgesind*], we are protected against the suspicion that there may be something basically wrong with our Western way of life. But the evils that had led to the two world wars and the atrocities committed during those wars cannot be regarded as the temporary sickness of a healthy body. How do we see the burning of witches compared to the lethal gassing of the Jews, or the *auto-da-fé*, compared to the liquidation of political opponents? The Socratic appeal to "know yourself" is once again accepted as valid and we ask ourselves whether we are not perhaps subject to an even greater extent than our fathers by misconceptions and superstitions. Is this period of development not perhaps a period of spiritual darkness? And is the war against superstition not perhaps a war against many of our most favourite convictions?²

Socrates's appeal, "Know yourself!", is the urgent appeal that Versfeld hears from the confusing times in which he writes. To know yourself, you have to know your era; you have to be aware of the convictions that you hold, which may have been handed down to you; you have to know which mental abilities you will use to

---

1   The letter, dated 30 August 1938, is kept in the Versfeld Collection in the Archive of the University of Cape Town Library (to which further references will be made as follows: UCT Archive, file 102, quotation from p. 11 of the letter). It is clear that at the time when he wrote this letter, Versfeld was already far removed from the Dutch Reformed Church in which he had grown up, but he had not yet joined the Catholic Church. He would eventually do this in 1943.
2   UCT Archive, file 107, quotation, p. 3.

respond to the Socratic appeal to improve your insight into yourself; you have to know the reasons for your personal decisions.

But what is the connection between this urgent appeal and "gods and idols"?

2. "Gods" and "idols"

Oor gode en afgode is a collection of five essays that were not originally preceded by an introduction. Nowhere does the author give us a clear idea of what the general theme or purpose is; rather, he wastes no time before he starts working. The confusing title is the only hint that the reader is given regarding the content.[3] I refer to the title as confusing, because the plural "gods" [*gode*] is often regarded as synonymous with "idols" [*afgode*]. What would we expect to find in a book titled *On Dogs and Hounds*? What is the meaning of the "and" in *On Gods and Idols* [*Oor gode en afgode*]? The reader will also notice that Versfeld postponed as long as possible explaining what he means with *idols*. Furthermore, if it is so important to talk about idols that they are mentioned twice in the title, it is strange that the first mention of a deity in the book is the reference to a God written resolutely with a capital letter and who exists only in the singular (*GA* 3). To complicate matters even further, in particular for those among our contemporaries for whom it has become difficult to count as far as this One, Versfeld still reminds his readers in the first chapter that, according to Augustine, "[w]hen you start counting the Trinity, you depart from the truth [...]. In a certain sense, it is not supposed to be reasonable [*redelik*[4]]" (*GA* 31). That it counts as reasonable whether a person utters the big three-letter word or not will be discussed later, but we cannot simply assume that all readers will have sympathy for the eradication of idols.

---

[3] In the foreword to a collection of essays titled *A Saraband of the Sons of God* (compiled in circa 1971), which was, however, never published in that format, Versfeld wrote: "I have always regarded the title of books as crucial. I have friends who write books and then struggle to find a title, but with me things work the other way round. I become enamoured of a title, and have no rest until I have constructed the book that belongs. This implies that the title has the validity of an image, and this immediately brings me into trouble with my fellow philosophers because they do not see the relevance of imagination to intellect" (UCT Archive, file 155). If this remark may be applied to *Oor gode en afgode*, from twenty years earlier, it might explain the obscure nature of the title.

[4] Probably "rational" is intended, because the term "reasonable" is reserved for a specific service – see discussion below.

In the case of gods and idols, we have a different situation: Versfeld is not only able to count them – there is a whole list of them throughout his book – but they lend themselves to normal, rational investigation. So important are these gods and idols and their whereabouts in Versfeld's assessment, that the title states that the book is about *them*.

One might well ask why Versfeld would choose the title *Oor gode en afgode* for a book that deals with something totally different – namely, the urgency of choosing a suitable way of life. Perhaps it was because it is only when we confront our idols that we become most aware of the urgency of the choice that needs to be made. This surmise becomes credible when we consider the fact that Versfeld's idols are not "mixed bathing", "girls who smoke", "the virtues and vices of the bioscope" or "other more or less unimportant issues" highlighted by a bigoted puritan cultural conservatism, but the glorification of one's own over-refined emotions[5] in politics (*GA* 54), certain states (*GA* 59), in particular the militarised nation state (*GA* 162), certain views on community (*GA* 78), the disproportionate desire for and love of certain things (*GA* 152ff.), and capitalism and the hoarding of money through the exploitation of others (*GA* 159). It should be noted that all Versfeld's idols are either political offences, or the supporting of social infringements. By giving his book the title *On Gods and Idols*, Versfeld agrees with Van Ockham: "[O]nly the first commandment is absolute; the others are occasional rules" (*GA* 55). All the other ethical principles are dwarfed or reduced to occasional rules by the command: "You shall not serve any of these socio-political gods before Me!"

---

[5] This claim is not clear. Versfeld's depiction of emotions in *Oor gode en afgode* is undeniably negative; however, it appears as if this negativity was motivated by his political concerns. An illustration of what he might have had in mind can be found in the letter he wrote to the editor of *Die Spantou* in August 1940, in which he expresses his disapproval of the Afrikaners' "self-adoration" and "self-pity", which he describes as idolatry (Letter in UCT Archive, file 19).

3. War, exploitation, racism. Critique of social and political violence

Although Versfeld, inspired by Augustine and Toynbee, views *gods* and *idols* together with *holiness* and *sin* as "fundamental historical concepts" (*GA* 150),[6] it is clear that, when referring to them, he has specific historical phenomena (rather than vague, moralising speculation) in mind. If one considers the era in world history during which this book was written (a period of approximately ten years prior to 1948), our initial impression of *idols* as a dull, world-foreign, fanatical term fades and we find ourselves in the midst of dramatic events on the international and national scenes that demand radical decisions about our attitude towards life.

Three aspects of this historical-political context of "the current political madness" (*GA* 64) deserve to be highlighted as excellent illustrations of the accuracy of Versfeld's critical insight.

1. On the reverse side of Versfeld's pronounced pacifism during World War II, we have the theme of *war*, which occurs throughout *Oor gode en afgode*. He had no illusions about the extensive and radical nature of war:

> Today a war can only be waged "successfully" by encouraging a totalitarian mental state of mind. This requires the abolition of democratic institutions, the censoring of news, the suspension of rational objectivity, free discussion of conscientious objections, the conscription of lives and properties, the increase in violence and fraud;

---

[6] In his unpublished autobiographical text, Versfeld states that "[i]n philosophy I have a preference for Plato, Augustine and Thomas [Aquinas], but for Augustine in particular. Our generation is saddled with the problems of time and history, and what Augustine taught me was the Christian interpretation of history and the role of the Church in the unfolding of time. These problems were greatly exacerbated by the war" ("Waarom ek Katoliek geword het ..." ["Why I Became a Catholic ..."], UCT Archive, file 59, p. 8). The exact date of this text is unknown. Parts of the text can be read in De Klerk, "Marthinus Versfeld: die man en sy denke". Following the death of Toynbee, whose thinking is described as neo-Augustinian (*GA* 134), Versfeld wrote a newspaper article about him, which included an important comment: "As mentioned many years ago in my booklet *Oor gode en afgode*, Toynbee should be counted among those who reacted to three centuries of Cartesian rationalism" ("*Toynbee het gesoek na die betekenis van die geskiedenis*" ["Toynbee searched for the meaning of history"], *Die Burger*, 27 October 1975, in UCT Archive, file 195. This is an implicit reference to *GA* 134).

in short, the heyday of exactly those attitudes that have the most destructive effect in a civilisation. To suggest that a war could be waged for the sake of civilisation is therefore contradictory. All wars diminish civilisation [*onbeskawend*]. Brutality can only be overthrown by acting in a way that shows the way to another world. (*GA* 102)

War is therefore more than an armed conflict *between* countries – the Second World War was a war waged *inside* different countries between a small and weak moral minority and the power of states that had replaced the conscience and the place occupied by God (*GA* 100). However, war is in fact only the explosion of the powers that are, under normal circumstances, boiling in the modern nation state. The direct relationship between the "national, centralised, all-powerful state" and "the atomic, independent individual" results in "a tendency to absorb the individua into the body of the state, which leads to the development of that strange modern beast, the conscripted, regimented person who joins the masses in their battle cry demanding freedom and self-expression."[7] Whence the urgency of a decision in favour of a way of life that can counteract this continuation of war by using different, non-violent means.

2. The urgency of the need to take such a decision features prominently in an equally central theme in *Oor gode en afgode*, namely Versfeld's concern about *exploitation*. His point of departure is that exploitation is the result of the fact that the accumulation of wealth has been made the highest good of a society (*GA* 73), and that this political fact has taken on the scope of a global imperialism (*GA* 71). Versfeld agrees with Plato when he points out that if the accumulation of material wealth is indeed the highest aspiration, all other things become subordinate to that aspiration. This necessarily means that the spiritual becomes subjected to the material, which results in some people being exploited by others. There are two forms of exploitation:

> First, the labour of some is exploited by others. They are treated like tools and their happiness, health, family relationships, etc. are either ignored, or treated with selfish premeditation. Second, their value as consumers is exploited. Consumers are encouraged to use those products that will ensure the maximum profit for their producers without giving any consideration to whether they will derive any real

---

[7] Quotations from pp. 1–3 of Versfeld's radio presentation titled "Die mens as sosiale wese" ("The Human Being as a Social Being") of 12 March 1944 (UCT Archive, file 107).

benefit from what they consume. The result is that the value of human life is generally diminished, which then leads to the recklessness which manifests itself in subsequent wars. (*GA* 73–4)

Thus the imperialist capture of nature with a view to its commercialisation gradually leads to the "exploitation of *human* nature, to man's alienation from himself, his denaturalisation in his own environment" (*GA* 129, also 88). In other words, it leads to the imperial conquest of the human being. For this reason, one cannot expect any modernist optimism about progress from Versfeld.

3. The exploitation and conquest of people, however, follow patterns according to which certain groups are largely on the receiving end. It is in this regard that we hear Versfeld speaking about *racism* in 1948:

> The whites accelerated their own exploitation through their exploitation of other races. Their ingenuity in the use of transport and explosives placed them in a position to use non-whites[8] as means for their own purposes. (*GA* 129)

According to Versfeld, this state of affairs can be explained by the narrowed understanding of human nature and the fatal linking of a race or nation to an inescapable destiny (*GA* 94); the temporarily contingent is elevated to become the decisive. In South Africa, however, racism is practised incoherently, as Versfeld asserted in a letter to the editor of *Die Burger* in 1939:

> To the lack of originality that forces us to imitate [*na te aap*] the German example to solve racial problems, we have to add the blindness that prevents us from seeing, with German clarity, that the oppression of the church is a logical accessory.[9]

In other words, those who purposefully maintain a consistent racist understanding of humankind and racist politics must necessarily view the Christian doctrine, according to which all people have intrinsic value, as a repulsive obstacle.

---

[8] At the time of writing, the term "non-white" still served as an alternative to racist phraseology.

[9] *Die Burger*, 13 January 1939 (quoted from the text in the UCT Archive, file 102, p. 2). This claim did not simply fall from the sky. A report titled "Germany – New Holy Land. 'ABC of the Heathen' Published", which appeared in the *Cape Times* on 11 February 1935, a cutting of which is preserved in the Versfeld archive (UCT Archive, file 195), relates the rise of an official Germanising paganism and the supersession of the Christian religion in Germany.

A decade later, during the first year of the National Party's "Christian National" rule, Versfeld insisted on the unavoidable tension, the "most radical difference" between nationalistic and Christian ethics. The latter is guided by

> a belief in the true unity of humankind: human beings have a common origin and a common purpose in God and may therefore not act in a way that suggests that they were not all created in His image. Therefore discrimination based on race, unilateral patriotism, participation in unjust wars, exploitation, etc. are sinful. (*GA* 97–8)[10]

While some readers of *Oor gode en afgode* might not like the terms *idols* and *sin*, the actuality – then and now – of what Versfeld touches upon here cannot be denied. Someone who does not believe that these three themes deserve our attention obviously does not have to read this book.

4. Urgency, time and incarnation

However, anyone who feels touched by the urgent appeal to address these types of violence (and others discussed in *Oor gode en afgode*) might want to reread what Versfeld says about *idols*. The reason for this can be found in both the theme of unjust subjection to violence (i.e., the three examples of "idols" discussed above) and the experience of a feeling of urgency. Realising the urgency of worrying questions is to be aware of the continuation of injustice and of the necessity to cling desperately to the existence of something valuable that is being threatened; it is being aware of the passing and loss of time; in short, it is taking *time* seriously. If one can accept this, and if the historical-political use of the term *idols* is borne in mind, it is easy to concede that "[i]dolatry is indeed an abuse of time, if we understand 'time' to refer to the succession of beings [*skepsels*]" (*GA* 150). Positively stated, this could read: "A person's duty during this existence is not to escape from time, but to develop a strong awareness of the urgency thereof – and never to misuse any of it" (*GA* 149).

---

[10]   In the letter addressed to Revd Conradie (1938), quoted in the introduction (above), Versfeld states his main objection to the Dutch Reformed Church: "I refer in particular to the church's attitude towards non-whites: the maintaining of the colour barrier, the repeated allegation that discrimination on the basis of colour is based on the will of God" (p. 2). Versfeld once again addresses this issue in *GA* 95 by explicitly taking a stance against this attitude.

It is, however, impossible to cultivate an awareness of the urgency of time as the succession of beings without taking a positive stance with regard to the material world (*GA* 145). According to Versfeld, idolatry is not the love and pursuit of people and things, but the love and pursuit of people and things with a degree of determination that is out of proportion with their actual value (*GA* 150). It is our love of and pursuit of people and things, in the right or wrong proportion, that form our character and shape our life stories. Ultimately, the things we love and the pursuit thereof structure all our relationships – the relationships between us and various things, and between us and other people and our institutionalised existence within societies (*GA* 151). The quality of the relationships that we establish with objects, other people and institutions determine our well-being, and Versfeld confirms that "for human beings the most important thing, in fact the only important thing, is their wellbeing" (*GA* 150).

In my opinion, this reference to the importance of people's well-being is of utmost significance in our assessment of Versfeld's claims regarding how we should live. In fact, I consider it to be even more important than his self-imposed comprehensibility criterion for the success of his argument, which consists of "making the content of our experience more easily understandable than could be achieved by the interpretation of any other point of view, and then to give our knowledge a broader context and deeper content" (*GA* 144). Versfeld's first aim, the criterion against which he wants to be measured, is not dogmatic faithfulness (although this is evidently important to him; see, for example, *GA* 69), but human well-being. In other words, his criterion is the success with which one can discuss the urgency of humanity and of human dealings with other humans and things throughout history. The acknowledgement of the value of human life is therefore as important as the correctness of his claims regarding – and in the name of – the Christian faith, and it would be futile to talk about human well-being if this does not include the well-being of all of humankind. This leads to a concern about the complete human being and all the dimensions of being human, including all aspects from the spiritual to the bodily life.

For Versfeld, the two criteria that he presents for the success of his work – one spiritual-theological (the comprehensibility criterion) and the other anthropological (the well-being criterion) – are as inseparable as the spiritual and corporeal aspects of human existence, which in turn are as inseparable from each other as the spiritual and physical aspects of the sacraments

(*GA* 148).¹¹ This inseparability therefore has both a theological and an anthropological tendency – in both cases it can be called "incarnation" or "embodiment" (*inkarnasie* or *vleeswording*).

For Versfeld, incarnation is perhaps the most comprehensive test for the acceptability of thought. "In a philosophical sense the Incarnation means that, among other things, time is real, our bodies are a means for human wellbeing and our temporary conduct has eternal meaning" (*GA* 147). In other words, in the absence of respect for incarnation, (a) the reality of time is compromised; and/or (b) people's corporeality, and therefore also their well-being, is disregarded; and (c) a disjunction develops between temporal conduct and its eternal significance.¹² This brief citation has brought us to a series of Versfeld's core themes in *Oor gode en afgode*, as well as in all his later works: (a) time and the need for virtuous conduct; (b) human incarnation as the key to non-reductionist anthropology; and (c) the tight link between the temporal and the eternal. However, these three themes are so closely intertwined that they are in fact only different perspectives on the same issue. This issue is called embodiment, incarnation or unity.

We will now focus on the issue of unity and deterioration in §5 of this chapter, before shifting our focus to the three core themes in §6.

---

11 I refer to the issue of the sacraments already here, not only because it is mentioned in the text of *Oor gode en afgode*, but because it clearly indicates the crucial influence exerted on Versfeld by Archibald Bowman, his promoter during his doctoral studies. Here I would like to remind the reader that during the last year in which he acted as Versfeld's promoter (1934), Bowman delivered his Vanuxem Lectures at Princeton and immediately afterwards, until the time of his death in 1935, was occupied with rewriting these lectures in book form. The lectures are titled *A Sacramental Universe*, and a fragment of the last lecture clearly shows that, under this title, he also reflected on the theme of human and divine incarnation. Those who are able to obtain a copy of Charles Hendel's introduction to Bowman's *The Absurdity of Christianity and Other Essays* (New York: The Liberal Arts Press, 1958) will find that it provides a useful introduction to Bowman's work. The last essay in this collection is the one to which I have just referred.

12 War, exploitation and racism are among the consequences of such a disjunction. However, it is important to note that this disjunction is a phenomenon that is often seen in modern Western cultural development. In a manuscript titled "Rationalism and Politics", which to my knowledge was never published and was most probably written during the early part of World War II (UCT Archive, file 18), Versfeld points out this broader disjunction between the rational and moral development of the West and refers to the development of the ability to carry out air raids.

5. Unity and decay

It might not be immediately evident that the issue of unity is the common factor in the three themes elaborated above: urgency, time and incarnation. The term *unity* elucidates the synonyms *incarnation* and *embodiment* by revealing the full scope of these terms. When Versfeld expresses the opinion that "the concept of unity is at the centre of the Christian consciousness" (*GA* 40, and cf. later *PO* 205), he does not only have in mind a specific representation of the Christian consciousness during the late Middle Ages, but also accepts the concept of unity as the measure that will direct his philosophical thinking in general. The unity with which he is concerned here corresponds with the three themes mentioned above: anthropological (body – soul, individual – humankind); practical (abstract rationality – practical reasonableness, personal existence – institutional existence); and metaphysical (temporal – eternal, secular – religious) (see, for example, *GA* 40). Furthermore, the anthropological, the practical and the metaphysical aspects of unity are linked by their reciprocal implications.

The decline, disintegration or decay that forms the dramatic background to the urgent appeal for a new orientation to life in *Oor gode en afgode* can be understood only with the aid of this representation of the Middle Ages:

> The decline of the Middle Ages was the disintegration of the concept of unity and the beginning of a multifaceted process of fragmentation: the dissolution of Christendom into nation states; the irreconcilable clash between the religious and the secular orders; the fragmentation within the Church, which was brought about by Protestantism, an anti-institutional religious movement. (*GA* 40)

This decline is also evident to Versfeld in the breach between the individual and the community, the idea of an original conflict between individuals (*GA* 53ff.) and between states (*GA* 87), the dissolution of human unity to become an irreconcilable body and soul, the loss of co-ordination between reason and emotion (*GA* 41), the separation of fact and value (*GA* 133ff.), the breaking up of the human knowledge enterprise into separate and divided sciences (*GA* 137) and so forth. The explanation of how and why this disintegration had to have violent consequences is one of the major golden threads in *Oor gode en afgode*, as I have already mentioned. Despite the historical manifestations of the catastrophes caused by this disintegration, the failure is also evident in certain "symptoms of decay" (*verrottingsimptome*) (*GA* 39) – which is how Versfeld refers to the philosophers of the post-mediaeval period.

No body of ideas is more suitable to make an effective diagnosis of the modern era than that of Descartes. Versfeld's study of this "father of modernity" earned him a doctorate in philosophy and also provided the material for his first book, titled *An Essay on the Metaphysics of Descartes* (1940). Throughout his work, Versfeld sets himself up as Descartes's doctor; on the very first page of his later book *Die neukery met die appelboom* (*The Trouble with the Apple Tree*) (1985), we can still read: "Descartes's world is a disintegration of multiple substances. *Things fall apart*. The Unity, not only of the Church, has fallen apart and we would use the fragments to build a new world" (*NA* 2nd ed. 19).[13] To a large extent, it is with Descartes's help that Versfeld seeks access to the philosophical development of the modern era. This can clearly be seen in *Oor gode en afgode* when, in his chapter on Rousseau, Versfeld makes sure to point out that Rousseau's intellectual genealogy can be traced back to Descartes (*GA* 39). Hobbes, Luther, Spinoza, Hume and Kant are in one way or another connected with this contamination.[14] It is no secret that in making this diagnosis Versfeld had been influenced by the neo-Thomist Jacques Maritain: "Maritain too had found it necessary to reckon with Descartes in order to reckon with modern philosophy and I don't expect I shall forget the force with which his *Three Reformers* burst upon me, nor the influence of his *Dream of Descartes*" (*Sum* 20). The three reformers referred to by Maritain were none other than Luther, Descartes and Rousseau.

Once the reader has studied the details of Versfeld's diagnosis of the philosophical "symptoms of decay" and the corresponding cultural-political catastrophes, it will become clear why he considered it appropriate to include the following appeal on the last page of his book: "In this disorderly world, in which it has become clear that our national idols have feet of clay, the re-assessment of our past becomes unavoidable" (*GA* 164). The first period of the past that, according to him, needs to be reassessed, is the Middle Ages. However, this does

---

[13] Versfeld had good reason for choosing the title "Descartes and Me" for his 1960 autobiographical essay – see *Sum* 13–24.

[14] It is interesting to note that although Versfeld refers to Nietzsche more than ten times, the purpose is seldom to associate him with the trend of decay – more often, Versfeld expresses support for Nietzsche's analysis of culture. It is also illuminating to note that whereas Versfeld remarked that "[i]n his statement of the facts Nietzsche was correct" (*GA* 133), six years later, in *The Perennial Order*, in the translation of the text from which this quote was taken, Versfeld states, more precisely: "As a diagnostician Nietzsche is superb. But it has been left to others to endeavour to overcome, in a positive way, the evils that he has laid bare" (*PO* 144). Paul van Tongeren explores the relation between Versfeld and Nietzsche further in Chapter 4.

not imply a return to the Middles Ages, which would be neither desirable nor possible. What Versfeld means – as he states more explicitly in the foreword to *Rondom die Middeleeue* (*On the Middle Ages*) (1962) – is that the Middle Ages was not only an era in history, but a "spiritual moment" and an important part of the tradition out of which we live. Therefore, knowledge of and a reassessment of that era is "something [...] that is essential to our self-knowledge" (*RM* page not numbered; this point will be examined further below, §7 and in Chapter 10, §7). Having been successfully reminded of the catastrophes that followed after the disintegration of the unity of the Middle Ages, we are therefore again confronted by the Socratic appeal: know yourself! In 1948, to know yourself meant (as Versfeld would still confirm today) not only to gain insight into modern thinking and social developments, but to go further back to the important treasure that shaped the Middle Ages, and to reassess and reflect on it. It is in this light that, in 1960, Versfeld described himself as philosophically "postmodern" (*Sum* 20).[15] In Versfeld's opinion, postmodern philosophy is a philosophy that, disillusioned by the modern development of philosophy and its cultural and political correlates, reconsiders the tradition (of the Middle Ages, but also of antiquity, modernity and contemporary thinking) in an attempt to obtain improved self-knowledge. In Versfeld's opinion, anyone who has any doubts about the influence of our mediaeval heritage only has to consider the

> idea of the generality [*algemeenheid*] of human nature, of the value of the individual, the necessity of freedom and the right to a conscience [...]. Their theoretical development took place in the Middle Ages, and all progressive political movements of the modern time are based on these ideas. (*GA* 90)

At the centre of this "theoretical development" we find the concept of *unity*.

Let us now look at the three aspects of the concept of *unity*, and how Versfeld attempts to gain insight into them by making use of mediaeval, and other, means.

---

[15] This philosophical self-typification also responds to the culture-critical opinion that he expressed in *The Perennial Order*, namely that "the 'modern period' is drawing to a close" (*PO* 205).

6. The concept of unity – Or, a philosophy of incarnation

To confirm the existence of a form of rationality that is unlike that with which we are familiar in modernity is one thing; to convince ourselves that it is, at the very least, worth taking up is something totally different. This is indeed a central theme in Versfeld's philosophy. If he wishes to rehabilitate the concept of unity or incarnation and make it the core concept of his "postmodern" thinking, he needs to restore rational credibility to incarnation in the philosophical sense, which entails "among other things, that time is real, that bodies provide the means for human wellbeing and that our conduct in time has eternal value" (*GA* 147). It seems to me as if this task is similar to the restoration of appreciation for the unity of reason (§6.1), the unity of being human (§6.2, and the unity of the secular and the religious (§6.3).

6.1 Wisdom, *prudentia*, or the unity of reason

In Versfeld's opinion, in the domain of reason, we appreciate time as real by restoring "the place and value of reason in our activity as a whole" (*GA* 2). Failure to restore the situatedness of reason, will detach it from human conduct and well-being. Following Aquinas, Versfeld makes an attempt, in the first chapter of *Oor gode en afgode*, to argue in favour of what he sees as the "true rationalism", in other words, he argues for the restoration of the unity of reason. In his attempt to get a grip on this unity, he uses various terms: *rationalism, rational, irrational, reasonable, not reasonable, unreasonable* and *super-reasonable*. While these terms are unfortunately not used unambiguously, his intention is nonetheless clear: the unity of reason is comprised of the unity between two types of reasoning – namely, that which is rational and that which is reasonable. Rational activities are those in which reason is used in a distant, abstract, general, conceptual or systematising way. Reasonable activities do not show these formal characteristics of rationality, but may nevertheless obtain approval from the mind by occupying a sensible place in life: we only have to think about the many things we do every day, activities that can hardly be regarded as irrational, even though they are not rational. Artistic activities are a good example.

Just as artistic reasonableness is not enough to get a person through life, abstract, systematising rationality also does not suffice. In fact, both are only reasonable insofar as they are given a reasonable place in our "activity as a whole" (*GA* 20). The kind of reasoning that ensures each activity of a rightful place, regardless of whether it is rational in the strict sense of the word or not, is the practical use of reason, good sense or *prudentia* (*GA* 21ff.). Practical reasoning is what is required to imbue all activities and kinds of reasoning with their reasonableness for one's life. Greeting people, ironing clothes, feeling guilty about transgressions, caring for animals, whistling tunes while walking, and planning a life project are all intrinsically non-rational activities, but they are nevertheless reasonable and not simply irrational. Doing mathematics, writing a computer program, and keeping a record of your income and expenses are intrinsically rational activities, but unless they are embedded in life in a reasonable way through the practical use of reason, they remain extrinsically non-reasonable and, in this sense, irrational (*GA* 6).[16] Each activity is allocated a place in the course of a person's life, and people who, through practical reasoning, succeed in effectively organising their lives and who act sensibly (reasonably) will enjoy well-being.

This basic distinction between rationality and reasonableness within the realm of reason is followed by a lengthy argument – first to indicate that poetic and artistic activities are generally reasonable, even though they are not rational, and then to show that, similarly, faith is reasonable even though in the strict sense of the word it is not rational. When I say that Versfeld argues for the reasonableness of "faith", I have to add that it evident that what he has in mind is belief in the traditional Christian doctrine (see, for example, *GA* 5, 22 and 30). It is, however, far from trivial to note that when Versfeld considers faith, and religion in general, as a type of knowledge, and when knowledge is here understood as the mutual appropriation of knower and known (*GA* 30), this type of knowledge applies to all "religious perception" (*GA* 25ff.). In this way, Versfeld's thinking, from an early stage, leaves room for reflection on other religious and spiritual traditions (see, for example, the discussion of the *Upanishads*, starting from *GA* 26) and his love of Eastern wisdom. Furthermore, it should be noted that the reasonableness of faith is made dependent on the prudence[17] by which one pursues one's own well-being, in accordance with the well-being criterion for the acceptability of philosophy

---

[16] In his review of *Oor gode en afgode* (in which only the first chapter is considered), Hennie Rossouw correctly emphasises the precise importance that Versfeld here wants to attach to reason when he states that "Versfeld's earliest understanding of philosophy was an attempt to – in the spirit of 'true reasonableness' – show respect for both the *central function* and the *relative place* of reason in the human existence" (Rossouw, "Die kuns van die lewe is om tuis te kom", 13).

[17] Note, however, that the practical reason is again later made dependent on a metaphysical view of reality (which is a philosophical articulation of tenets of religious faith – see *GA* 37). In other words, an intimate dialectic exists between practical reason and the combination of metaphysics and faith.

as proposed by Versfeld himself (*GA* 150, discussed in §4, above). It is for this reason that Versfeld's metaphysically worded insistence on the unity of reason, which leads to his insistence on the importance of practical reasoning, should not be understood as dooming him to inflexible rigidity. It is precisely through practical reasoning that the metaphysically oriented individual can respond to the changing and time-bound demands of concrete events: practical wisdom or *prudentia* is, according to Aristotle's understanding of *phronesis*, "the ability to see the appropriateness of a principle within the inexhaustible variety offered by reality, and to apply it" (*GA* 56).[18]

I leave it to the reader to evaluate the details of Versfeld's ideas about the reasonableness of faith and religion. However, it should be pointed out that, with this, Versfeld attempts to restore two aspects of the unity of reason. In the first place, he is concerned with the co-ordination of all the different types of reasonableness among themselves, and between reasonableness and a person's life, so that about any activity it can be said: "If it can be incorporated into life by reason, it can be called reasonable, even if it is not knowledge acquired through concepts" (*GA* 22). Thus, the reality of the temporal nature of reason is also taken seriously; contemplation on reasoning cannot be separated from reflection on practice. This then is the orientation from which Versfeld opposes the separation of fact and value, resulting in an unfair emphasis placed on the narrow definition of rationality, and detaching the ability to judge from the sphere of human reasonableness (cf. *GA* 133ff.).

Second, when you think about practice, you reflect on time and on the course of your own life and the relationship between your life and the lives of others – in other words, you necessarily think historically.[19] However, since every representation of the historical course of events requires selection of what is narrated, such historical representation is dependent on a wider perspective from which selection can be done sensibly (*GA* 140). For Versfeld, this perspective is metaphysical, and it is this overarching metaphysics that not only keeps fact and value together, but also saves the various sciences from an irreconcilable

---

[18] Virtue, as the intelligent approach that helps us to decide, in concrete cases, how to live an ethical life, is also discussed in *Oor gode en afgode* (e.g. *GA* 50). The gender-specific term *manliness* [manlikheid], which is often used (*GA* 46, 81, 98), is hardly acceptable today. However, based on its etymological origin, this term should perhaps rather be understood as, and replaced with, *virtuosity* (*vir*: Latin for *man*).

[19] Throughout his work, Versfeld emphasises an essentially Jewish legacy of the otherwise Greek thinking of Christendom, the Middle Ages and the European culture: the ability to think historically (cf. *GA* 147ff.).

multiplicity, and thus also saves reason from one-sidedness (*GA* 4, 92ff.). Thus, human finitude does not invalidate the practice of metaphysics, but rather encourages metaphysical thinking. It is for this reason that Versfeld continued to spend time reflecting on the nature of metaphysical thinking, because deep down metaphysics is not the possession of truth, but the love of truth:

> [Metaphysics] exists as a question about itself, and for this very reason it knows that it is not the answer to its own question. It seeks its own being *qua ens* and is well aware that its *adequatio* can never exhaust its own essence. It always points beyond itself to a wisdom which *is* its own being, and without this reference to transcendence it would not be what it is. By keeping itself open, it keeps the special sciences open to their own progress. ("Talking" 17–18)

In essence, this corresponds with what Versfeld says in *Oor gode en afgode* (*GA* 4, 135, and 137).

6.2 Body and spirit: On anthropological unity

These thoughts on the unity of reason and on the central role of practical reason should already serve as an indication that Versfeld viewed the unity of the human being as extremely important. The contours that he gives to this unity may be read about in *Oor gode en afgode*. However, it may be useful to point out that here, once again, two aspects of the unity of the human are at stake.

On the one hand, Versfeld is concerned with the unity between body and spirit. Since it is the body that makes humans temporal beings involved in worldly matters, the body is of the greatest significance for ethics:

> The human being as a moral being is an embodied being who is in touch with the world of historical and incidental details through his/her senses, and influences the world through conscious decisions expressed in the form of bodily actions. (*GA* 47)

A hypothetical disembodied person would not be able to act sensibly and would not understand the urgency of the passing of time.

On the other hand, we have the unity of individuals and humankind (*GA* 40ff., 139). People are not only incarnated in a body, but also in humanity. An essential part of Versfeld's political philosophy is the emphasis he places on multiple institutions and collectives in which people participate – like a body made up of various organs – rather than on the direct link between individuals and the state. Furthermore, just as Versfeld's high regard for the body does not comprise an anthropological reduction to a mere body, he also does not reduce the individual to a mere citizen of a state. He subscribes to Augustine's instrumental view of the state in that the individual may be part of the state, but the state has a duty to serve individuals and assist them in rising above the functioning and values of the state (*GA* 82).

6.3 Analogy of the unity of the secular and the spiritual

We now come to the third form of incarnation or the concept of unity: the unity between the temporary and the eternal or, as Versfeld says, the fact that "temporary behaviour has eternal meaning" (*GA* 147). As suggested in the discussion in §6.1 above, it was evident to Versfeld that practical reason spontaneously leads to faith and metaphysics. However, according to him, following Aquinas's example, this does not imply the surrendering of life to irrationality or obscurity. To determine the reason for this is of central importance in all Versfeld's work. At least three reasons can be given. First, because he is of the opinion that faith, even though it is a gift and a mystery, is also a form of *knowledge*, in particular knowledge of something that has an "ontological status" that differs from that of humankind (*GA* 30). It is for this kind of knowledge that his arguments about the acceptability of religious perception must serve as justification. Second, because practical reason demands and approves our continuous practising of a *human faith*[20] (*GA* 32) and, to a large extent, our social existence is made possible by this kind of faith. Third, because Versfeld was convinced that what is believed "is rooted in nature"; in other words: "It is the natural life that helps us to understand supernatural life and makes us amenable to it" (*GA* 32). This is simply Versfeld's concise formulation of the idea of *analogy*, which he calls the backbone of "our Mediaeval culture" (*GA* 35) and advocates as the only protection against naturalism (*GA* 34), in other words, against the reduction of reality by a natural scientific mindset.[21]

---

[20] The example of this given by Versfeld, which was derived from Bowman, is that "Pasteur's conviction that fermentation is caused by a microscopic organism, was in his case a truly reasonable conviction; in my [Versfeld's] case it is a belief" (*GA* 9).

[21] "The religion of the Middle Ages was characterised by an acknowledgement of bodily things, and also of the sacraments by which people are incorporated into the mystical body, which is the carrier of their historical fate. Under the Cartesians (at least), the new physiology isolated the body from the spirit and history as coherently functioning matter, as a machine, which in turn became the model for interpretations of the body!" (*Wat is kontemporêr?* 20).

I would like to focus on this last point – Versfeld's appropriation of the concept of analogy, because in my opinion this is one of the most typifying characteristics of his work. This is how he explains this principle in *Oor gode en afgode*: "Human love is filled with foretastes of God's love, and those who are prepared to face nature without prejudice will find themselves on the threshold of the temple" (*GA* 32). By claiming that an analogy exists between something earthly and something spiritual, it is stated that while a similarity does exist between them, the difference between them is not denied, with the result that the difference serves to highlight the similarity, and vice versa.[22]

Once one understands how important this figure of thought is to Versfeld, its use in multiple variations becomes obvious. Even before *Oor gode en afgode* was written, an essay written by Versfeld and included in *Die berge van die Boland* (*The Mountains of the Western Cape*), co-written by Versfeld and W.A. de Klerk, discusses a "few major climbs on Table Mountain," and it would be wrong to assume that he is merely expressing himself lyrically when he says that "rock climbing is much more than a form of physical exercise. It is a spiritual experience".[23] While in *Oor gode en afgode* Versfeld does not yet articulate the separation or tension in the analogy – "the earthly is filled with foretastes of the heavenly" – he compresses this relation in his later work, so that miraculous phenomena are almost identified with the secular. In *Food for Thought*, he says: "[t]he secular is the miraculous" (*FT* 89).

Here it would be wrong not to take note of the analogy and to regard the expression as a mere metaphor or a statement of identity. For this reason, I refer to this kind of statement as an analogical symbol or an analogical spark, hoping that it will evoke ideas of a difference, a tension, a connection and a sudden mutual clarification.[24]

[I]t is the ordinary which is the extra-ordinary (*PP* 1).

Paradise is wherever you feel at home, and the gate of heaven is your own gate. (*NA* 2nd ed. 38)

---

[22] A detailed discussion of the mediaeval concept of analogy can be found in chapter VI of *Rondom die Middeleeue* (*RM* 82–92).
[23] Versfeld and De Klerk, *Die berge van die Boland* ([1947] 1965), 29.
[24] Speaking about this figure of thought used by Versfeld in this way seems more correct than to assert that the separation of transcendent and immanent is revoked by incarnation – as I did in my 1999 article, "Sanctus Marthinus laudatory philosophicus", 94 (now Chapter 7, below).

> If you want to convert an atheist, get him to clean the carrots well. (*FT* 20)
>
> The cook, even the domestic cook, is a priest or a priestess. (*FT* 20)
>
> If your cooking is play and not work, it will smell of Paradise. The resurrection starts in the cooking pot, because man is what he eats and because what he is, his substantial existence, is in its uniqueness touched with eternity. (*FT* 93)
>
> Being able to talk to God is being able to talk to the world. (*KK* 8)
>
> When we play, we become united with God's creative imagination. (*KK* 97)
>
> [Y]ou are a priest when you roast the leg of mutton [...]. Kneel down when you light the fire" (*TD* 109).

This originally Catholic way of thinking facilitated Versfeld's openness with regard to the Eastern religions and wisdom; the advice that "[i]f you want to levitate, buy a step-ladder" (*PP* 67) summarises the lesson contained in an Indian story. Similarly, the statement, "your spiritual life is your biography, your lifestyle. Spiritual life is being yourself. It is your ordinary life" (*ACCG* 10), is based on a Zen story and can be found in Versfeld's commentary on the Christian philosopher Augustine:

> If the bread of the Eucharist is not the same bread as that with which he feeds his family it is of no use. [...] Your spiritual life is your ordinary life: washing dishes, cooking supper, going to a concert or a shop. You can't "find yourself" by walking out of all this. Prayer is cutting bread. (*ACCG* 9)

This is clearly the culmination of a thought process that attempts to overcome the disintegrated oneness of body and soul, of value and fact, of theory and practice, of reason and faith, and of humans and nature. This is done on the strength of the concept of unity, or in imitation of the idea of incarnation to which the Christian sacrament (*GA* 90, 148) is a key: "This is my body". Although we are clearly dealing here with a figure of thought and not with a figure of style, I am inclined to imagine that this analogical symbol or spark played a major role in the high regard in which Versfeld was and is held by poets, novelists and scholars of literature. The openness that it reveals with regard to the miraculous nature of everyday phenomena, and the celebration of the apparently banal, imbues Versfeld's text with a unique poetic quality (I will demonstrate this in more detail in Chapter 7, §§3 and 4 and Chapter 10, §4).

7. Reception and continuation

In *Oor gode en afgode*, we do not yet see the calm playfulness that is characteristic of later texts. In 1948 the reader makes the acquaintance of an author driven by the passion of a recent life choice who is urgently seeking alternatives to a decaying world. Despite the confidence he shows about his discovery of, and excitement about, a strange old wisdom, the author of *Oor gode en afgode* finds himself at the beginning of a journey of development on which he not only seeks insight into his themes, but also searches for the correct language and register in which to reflect on it.

He was also a thinker who still had to decide how he should respond to his readers and critics. Some of them shared his concerns; others would have preferred that he act as an advocate for other issues or sympathies; and yet another group was impressed by the strangeness of his approach or use of language.

In a radio review broadcast on 17 March 1949, Tjaart Büning praised the author of *Oor gode en afgode* for his "probing" work in which he creates a bridge between the Middle Ages and the twentieth century, between Aquinas or Anselm and contemporary thinkers, to reflect on "some of the core problems of our disrupted world". Even though Büning considered the last two essays to be less convincing than the first three, he characterised *Oor gode en afgode* as follows:

> This is an interesting collection of essays that stimulates serious reflection. Despite the author's occasional disturbing tendency to become preachy and somewhat fanatical [*dweperig*], one can generally agree with him if one subscribes to his point of departure. Versfeld reads mainly English texts, which probably explains why his Afrikaans, although quite satisfactory, is not always idiomatically correct.[25]

---

[25] Radio talk by Tjaart Büning, broadcast from Johannesburg on 17 March 1949 (UCT Archive, file 205, quotations on pp. 1 and 2).

Three points that are evident from the above are the seriousness and importance of Versfeld's thinking, which is commended, the doubt that exists concerning his (probably mediaeval, Christian philosophical) point of departure, and his language use.

Although H.G. Stoker's 1949 review[26] of *Oor gode en afgode* was clearly written from a Calvinistic trench, it echoes Büning's more impartial review:

> Dr Versfeld's five incisive and enthusiastically written popular philosophical essays require us, as Calvinists in this country, to consider where we stand in relation to Rome, in particular since they are written in Afrikaans (albeit interspersed with acceptable and original Anglicisms). The frank and courageous faith language employed by this thinker in his criticism of the increasingly heathen spirit of our time deserves to be fully recognised. He is not ashamed of his faith, which is the fertile ground from which his philosophical thinking develops. These are the words of a confessing Christian. His thinking is closer to ours than that of Kant, Rousseau, Nietzsche, Hegel or Whitehead. The work contains many ideas that we can accept as they are, or differently formulated. However, we reject the specific Catholic-philosophical principles on which it is based and which bind it together. I regard Versfeld as a Christian and a keen-witted philosopher, and would like to recommend this book to our readers. I enjoyed reading it and also learnt from it. However, anyone who is aware of the increasing influence of the Roman Catholic Church in this country will realise that it has to be read with discrimination. This book enriches our Afrikaans philosophical literature.

The dilemma that Stoker faced is evident: here we have a serious, well-informed, openly Christian philosopher from whom one could learn, but whose Roman Catholicism creates a cacophony in the traditional Afrikaans-Calvinistic ear. It is evident from many of Versfeld's autobiographical descriptions that this review by Stoker reflected the reaction of many of his contemporaries to the author's early thinking.

Although I cannot judge whether such a strong English overtone is audible in Versfeld's 1948 book, I found interesting material in the archive that cast some light on this question. The typed text, "A Moral Philosopher Looks at

---

[26] Review in *Koers*, February 1949, 4 (my page reference here refers to Stoker's typed text sent to Versfeld by Nasionale Pers – UCT Archive, file 205).

His World"[27] corresponds in part with chapter 3 of *Oor gode en afgode* and is definitely older. There is also an early text titled "Morals and Machines",[28] the first part of which largely corresponds with chapter 4 of *Oor gode en afgode*. Finally, I discovered a text on Rousseau,[29] the beginning of which shows strong similarities to chapter 2 of *Oor gode en afgode*, but then continues with a more detailed discussion. I suspect that this was a lecture he had prepared before he wrote *Oor gode en afgode*. From this, it could be derived that probably more than half of the book had originally been written in English before being translated into Afrikaans. The archived material further revealed that Versfeld rarely wrote notes in Afrikaans as most of this material – consisting of notes or manuscripts for his lectures – had been written in English. We should therefore assume that when he wrote, Versfeld thought mainly in English – at least during the 1930s and 1940s. However, it appears that in the foreword to his second book on philosophy published in Afrikaans, *Rondom die Middeleeue*, Versfeld justified his use of Afrikaans to his critics as follows:

> [In Afrikaans philosophical writing] we tend to rely on German and Dutch, sometimes with disastrous consequences, while we tend to shy away from English. However, regardless of whether we are aware of it or not, we are strongly influenced by English and this, from all sides. To deny this and to pretend that such influence does not exist, is to cause an inner conflict and then to suppress it, sometimes with almost neurotic consequences. It would not harm us if we chose to write in Locke's style rather than in Hegel's, which would prevent the average person's interest in philosophy from being smothered to death by big loads of big words. (*RM* foreword, not numbered)

However, the acceptability of philosophy does not depend only on its style. An intense involvement with the history of philosophy is typical of Versfeld's lectures and published works. By so doing, he gave a concrete response to what he regarded as the unavoidable re-evaluation of history (*GA* 164). *Oor gode en afgode* does not offer a master plan for undertaking this in-depth exploration

---

[27] UCT Archive, file 19. This text was probably written during the early 1940s.
[28] UCT Archive, file 23. This text was probably written at the latest in 1949 and refers to another version of the same text written two years earlier. It is therefore quite possible that an earlier English version of this text existed before the publication of *Oor gode en afgode*.
[29] UCT Archive, file 34. This English text on Rousseau cannot easily be dated, but since both the manuscript and the typed version have been preserved, it is highly likely that it is the original version, which would correspond with Versfeld's custom.

of the history of philosophy, but several important lines of investigation run from this book through his subsequent work. In the first place, a line runs from *Oor gode en afgode* directly to *The Perennial Order*. Chapter 10 of the latter is a slightly rewritten version, but is largely a translation of chapter 5 of *Oor gode en afgode*, which deals specifically with the philosophy of history. Furthermore, *The Perennial Order* (like almost all his other books) is a clear effort to immerse himself in the reappropriation of mediaeval thinking. *Rondom die Middeleeue* (*On the Middle Ages*) is Versfeld's most comprehensive discussion of mediaeval thinking, but we should not forget that, already in 1958, he had published a well-received commentary on Augustine's philosophy – *A Guide to the City of God* – and that his thoughts about mediaeval philosophy are clearly reflected in his last complete collection of essays, *St Augustine's Confessions and City of God* (1990) (on the relation between these two books, cf. Chapter 10, §1).

The philosophy of antiquity, represented by Socrates, Plato and Aristotle in *Oor gode en afgode*, was also to receive Versfeld's direct attention. His preference for Plato is evident in the titles: *Plato. Die simposium of die drinkparty* (*Plato. The Symposium or the Drinking Party*) (1970) and *'n Handleiding tot die Republiek van Plato* (*A Guide to Plato's Republic*) (1974). In addition to these, one also has to consider numerous essays written by Versfeld, including his inaugural speech delivered at the University of Cape Town (1971), which was published in *Persons* under the title "The Socratic Spirit". Versfeld's interest in Buddhism and the wisdom of the *Upanishads* already came to the fore in *Oor gode en afgode*, and many essays included in his subsequent collections are devoted to Eastern thought. His translation and introduction of *Die lewensweg van Lao-Tse* (1988) into Afrikaans clearly shows his interest in Eastern traditions. This theme will be dealt with in detail by Kobus Krüger in Chapter 6.

Versfeld's strenuous efforts to get a proper grip on modern philosophy that preceded the twentieth century is evident from his lectures kept in the University of Cape Town archives and the frequent references to philosophers from this period found in his books. However, he saw no need to devote a monograph or commentary to any specific figure, with the exception of Descartes, in *An Essay on the Metaphysics of Descartes* (1940), to which, to a large extent, *Oor gode en afgode* already attempts to respond. Versfeld's most thorough discussion of twentieth-century philosophy can probably be found in *The Mirror of Philosophers* (1960).

In all his thinking via his contemplation of the history of philosophy, the issue remains the *problems discussed* by all those philosophers. Versfeld does not aspire to know philosophy, but wants to respond to the appeal: Know yourself! It is for this reason that he also wants to get to know the world around him.

The themes from *Oor gode en afgode* that are highlighted in this chapter are reformulated and repeatedly contemplated in Versfeld's later books. The urgency of the post-war book did, however, make way for a calm, meditative tone; the confidence of the newly converted is replaced by an appreciative, poetic attention to the commonplace and the earthly (but I will comment on this change in Chapter 10, §4); the insistence on a Christian science is transformed into a serene Socratic ignorance; the call for a courageous decision fades away and makes way for hospitable humour. And yet, when we read the first page of his last book, *St Augustine's Confessions and the City of God*, we are still unmistakably dealing with the author of *Oor gode en afgode* – the theme of decline invites reflection on the contemporary world with a reference to Augustine:

> The reason for this book is the relevance to us of Augustine's life, thought and political situation. His soul was dying, so is ours. His Rome was collapsing: so is ours. [...] We need some participation in a vision which could make sense of a perilous and breaking world. Perhaps our Rome is also crumbling, and through the cracks we may catch a ray from the *City of God*. (*ACCG* 7)

This is followed by the themes that are so characteristic of Versfeld's thinking: time, incarnation, everyday experiences, God, the unity of humankind, reasonableness, the futility of inequitable capitalism, quality of life, food, politics, the environment – and he takes time to contemplate each of these, as if with the beads of a rosary.

However, adherence to certain themes is not necessarily a reason for recommending a philosopher's work. Eventually, we have to get to what Versfeld considers to be the really important issues in *Oor gode en afgode*, and how he worked on these issues: are the arguments convincing? The purpose of this chapter is not to answer this question. Each reader will have to decide individually how the book should be received. In Chapters 8 and 9 I will offer two general appreciations of his work from two different perspectives. However, a few questions are already in order here.

Regardless of how convincing the burning issues raised by the author might be, the way in which he deals with them will necessarily give rise to a number of questions. If it is altogether understandable that, during World War II, a person would have been shocked by the illness of Western culture, does that mean that the essence of modernity has thereby been completely unmasked and that the entire project of modernity should be declared bankrupt? At the same time, one would have to determine whether the inexorable cultural criticism of the modern world (such as that of Versfeld) cannot perhaps provide an alibi for a generally conservative cultural politics.

The call to make a decision – based on the decay of Western civilisation and which, in Versfeld's opinion means that, like the first Christians, we (in 1948) "live in a time of moral radicalism" (*GA* 100) – could lead to conflicting practical implications. On the one hand, he envisages the necessity of a catacomb existence (*GA* 103) for a moral-religious creative minority or elite, or a Christian proletariat characterised by social marginalisation (*GA* 156, 160). On the other hand, he advises against withdrawal from the world and insists that we should participate in the political world, among other things through institutions in order to improve them (*GA* 149).

A number of questions relating to how, and with what degree of evenhandedness, Versfeld interprets the history of ideas deserve to be answered. An important detail from Augustine's and Rousseau's works respectively could be used as a test. About Augustine we are told that "he was overwhelmed by a positive meaning of the concept of incarnation" (*GA* 146), and throughout Versfeld's works we repeatedly see this pronouncement in a variety of formulations. But should this positivity not be related to the abundant remarks throughout the *Confessions* that clearly show how disgusted Augustine was with his own body? The state that was inspired by Rousseau's political ideas may have produced the Terror, but it also institutionalised human rights. And should one not welcome it if what has since been achieved in that state for the emancipation of women could be equalled by a certain Middle Ages–inspired institution of our world…?

The idea that people are shaped by history does not seem too strange to modern thinking, at least not since Hegel. However, it is important to reflect on how we are shaped by history – in particular by the history of mediaeval thinking. Who, in the South Africa of 1948 and today, was shaped by mediaeval history, and how? In which ways do many South African citizens, who have no direct cultural heritage from the European Middle Ages, live indirectly out of that period? Or how, and on which grounds, could the Middle Ages be presented to them as a past out of which they could live? The preservation or reactualisation of the idea of the unity of humankind (as it was viewed in mediaeval Christendom) should certainly take into account the total transformation of the composition of the problem of unity as it became clear to Europeans following the discovery of the New World. Would it not have been necessary to offer a thorough discussion of the complexity of the unity of a global human population characterised by numerous cultural and religious traditions – if not to establish the validity of the idea, then at least to reflect on what it means in practice?

This naturally brings us back to the two criteria applied by Versfeld himself to measure the success of his work: the criterion of comprehensibility and the criterion of well-being. One would have to establish whether any Christian history or any other Christian science (in the terms in which it was defined by Versfeld) has ever been practised, and to what extent it could legitimately be claimed that it was superior to other efforts to understand the world, and if so, how it was done. Perhaps even more important, when evaluating *Oor gode en afgode*, one would have to ask what contribution the book, or the implementation and application of the ideas contained in it, have already made to the advancement of human well-being, or what contribution it might be able to make in what could reasonably be seen as its potential sphere of influence.

Are the monstrous political catastrophes and the inconceivable scale of human suffering during the twentieth century merely symptoms of a diseased Western civilisation (and probably, here and there, also some other civilisations)? Would it be possible to heal the world of these pathologies so that the continuity between human actions and divine actions could again be restored or at least be analogically related? Besides the question asked by believers (at least since the ancient Jews, whose sense of history Versfeld praises) – namely, "Where is God in suffering?" – one would also have to ask: if something like an analogy between the earthly and the heavenly ever really existed, was it not brought to an end by the unimaginable scale of violence of the past century? Or would practical reasoning perhaps suggest that – maybe for God's sake – we should declare the metaphysical belief of an analogy between the human and the Divine to be unreasonable and continue living as if it would make no sense to hold on to the reality of a God?

Should one nonetheless persist in thinking inside the framework of the Christian faith, one would probably also have to ask: is it still possible, realistic or reasonable to develop an interpretation of the Christian faith that does not seem to consider the development of the historical-critical study of both biblical and ecclesiastical documents of faith worthy of any discussion? And if the metaphysical way of thinking about reality is declared to be the only way to give intelligent articulation to the meaning of human existence and to complement the reflective search for meaning, should it not be extremely important to determine how, in the twentieth century, the proliferation of non-metaphysical philosophies of meaning can in any way whatsoever succeed in thinking about meaning, and should the value of these findings not be thoroughly contemplated? This question becomes even more pressing when we consider the fact that so many of these philosophies, each in its own way, radically engages temporality and embodiment.

It would be possible to expand the list of questions relating to *Oor gode en afgode* much further. The many instances throughout Versfeld's work where *he* reconsiders certain themes in different ways confirm the fact that such questions deserve our attention. This does not necessarily mean that *Oor gode en afgode* failed, but it could be seen as an indication of the importance of rethinking the themes that are dealt with. However, to determine how successfully *Oor gode en afgode* examines these issues, a thorough study of the book is essential, and I would like to invite you to do just that![30]

---

[30] I would like to thank Liesl du Preez, Andrew Nash, Willie van der Merwe, Ruth Versfeld and Francois Verster for their valuable advice in writing this text.

CHAPTER 4

VERSFELD AND NIETZSCHE: STRANGE BEDFELLOWS

By Paul van Tongeren

1. Introduction

Although there are not many places in Martin Versfeld's writings where he refers to the German philosopher Friedrich Nietzsche, the passages that do so are worth considering, and – most remarkably – are generally very positive. Undoubtedly, other authors are much more important to Versfeld, among whom not in the least is Saint Augustine, the one whom Nietzsche called "a slave who, without deserving it, has been pardoned and elevated [...], who lacks in a truly offensive manner all nobility of gestures and desires",[1] and whom according to Nietzsche, belongs to the "born *enemies of the spirit*".[2] Such designations must have offended Versfeld, and there are many more examples to give where the two thinkers seem to go in opposite directions. And yet, Versfeld seems to consider Nietzsche as a companion, at least for part of the way of his philosophy. One wonders why. In this chapter, I describe a few examples of this unexpected companionship and only at the end will I suggest an answer to this question.

---

[1] Friedrich Nietzsche, *Beyond Good and Evil*, trans. W. Kaufmann (New York: Vintage, 1966), §50. All references to Nietzsche are to section numbers, where necessary completed by page numbers.
[2] Friedrich Nietzsche, *The Gay Science*, trans. W. Kaufmann (New York: Vintage, 1974), §359.

2. Sounding out idols

In 1948 Martin Versfeld published a book with the title *Oor gode en afgode* (*On Gods and Idols*). Nietzsche's *Götzen-Dämmerung* (*Twilight of the Idols*) had appeared sixty years earlier. At least the similarity of the two titles suggests a related interest and commitment. Both authors speak of idolatry and find it where contingent and timely things are eternalised and taken to be absolute.

For Versfeld, there are mainly two idols to unmask: the nation state and the human being. It is immediately clear that it is of course not the state as such, let alone the human being as such, that is an idol. They are, however, made into idols by "an idolatrous nationalism" (*MP* 181) or by an equally idolatrous humanism. It is the idolatry that makes the idols: "In the phenomenon of nationalism, a historical coincidence, i.e. a particular, transient type of social structure is being made into the primary source of values, and thus into a God."[3] Atheistic humanism "is an act of pride, or self-deification" that begins when the human being mistakes "the image for the original" or "mistake[s] himself for the source of his own light, and give to himself the worship due only to the Original" (*MP* 178).

In *The Mirror of Philosophers* Versfeld seems to hold Rousseau responsible for this "idolatrous nationalism". As a positive counter-model, he most often refers to St Augustine's *De Civitate Dei*, in which the famous distinction between the terrestrial and the celestial realm is precisely meant to warn against this kind of idolatry. The idolatry of atheistic humanism is, according to Versfeld, actually as old as history: it "is the original sin, or fall of man".

Nietzsche attacked the idols of his time from his first publications. But gradually his criticism becomes more radical. In his early *Lectures on the Future of our Educational Institutions* and the *Untimely Observations* he mainly focuses on the idols of his time, but from *Human, All Too Human* on, he increasingly unmasks the great values of philosophy – morality and religion – as human fabrications. And in the preface to his *Twilight of the Idols*, he declares that the idols he targets

> this time they are not idols of the age but *eternal* idols which are here touched with the hammer as with a tuning fork – there are no more

---

[3] "In die verskynsel van die nasionalisme word 'n historiese toeval, naamlik 'n partikuliere, verganklike tipe sosiale struktuur tot die primêre bron van waardes verhef, dit wil sê tot 'n God." *GA* 200 (all translations from writings in Afrikaans are mine – PvT).

ancient idols in existence [...] Also none more hollow [...] That does not prevent their being the *most believed in*; and they are not, especially in the most eminent case, called idols [...][4]

And precisely here our two authors seem to go in radically different directions. For Versfeld, every idolatry is blasphemy and an offensive denial of the only true God. To protect ourselves against this kind of idolatry, we need a reference to "a supernatural reality" ("'n bonatuurlike werklikheid", *GA* 130), a "belief in a primary reality" ("geloof aan 'n primêre realiteit", *GA* 136) and even a commitment and devotion to the "Church" and its "sacraments" ("sekere sakramente", *GA* 130f[5]) in which the reference to this primary reality is safeguarded. Versfeld refers to doctrine of the Church as the mystical body of Christ, a reference that is made explicit in *The Mirror of Philosophers* (*MP* 180). In the chapter "A Season in Hell", he describes the history of modernity from Rousseau onwards as the gradual fragmentation of the unity of this mystical body, which has, according to him, caused the downfall of Christianity and the rise of nihilism. Only an absolute (and thus supernatural) perspective can "put in perspective" all human (all too human) constructions. Only a supernatural morality can bind the state to its instrumental meaning (cf. *GA* 120f), safeguard the dignity of individual human beings, protect them against an "annihilation [...] in a collectivity" (*MP* 184[6]), but also save them from an idolatrous self-aggrandisement.

It is, however, precisely this supernatural morality and its divine foundation that is, according to Nietzsche, the "eternal" idol that is usually not called an idol. He clearly asks a rhetorical question when at the end of section 344 of the *Gay Science* he writes:

> [...] what if this [i.e., "that Christian faith which was also the faith of Plato, that God is the truth, that truth is divine"] should become more and more incredible, if nothing should prove to be divine any more unless it were error, blindness, the lie – if God himself should prove to be our most enduring lie?

---

[4] Friedrich Nietzsche, *Twilight of the Idols*, trans. R. Hollingdale (London: Penguin, 1990), Preface, 32.
[5] Cf. also Versfeld's critical comment of Protestantism's "loss of the idea of incarnation" as is shown "in its thought on the visible Church, the sacraments and papacy." ("Tweegesprek tussen Marxiste en Christene", in *BU* 89–108, here 95).
[6] Cf. also Versfeld, "Philosophy of morals," in *PO* 95–143: "But this very submission [i.e., man's submission to 'divine authority'] bestows on him a dignity which no man can take from him" (*PO* 137).

Both authors want to sound out idols. But what, for Versfeld, is the criterion for the discernment of "that famous hollow sound which speaks of inflated bowels"[7] is, for Nietzsche, itself hollow instead of holy. What, according to Versfeld, is the protection against "nihilism" (an important concept for both, on which I will elaborate further below) is, for Nietzsche, itself deeply nihilistic:

> No doubt, those who are truthful in that audacious and ultimate sense that is presupposed by the faith in science *thus affirm another world* than the world of life, nature and history; and insofar as they affirm this "other world" – look, must they not by the same token negate its counterpart, this world, *our* world?[8]

One wonders whether they really hear the same thing when they "pose [their] questions [...] with a *hammer*".[9]

3. Man, morality and metaphysics

In terms of traditional philosophical disciplines, Versfeld and Nietzsche both worked mainly in the fields of anthropology, moral philosophy and metaphysics, without of course separating these from each other. Versfeld situated the special place of the human being in the whole of nature on metaphysical presuppositions and he elaborated the moral implications of this. For Nietzsche, the relation between the three is first and foremost a critical one: metaphysics and morality are shown to be human fictions meant to protect and promote a particular ("sick" or "weak") type of life. Nevertheless, he too frames this statement in some sort of a metaphysical hypothesis about the world as will to power and connects it to some kind of anthropological definition; his vocabulary of sickness and health, moreover, does not leave any doubts about the practical implications of his understanding of the human being.

Although Nietzsche wants to "translate man back into nature" and to recognise "the horrifying basic text of *homo natura*" under the "flattering colors

---

[7] Nietzsche, *Twilight of the Idols*, Preface.
[8] Nietzsche, *Gay Science* §344.
[9] Nietzsche, *Twilight of the Idols*, Preface.

and make-up" of morality and metaphysics,[10] this doesn't alter his view of the human being as different from the rest of nature. Nietzsche's "definition" of the human being reads: "[...] man is the *as yet undetermined animal*"[11]. This distinguishing characteristic is, however, radically different from the ones that Versfeld identifies: intelligence and self-consciousness. Versfeld refers to the famous expression with which Aquinas resumes Aristotle's doctrine: *anima humana quodammodo omnia*[12] to indicate the "*capacity* which distinguishes man from other objects in nature". He adds "that the human mind not only contains its own and other bodies, but that it also contains itself. [...] It has a being for itself, enters into a relation with itself, and knows itself for itself in the very moment that, by knowledge or perception, it receives into itself a tree or a star." (*PO* 97)

It is clear that what singles out the human being among the rest of nature is for Versfeld a surplus, something (a capacity) which the human being has while the rest of nature does not. For Nietzsche, on the contrary, it is rather a defect that characterises the human being. The human being is "more sick, uncertain, changeable, indeterminate than any other animal, there is no doubt of that – he is *the* sick animal".[13] Certainly, this defect is the reverse of something positive: the human being "has also dared more, done more new things, braved more and challenged fate more than all the other animals put together: he the great experimenter with himself, discontented and insatiable".[14] But these great possibilities are based on a defect. Nietzsche's description, in the second section of his *Genealogy of Morals*, of the process in which the human being, the "animal *with the right to make promises*", was "bred", starts with a loss: the loss of a necessary condition for happiness,[15] i.e. of forgetfulness.[16]

---

[10] Cf. Nietzsche, *Beyond Good and Evil* §230. N.B., the word "horrifying" ("schreckliche") was dropped by Kaufmann in his translation!
[11] Nietzsche, *Beyond Good and Evil* §62.
[12] Cf. *PO* 97: "To make the statement: I am insignificant because I am swallowed up in the stellar spaces, is to overlook the fact that this statement is possible only because the stellar spaces are, in a way, swallowed up in us." Cf. Sancti Thomae Aquinatis, *De Natura Materiae*, cap. 3: http://www.documentacatholicaomnia.eu/03d/1225-1274,_Thomas_Aquinas,_De_Natura_Materiae_et_Dimensionibus_Interminatis,_LT.pdf [last access 8 August 2020].
[13] Friedrich Nietzsche, *On the Genealogy of Morals*, trans. W. Kaufmann and R. Hollingdale (New York: Vintage, 1969) §III.13.
[14] Nietzsche, *Genealogy of Morals* §III.13.
[15] Friedrich Nietzsche, "On the Utility and Liability of History for Life," in *Unfashionable Observations*, trans. R.T. Gray (San Francisco: Stanford University Press, 1995) §II.1.
[16] Nietzsche, *Genealogy of Morals* §II.1.

Different as these two interpretations of the human being sound, they are related, among other ways, in the respect that both point to a practical and normative implication. Both stand in the tradition of the doctrine that prescribes the human being to become what it is. Versfeld writes that "[t]his 'self-occupation', which is also a capacity of being occupied with himself, is what marks man off as *human*. It is in this capacity that he is the object of ethics" (*PO* 97). For Nietzsche, on the contrary, the human's being "*as yet undetermined*" is the basis for his criticism of Christian morality that determines and identifies the human being with one particular type, and in that sense Nietzsche's definition of the human being includes the demand to maintain this "non-determination" and so to prevent full "animalization".[17] This definition allows him in any case to distinguish between higher and lower types of self-realisation. The higher ones most comply with humans' undetermined status, that is, those who are most open to many possibilities.[18] I will return to this difference regarding the normative implications of their respective anthropologies, after considering another point of similarity and conflict between our two thinkers.

Versfeld connects his definition of the human being as distinct from the rest of nature with a criticism of naturalism and subjectivism (both with respect to morality) for which he claims to have Nietzsche at his side. The combination of naturalism and subjectivism may be surprising; for, whereas naturalism seems to reduce the human being to a natural object, subjectivism reduces objectivity (at least the objectivity of moral judgements) to subjective perceptions and interpretations. But Versfeld points out that subjectivism really is just a variant of naturalism, and precisely for that he seems to rely on Nietzsche.

Subjectivism denies that moral judgements have anything to do with real qualities in the objective world. They only express the preference of the judging subject and the more resolutely these judgements are brought forward, the more they command others to act in conformity with these judgements. Moral judgements are commands; they express "the will do dominate over others without regard to anything except its private urges, and morality is transmuted into immorality" and, according to Versfeld, "[n]obody has been more consequent than Nietzsche in drawing the right conclusions from subjectivism" (*PO* 123).

---

[17] Cf. Friedrich Nietzsche, *Human, All Too Human. A Book for Free Spirits*, trans. R. Hollingdale (Cambridge: Cambridge University Press, 1986) §247; *Beyond Good and Evil* §203; and *Twilight of the Idols* §IX, 38.

[18] Cf. Paul van Tongeren, *Reinterpreting Modern Culture. An Introduction to Friedrich Nietzsche's Philosophy* (West Lafayette: Purdue University Press, 2000), 199–201.

This does not yet show subjectivism to be a variant of naturalism. That becomes clear, however, as soon as we ask why someone (or ourselves, for that matter) would utter a moral judgement. There would be no justification for my commanding, which would not repeat the same verdict. Saying that it is good to command would amount to commanding somebody (or even everybody) to command – "[t]o say that it seems good to me to command can only mean that I command myself to command, which is no reason at all" (*PO* 123). This leads Versfeld to the conclusion that subjectivism reduces moral judgements to nothing other than facts of nature: they "would then have to be located in the sub-rational arcana of human nature, and in the act of commanding a man would become a slave to his irrational desires". And, according to Versfeld, "here again it is Nietzsche who has the courage to go the whole way" (*PO* 123).

For a subjectivist, acting becomes behaviour; acts and decisions are reduced to events, which can be explained without making an appeal to reasons and final causes (*PO* 103). And so the subjectivist loses the subject, because it is nothing but a link in a chain of causes and effects. Subjectivism finds itself back as materialism and relativism (*PO* 125), and "[r]elativism in morals inevitably means absolute authoritarianism in law and in government" (*PO* 140). Nietzsche does indeed criticise the idea of a free subject as originating in creative acts and judgements and he interprets the act of willing as a complex organisation of commanding and obeying:

> "Freedom of the will" – that is the expression for the complex state of delight of the person exercising volition, who commands and at the same time identifies himself with the executor of the order – who, as such, enjoys also the triumph over obstacles, but thinks within himself that it was really his will itself that overcame them. [...] What happens here is what happens in every well-constructed and happy commonwealth; namely, the governing class identifies itself with the successes of the commonwealth.[19]

But he also criticises what Versfeld uses as a protection against this subjectivism: the idea of "an ultimate Intelligence" and the recognition of "absolute principles of good and bad" (*PO* 143). That is exactly what Nietzsche calls

---

[19] Nietzsche, *Beyond Good and Evil* §19.

the worst, most durable, and most dangerous of all errors so far [...] namely Plato's invention of the pure spirit and the good as such. [...] To be sure, it meant standing truth on her head and denying *perspective*, the basis condition of all life, when one spoke of the spirit and the good as Plato did.[20]

In as far as Nietzsche criticises naturalism, it is not because he would *not* "translate man back into nature" or recognise "the horrifying basic text of *homo natura*" from under the "flattering colors and make-up" of morality and metaphysics.[21] On the contrary: he opposes standard naturalism, because it misunderstands itself and thinks of "nature" as something that proceeds according to laws – in other words because of its "naïvely humanitarian emendation and perversion of meaning"[22] Nietzsche does not oppose some kind of moral objectivism over the criticised subjectivism and naturalism, but rather a different kind of naturalism. Nietzsche is not an anti-naturalist, but he is a naturalist with another interpretation of nature than standard naturalism. Nature is, according to Nietzsche, rather "the tyrannically inconsiderate and relentless enforcement of claims of power".[23]

Both for Versfeld and Nietzsche, morality demands from the human being some kind of conformity with nature. For Versfeld, this implies an adherence to "the natural law theory of morals" (*PO* 134). Nature is, as the creation of an "ultimate Intelligence", well-ordered. And human beings are, through their intellect, able to recognise this order, to know the "absolute principles of good and bad" implied in this creation, and to conduct their lives according to these principles. Since human beings *can* in fact overstep the limits set by nature, they have a *duty* to do what the rest of nature cannot but do.

For Nietzsche, on the contrary, nature is will to power, and "will to power" is always shorthand for the struggle of conflicting wills to power.[24] Moral judgements and moral theories, but also scientific or philosophical theories of nature, are themselves such conflicting interpretations through which this will to power realises itself. If there is a moral demand included, it is the demand to become homologous to nature as will to power, which is to realise oneself as a

---

[20] Nietzsche, *Beyond Good and Evil*, Preface.
[21] Nietzsche, *Beyond Good and Evil* §230.
[22] Nietzsche, *Beyond Good and Evil* §22.
[23] Nietzsche, *Beyond Good and Evil* §22, 30f. Cf. also P. van Tongeren, "Nietzsche's Naturalism," in *Nietzsche and the German Tradition*, ed. Nicholas Martin (Bern: Peter Lang, 2003), 205–215.
[24] Cf. P. van Tongeren, *Reinterpreting Modern Culture. An Introduction to Friedrich Nietzsche's Philosophy* (West Lafayette: Purdue University Press, 2000), 154–165 and 220–228.

struggle of conflicting wills to power: "The highest man would have the greatest multiplicity of drives, in the relatively greatest strength that can be endured. Indeed, where the plant 'man' shows himself strongest one finds instincts that conflict powerfully [...], but are controlled."[25]

And yet, even when Versfeld claims that "there can be no morality where absolute principles of good or bad are not recognised", and while referring to the radical nihilistic consequences of this position, he does not criticise Nietzsche, but writes: "There is much here to learn from Nietzsche" (*PO* 142f). How to understand this strange affection for the thinker who seems to be his antipode?

4. Nihilism

One way to answer our question would be to suggest that Versfeld refers to Nietzsche as the one who describes the dangers and the problems we face and who therefore shows why we should make up our minds and take measures. Nietzsche would be the diagnostician of the disease that Versfeld is trying to cure. That is the suggestion that Ernst Wolff makes in his introduction to the new edition of *Oor gode en afgode*, and he refers to a passage in that book where Versfeld writes that "Nietzsche was right in his observation of the facts" (*GA* 2nd ed. 22 and 174). He not only described the facts correctly, but also saw their connection in the constellation of nihilism of which they were the symptoms, and analysed the origin of "this uncanniest of all guests" that "stands at the door".[26]

In "The Philosophy of Morals" Versfeld writes in a footnote:

> The best definition of nihilism has been given by Nietzsche. A nihilistic universe is a universe without a goal, which holds no answer to the question: why?, which has in short no "finality". Nihilism is a radical denial of value, of intelligibility, and desirability. It is the conviction that there is no point in anything that happens. (*PO* 105)

---

[25] From the unpublished notes: Friedrich Nietzsche, *Sämtliche Werke*. Kritische Studienausgabe in 15 Bänden, ed. G. Colli and M. Montinari (Munich and Berlin: DTV and De Gruyter, 1980) 11, 27 [59]; Friedrich Nietzsche, *The Will to Power*, trans. W. Kaufmann and R. Hollingdale (New York: Vintage, 1968), §966.

[26] From the unpublished notes: Nietzsche, *Sämtliche Werke* 12, 125 2 [127]; Nietzsche, *Will to Power* §1.

Nietzsche has defined this disease, "predicted" (*GA* 134) its appearance as well as the consequences it will produce, and put the finger on its symptoms. It is almost as if Versfeld considers himself to be a successor of Nietzsche. Versfeld will start the cure for the disease that the Nietzsche diagnosed: "[a]s a diagnostician Nietzsche is superb. But it has been left to others to overcome, in a positive way, the evils which he has laid bare."[27]

There are, however, some problems with this suggestion. Although Versfeld is inclined to identify rather Descartes and Rousseau as the primary suspects who caused the rise of nihilism, he certainly knows that Nietzsche not only describes the disease but also seems to approve and even promote the underlying causes of it: the "contempt of truth and duty" (*GA* 173) and the proclamation of the death of God. And Versfeld certainly knows that his own proposals for how the threat of nihilism could be forestalled or averted, differ radically from what Nietzsche has suggested.

Against the proclamation of the death of God, Versfeld develops a "Christian philosophy" (*GA* 136f); against the separation of "fact and value", he refers to J. Maritain's presentation of Christ as the unity of fact and value (cf. *GA* 175), and to the Church as the mystical body of Christ;[28] against "the uprooting of the belief in a primary reality" (*GA* 136f), he affirms a metaphysical unity; against the thesis "that there is no natural distinction between good and evil" (*PO* 138), he departs from the belief in "a supernatural morality" (*GA* 141). And at the basis of all these oppositional claims is a fundamental difference regarding the meaning of this concept of "nihilism".

For Versfeld, nihilism is something to be condemned and to fight against. For Nietzsche, on the contrary, it is an unavoidable event.[29] Moreover, the history of European culture is, according to Nietzsche, the historical unfolding of nihilism. Platonism and Christianity have admittedly been able to hide the absurdity of life for a long time. But they have only managed to do so with the help of the fiction of a true world, beyond the actual one. This fiction is itself deeply nihilistic because it founds the meaning it construes on the denial (annihilation) of the world of the senses. It is the product of Socrates's questioning, which always uses the distinction between *doxa* and *episteme*, between what seems to be the case and

---

[27] *PO* 144, as quoted in Ernst Wolff's introduction to the new edition of *Oor gode en afgode*, 22.
[28] Versfeld, "Die moderne humanisme," in *BU* 109–123, here 118f.
[29] In the rest of this paragraph, I briefly summarise what I have developed extensively in my *Friedrich Nietzsche and European Nihilism* (Newcastle upon Tyne: Cambridge Scholars Publishing, 2018), esp. chapter III.

what really is, between apparent and true reality. Socrates's search for truth, his truthfulness, has finally turned itself against its own presupposition and unmasks this true reality as its own fictional construction. The ultimate phase of this self-undermining Socratic questioning is experienced as an antagonism: we can no longer believe in the fictions that we need in order to survive. Human beings, at least since Socrates, cannot but search for meaning; in their search, however, they finally discover that it is the question itself that condemns them to misleading or fictional ideals. In the famous Lenzer Heide note on *The European Nihilism*, Nietzsche writes:

> We now notice in ourselves needs, implanted by the long-held morality interpretation, which now appear to us as needs to untruth: conversely, it is on them that the value for which we bear to live seems to depend. This antagonism – *not* valuing what we know, and no longer being *permitted* to value what we would like to hoodwink ourselves with – results in a process of disintegration.[30]

And that is what Nietzsche in *The Gay Science* describes as the

> inexorable, fundamental and deepest suspicion about ourselves [...] that could easily confront coming generations with the terrifying Either/Or: "Either abolish your reverences or – *yourselves*!" The latter would be nihilism; but would not the former also be – nihilism? – This is *our* question mark.[31]

From this perspective, Versfeld's call for a Christian philosophy, a supernatural morality and an objectivist metaphysics sounds like the typical restorative form of what Nietzsche calls "passive nihilism": the longing for what is forlorn, rather than the therapy that would seamlessly fit Nietzsche's diagnosis.

---

[30] From the unpublished notes: Nietzsche, *Sämtliche Werke* 12, 5 [71] section 2 (my translation).
[31] Nietzsche, *Gay Science* §346.

5. Conclusion

The question therefore remains: how could Versfeld, often a perspicacious and attentive reader of the history of philosophy, be so positive about Nietzsche, who clearly goes in a completely different direction? How could he neglect everything in Nietzsche that did not fit his own philosophy and almost reduce Nietzsche's philosophy to a question to which his own thinking could be the answer?

We probably need more than only Versfeld's published writings as they have been researched for this article to find a solid answer to these questions. Maybe his private notes can tell us more about this affinity against his better judgement.

Or should we say that the affinity *is* the better judgement? That affinity has – without doubt – to do with something that Versfeld mainly showed in other publications than the ones I used for this chapter. He does not need to refer explicitly to Nietzsche to show that affinity when he writes about cooking and a variety of sensual experiences in *Food for Thought* and in the essays collected in *Klip en klei*, or when in *Die neukery met die appelboom*, he replaces Heidegger's "being there" with "being here", and writes that "heaven is where one is at home and no longer endlessly on the run".[32] In other words, I think that Versfeld and Nietzsche share a very basic sense of the "here and now" and the way our senses connect us to the world in which we live. In Zarathustra's call to "remain faithful to the earth",[33] Versfeld might have recognised a kindred spirit, with whom he made friends. And that friendship went deeper than philosophical disagreements.

---

[32] "Die hemel is daar waar jy tuis is en nie in 'n ewige ontvlugting betrokke is nie." (*NA* 2nd ed. 70)
[33] Friedrich Nietzsche, *Thus Spoke Zarathustra*. In *The Portable Nietzsche*, trans. W. Kaufmann (New York: Penguin, 1976), the first part: "On the Gift-giving virtue," §2 (188).

CHAPTER 5

GRASPING THE TRUTH FROM WHERE WE ARE

1. Introduction: Flux, stability and where we are

Who we are as humans is arguably the most pervasive theme in the thought of Martin Versfeld. In the concluding remarks to his *Essay on the Metaphysics of Descartes* (1940),[1] he deplores Descartes's egocentric self, which is isolated from the body, others and the world to such an extent that any relation between them remains merely accidental to what the ego essentially is. Half a century later, Versfeld chose the title *Sum* (*I am*) for a selection of his essays, which serves as "a sort of biography". Situating this thought between the rejection of Descartes and the adoption of Socrates and Thomas Aquinas, he favours the "consonance" of oneself with oneself, others and the environment (*Sum* 7). Roughly between these two texts, his 1971 inaugural lecture at the University of Cape Town is devoted to the Socratic quest of "knowing thyself" and was chosen to open a book entitled *Persons*.[2] When the first page of *Our Selves* then opens with the Socratic call to know yourself, and frames this injunction straightaway with a critique of Descartes's notion of the ego and approval of certain points of the thought of

---

[1]   Marthinus Versfeld, *An Essay on the Metaphysics of Descartes* (London: Methuen, 1940), chapter XI, especially 148–150. This book is the published version of Versfeld's doctoral thesis, completed in Glasgow in 1934, and represents his earliest independent work.
[2]   Marthinus Versfeld, "The Socratic spirit," in *Persons* (Cape Town: Buren, 1972), 1–15.

Augustine and Aquinas, one easily recognises the architect of this building by its façade, the design of which – as Versfeld explains – is an autobiographical act (*OS* 93).

Yet, such an architectural image may attribute more stability and structure to this collection of ten essays than it actually has. By the time the essays were published together in 1979, some of them already had an eventful career behind them. "On Justice and Human Rights" first appeared in 1960[3] and was therefore in circulation two decades before the appearance of *Our Selves*. "The Human Vision" might be equally old.[4] Some essays tell a different story. "St Thomas, Newman and the Existence of God" appeared in 1967,[5] and a version of it was later chosen to become a chapter in *A Saraband of the Sons of God*.[6] But *A Saraband of the Sons of God* never saw the light of day. Two other essays from *Our Selves*, "Reflections on Evolutionary Knowledge"[7] and "On Justice and Human Rights", were set to become two of the five chapters of Versfeld's *Towards an Existential Political Philosophy*.[8] But *Towards an Existential Political Philosophy* was never published either. Furthermore, whereas some of the separate chapters were, then, previously assigned to be read in association with chapters other than their neighbours in *Our Selves*, there is reason to believe that "The Desirability of Desire" was initially not planned to be included in *Our Selves*, and three other essays were.[9] From this information it is manifest that *Our Selves* had been simmering for a long time before it was dished up in its current format and we can understand why Versfeld could later say that, "For me, making

---

[3] Marthinus Versfeld, "On Justice and Human Rights," *Acta Juridica* 1 (1960): 1–10.
[4] The fact that a typed copy of this essay appears with other essays from the late 1950s (in the Versfeld collection in the University of Cape Town's Archive, file 59) allows one to situate it with some uncertainty in the same period.
[5] Marthinus Versfeld, "St Thomas, Newman and the Existence of God," *New Scholasticism* 41 (Winter 1967).
[6] The selection of essays on authors such as Augustine, Rousseau, Kolbe, Chesterton, Aquinas and Newman was probably compiled around 1971 and can be found in the UCT Archive, files 155, 156 and 157.
[7] Published initially in the *International Philosophical Quarterly* 5, no. 2 (May 1965): 221–247.
[8] The complete typescript of this book is in the UCT Archive, file 68. It was probably compiled sometime after 1966 and before 1972. The three other essays of this book would have been "Metaphysics in Our Time", "Augustine and the Politics of Time" and "Law and the Idea of the Contemporary"; they can be read in other publications.
[9] This claim is made on the basis of the content of file 136 in the UCT Archive: it contains a mix of manuscripts, typescripts and article offprints for nine of the ten chapters of *Our Selves*, plus three other essays.

soup is rather like writing; my mind is a rag-bag, bits occasionally cohering to form some sort of unity" (*FT* 13). Ten essays, amended over two decades and flowing into an occasional coherence, would come closer to a description of this collection.

This detail on the boiling process from which *Our Selves* originated is not of marginal interest to understanding the book; in fact, it confronts us with its central concern. And if it is permissible to remind guests of the laurel leaves that infused a dish, but were removed before serving, I may cite one of the discarded passages that were intended to give flavour to two of the essays of *Our Selves* and claim that it significantly informs the thought of this volume:

> All things pass, as Theresa of Avila so often said, and though we reach out from the flux to grasp a stability which is the common aspiration of all men, yet the point from which we reach out is different for every man and for every generation, borne on as they are by the sweep of the creative process. We see the truth from where we are.[10]

According to this noteworthy clarification, the process by which Versfeld's book was formed can be said to bear the traces (cf. *OS* 21) of the flux of time – the time of the personal life of a man called Martin, to whom these texts refer retrospectively. Through the eventful formation of the book, its author continually attempted to make sense of his own contingent situatedness and in this way persistently affirmed the soundness of aspiring to find "a stability". "A stability" is not the perspectiveless, one-size-fits-all truth, but a truth that belongs to someone, who in turn belongs to a social reality, and by extension, to a history and to a world and ultimately to a "creative process". Conversely, this is not an à la carte truth chosen at will either, but a creative force in which one can participate – such is the stability that Versfeld will attempt to uphold and illuminate in dialogue with a series of authors, represented in this citation by St Theresa.

Since all of the themes of the book are in one way or another related to this basic orientation with respect to "where we are", it would be in order to say something more about it.

---

[10] Cited from the second paragraph of the "Preamble" of *Towards an Existential Political Philosophy* (UCT Archive, file 68).

2. Anthropology as first philosophy

Our Selves is a book of philosophy and it is therefore of no mean importance to notice what Versfeld girds himself for when he puts on the philosopher's mantle: "Philosophy ought to start with anthropology in the Continental use of the term. What comes first is not theory of knowledge, but the problem of the being of man", he writes in the opening sentence of "The Importance of Being Human", and adds, "We shall appreciate this better the more clearly we see how anthropomorphic all our knowledge is" (*OS* 24). If one counts well, it follows from this remark that philosophy, even philosophical anthropology, always comes, at best, second: first is the problem of being human, then comes reflection on this problem. Consequently, one does best to start philosophy by thinking about the human being and not about epistemology, since one risks failing to see how the problem of being human shapes knowledge. Another way of putting it would be to say that all philosophical claims, in fact all truth claims, derive their nature, meaning and significance from their setting in human life. The same holds for whatever one desires to achieve with truths: conducting politics, developing technologies, promoting culture, and even practising religion.

Hence the need for a book that contemplates ourselves as human beings. Now, Versfeld chose for the title of his collection of essays to separate "our" and "selves". "Selves" is a noun, the plural of "self", which the reader will see can be used with a small or capital S, and the title qualifies "selves" by the possessive pronoun in the first person plural, "our". These snippets of linguistic elucidation suggest that there is more than one self for each human being, the association with which is to be understood as a kind of "possession" or "having" and that one does better to consider this having of selves as something that concerns *us*, and not only *me*. In this way the title leads to the central tenet of Versfeld's thought on the self: everybody has the choice between two divergent forms of existence, or to put it more bluntly: "[...] we have two selves, and it is fatal to choose the wrong one" (*PP* 2nd ed. 70). When Versfeld roots philosophy in the problem of being human, he therefore derives the significance of all aspects of reality – be it political, technological, cultural or religious – from the decisive question concerning the quality of one's self and of the ways in which you have your self with others.

If the one option is for the I, self or ego and a life guided by grasping desire and *samsara*, the other option is for the real self, the Self, the person who exercises generous desire and follows the Tao or finds union with God. The reader will not find it difficult to trace the detail of this distinction throughout the book. Yet, one should guard against seeing this as a simple split between a narrow and a broad way. We should rather see two modifications of the same human existence, the difference located in the variation of the attitude one adopts towards one's incarnation in a body, a society and an environment. A first approximation to these two attitudes is provided by the existential distinction between recognition and disregard for transitive *being*: I am my body, I don't merely inhabit it (*OS* 28ff.); I am with others, they are not merely added to me (*OS* 80); I am my world, it doesn't merely contain me (*OS* 105). And hence, any attitude towards human existence that disregards these aspects of one's existence by reducing the human being to either mind or body, and humanity to a collection of individuals or by alienating the world from the people, is calling for personal, sociopolitical and environmental pathologies associated with the distortion of the real self.

But one comes closer to Versfeld's sophisticated reinterpretation of incarnation in *Our Selves*, by recalling the possessive pronoun in the title, "our", which applies to both of our selves. As a matter of fact, Versfeld reveals that the transitive notion of being can itself be considered a form of having – having as something more primitive than legal ownership (*OS* 109); *having as attachment through desire or love*. Our desires constitute the very nature of our temporality that is lived as much bodily as mentally and therefore are the energy of the delight one can have in oneself (*OS* 5f., 9). Desires are "post-social" – we are directed at the world in a socially constituted manner – and the quality of our loves determines the quality of our relations to others (*OS* 7, 39). And if life is "an activity which makes things surrounding the living being relevant" (*OS* 101), it is because through loving and desiring we are incarnate in a sphere of relevance; one possesses one's self by possessing the world (*OS* 104). Having, as the nature of one's loving or desiring, is what makes a self, whether it is more the real and decisive Self or the superficial and pathological mutation of it. Consequently, sinking into, or hardening into the grasping ego is then at the root of the sociopolitical misery presented throughout the book.

Despite this schematisation of two attitudes towards one's existence, which is needed for the diagnostic criticism of the ego, nothing is further from Versfeld's intention than a coarse moralism based on a denial of the difficult link between the two selves. Finding the true and decisive Self cannot mean bringing an end to the ego, because the very attempt to escape from the small self is itself an act of perseverance in the small self, or the desperate effort to escape the grasping ego and the deformed world that its action creates, is still a grasping of the ego.[11] If, according to Buddhism, "Nirvana is *not* total extinction but the extinction of the grasping ego" (*OS* 12), Versfeld still affirms the Buddhists advice: "let your *samsara* be your *nirvana*" (*OS* 49). Or, to translate the same principle into more Augustinian parlance: "at the heart of every desire, no matter how sinful, there is a seed of the divine radiance which can be set free" (*OS* 45). And hence, therapy consists, not of uprooting, but of elevating warped desires (*OS* 47). That is why Versfeld could claim that the essence of the most severe religious practice, ascesis, "is not struggling or straining but relaxing into what we are" (*OS* 21).[12]

This is an important point, especially when bearing in mind those people for whom this talk of finding a true self might sound too much like torturous abnegation or misty esoterica. Seeking the true self is not levitating above the common reality of daily life, but the submerging into the reality of that life itself: even in things as plain as washing dishes (*OS* 6).[13] Simply formulated, the true self is "our concrete individual being historically situated in the world" (*OS* 157). This particular situatedness is exactly the fact that has to be assumed in order to think (*OS* 157), or as Versfeld elaborates:

> We must, then, accept ourselves as we are, limited and embodied, and really connected with other beings including sensible beings. We seek to make sense of what we so accept not for the sake of any arbitrary assumption to be proved but simply in order to be able to accept ourselves as we are. (*OS* 165).

Our situatedness is the "where we are" from which we see the truth (as in the citation discussed at the end of §1), but since it is the never completely recoverable source of relevance of thought, it will forever remain a mystery (*OS* 88). Hence Versfeld's assertion concerning philosophy in his inaugural lecture:

> I must confess at once that I do not know what philosophy is. This sometimes embarrasses me before the innocence of students, but not before those who have come to realise that the things by which we live

---

[11] Or again, "[d]odging out of *samsara* is a *samsaric* dodge", *ACCG* 10.
[12] This is the locus in *Our Selves* in which to look for an elucidation of the idea that "the secular is the miraculous", what I have called elsewhere the analogical difference or the analogical spark (see Chapter 3, §6.3). For examples of this philosophical fingerprint of Versfeld in *Our Selves*, see *OS* 6, 14, 20f., 47, 49 and 68.
[13] See also *ACCG* 10: "Spirituality is not found by withdrawal from the world but by the indrawal of the world."

are the things about which we know least. We do not know what life is, or what knowing is, or what truth and goodness are. Or if we do know we can't say it [...]. (*Persons* 1)

Anthropology as first philosophy is philosophy that thrives from *that by which we live*; from the abyssal and unknown depths of our existence (*OS* 65f.).

3. Traditions and cultural criticism

One has to recognise that this decentring or unsettling of philosophical reflection by the singular human life calls for an appropriate relation to the (often one-sided) history of thought by which any contemporary philosopher has been schooled to think. This quest for a fitting relation to the history of thought is the reason for the surprising intertwinement of traditions of thought from which Versfeld draws in *Our Selves*: first the Greeks (especially Plato, e.g., *OS* 3, 7, 43, 111f.), then biblical theology (e.g., *OS* 51ff.) and its mediaeval reception (which is already a combination of the former two), especially that of Augustine and Aquinas (see, for instance, Augustine's theory of desires, *OS* 39ff., and Aquinas's theory of knowledge, *OS* 130ff.). But *Our Selves* opens with a burst of oriental wisdom – especially Buddhism (most of the first two chapters of *OS*), but also Taoism (*OS* 10, 34, 38, 70), a bit of Hinduism (e.g., *OS* 2, 15), and Jewish mysticism (e.g., *OS* 46f., 50f.).[14] Lastly, there is a distinct line of existentialism and/or phenomenology, which is quite surprising if one considers Versfeld's general critique of modern philosophy.[15] All of these strands are woven together in an intricate dialogue in which Versfeld does his best to respect the differences even while driving at his most central idea: from all of these bodies of thought, we

---

[14] Placing Jewish mysticism in the same basket as the variety of expressions of Eastern wisdom is somewhat artificial. However, Versfeld had the impression, at least from the mid 1970s, that he witnessed a boom in Western interest in oriental thought and later clearly associated Jewish mysticism with it. In fact, we are thinking primarily of Baal Shem Tov, often in Buber's rendering of his life. See especially "A Western Sunrise" in *PP* 54–61.

[15] Readers of Versfeld's *The Mirror of the Philosophers* (1960) will remember that he explains that his friend Johan Degenaar compelled him to rethink his formulation of an up-to-then primarily neo-Thomistic and neo-Augustinian philosophy (*MP* 43). Whereas this acknowledgement leads to a discussion on Kierkegaard, and Versfeld retains a certain distance with respect to phenomenological interpretations of Christianity, it is probably to this book that his appreciation for the phenomenological tradition should be traced.

can learn something of the perennial philosophy (*OS* 90, 100); from all of them, there is substantial instruction to be drawn, regarding the function of philosophy "not to discover new truths but to explicitate the truth which is given with us in our own existence" (*OS* 165).

If there is a need for such "explicitation" in philosophy, it is because of the particular situation in which Western modernity has brought itself and large parts of the world. This calamity – which is nothing but the negative diagnosis persistent in all of Versfeld's work[16] and the background against which his preoccupation with what we are is to be understood – is the nominalist revolution and the decay of the mediaeval unity. One can read the features of this process of decay at different places throughout *Our Selves* (see in particular *OS* 58ff.). The tendency to separate body and mind is accompanied by overconfidence in the capacity to see what is going on in the mind, as well as the fragmentation of human reason and the unrealistic emphasis on certain aspects of this reason (*OS* 59). The separation of mind and body is replicated on a larger scale in the tendency to exaggeratedly separate society and nature (*OS* 58). To this is linked the excessive development of the masculine urge to dominate, enforced by science and technology (*OS* 61) and the reduction of natural and human processes to mechanics (*OS* 64). These negative developments, supported by advertising, fuel consumption (both of which result in the widespread distortion of desires) and therefore stand in the service of capitalism (*OS* 59). The latter requires asceticism[17] as well as individualism, which in turn facilitates the exploitation of nature and other human beings and the reduction of value to monetary value.

I leave the reader to discover how Versfeld develops the connection between these phenomena – and to decide to what degree they could be said to be harmful developments with respect to the European mediaeval condition of life. What has to be noted is that all of these phenomena are presented as sociopolitical symptoms of disregard for the perennial philosophy, but more profoundly, of the illness of the grasping ego gone rampant. These symptoms of the decay brought about by modernity can equally be traced in the work of such modern philosophers as Descartes, Bacon, Machiavelli, Rousseau, Hobbes, Hume, Kant, Hegel and Marx, who form a tradition of thought from which Versfeld wishes to save the contemporary world. If there is in *Our Selves* a complex dispute between

---

16   As evident already in *GA* 40. See also Chapter 3, §5 and Chapter 7, §2.
17   Cf. *OS* 62: "A deep contradiction reveals itself: money may be for pleasure, and rest on the production of pleasure-giving objects, but to make a lot of money you must take time off from pleasure. Indeed, you must be ascetic. You must drive yourself along the strait and narrow road which leads to acquisition."

proponents of Greek, Christian and oriental thought on the one hand, and the modern philosophers on the other, it is not as a childish fight among schools but a contest in which the health of society is at stake.

This point may be overlooked, since so much in the book is developed around the question of the two selves. But careful examination will reveal that the human being in society with others and with the environment is equally at stake in *Our Selves*. Not only does the violence of modern sociopolitical life form the core of Versfeld's diagnosis to which he responds, but as he learned from Augustine, ethics and politics should be seen to have immediate mutual implications (*OS* 41), which could be traced in people's reflection on desire and on justice (*OS* 41, 82).[18] The reason for the indissociable link between ethics and politics is the sociopolitical constitution of the world (*OS* 121). Moreover, the well-being of the body politic, a just social fibre, is created by the collective effect of healthy personal relations (*OS* 107).

4. Using a thorn to take out a thorn, and throwing both away

In accordance with his view that philosophy is not intent on discovering new truths, but on the "explicitation" of what is given (as explained above), one doesn't find the author of *Our Selves* working on the construction of a novel philosophical system. He much rather attempts much rather to call us back to something from which we cannot escape and of which he is not the author. The value of his writing is situated in the translation of the perennial philosophy for a specific context, according to the needs of this context. Hence the independence of Versfeld's thought consists precisely in his writing from where he is. Two salient features of his manner of working follow from this orientation and situation of his work – let's call them reduction and detachment.

---

[18] Writing his review (in *African Book Publishing Record* VI, no. 3/4, 1980) of *Our Selves* from South Carolina, Daniel Sabia seemed to miss the significance of this point. Although the reviewer understands the enrootedness of all the concerns of Versfeld's book in human existence, he fails to see that the entire ethics of the self developed in these essays is a politics of the self as access to the society and world in which the self is to live.

4.1 Reduction – Using a second thorn

There can be no doubt about the central importance of religious thought – in particular the Catholic thought of God – in the entirety of Versfeld's works. And yet, it is not so simple to say flatly that his philosophy is Christian. Versfeld is quite clear on this in an earlier draft for the first paragraph of "The Yin and the Yang in Christian Culture" (*OS* chapter 5):

> Being known to be officially a Catholic in the regions where I live, I am sometimes asked: you're a Catholic, aren't you? I can never reply without a considerable degree of hesitation. I have pondered over this hesitation. I have come to the conclusion that this pondering has sufficient significance to be made public.
>
> This isn't quite as personal as it sounds. We are all under the influence of the Christian ethic and spirituality. We inevitably go on being Christian as Chinese go on being Confucian, no matter what sea-changes have occurred. The Marxist, for instance, continues to be dynamised, of historical necessity, by much of what he explicitly rejects. You can take stock of where you are, but you cannot step out of it.[19]

In other words, for Versfeld, thought about being a Christian, and his own thought in particular, has to acknowledge the general cultural shaping it has undergone by a certain Christian heritage, but has to do so in two divergent ways: one that recognises the failures, weaknesses and violence of this tradition; the other that explores the true core of assumed Christianity. We find a number of forms of existence of Christianity that are rejected by Versfeld, and the reader can learn much of the author's cultural criticism from this: he rebukes fundamentalist and moralist Protestantism (*OS* 59), the body-despising, institution-rejecting and business-minded Puritan individualism (*OS* 36, 62), some of the "superficial fools who write books on apologetics" (*OS* 157), of course Cartesianism, in which God comes only to a solitary, ahistorical, disincarnate and world-doubting mind (*OS* 157, 164), and the political compromise and moral policing of some popes and the curia (*OS* 54f., 57).

---

[19] In UCT Archive, file 135. Although these two paragraphs are crossed out, I consider them to state in a more personal and specific manner what is written in more general terms in the final version of the text, and partially to overlap with it (*OS* 52).

But just as it is, therefore, not that simple to say that Versfeld is a proponent of Christianity, so it is, in his mind, not self-evident to deny a certain Christianity that energises his non-Christian contemporaries. What Versfeld intends to do is to find what is precious in both confessing and cultural Christianity. However, this statement should be qualified, since for Versfeld it is not a matter of Christianity as opposed to other religions (as can be seen in particular in *OS* chapters 1 and 2), or of faith in opposition to reason (see in particular *OS* chapters 8 and 9). In fact, the other religions and spiritual traditions and the use of reason are vital for calling us back to that something from which his thought draws: "that by which we live" (or ought to), that which the perennial philosophy attempts to explicate truthfully.

The different traditions of religion and thought from which Versfeld borrows in *Our Selves* all serve to lead us back to this mysterious and elusive core. It is not to introduce a new and truer thought or religion that Versfeld engages with Buddhism or Taoism, but "for many of us at any rate, it would be wiser if these Eastern ideas served to remind us of things that have been forgotten or have gone stale in our own tradition, and brought new life to them" (*OS* 69) – this "own tradition" being our Christian past of which we cannot rid ourselves (*OS* 52, 68, 162). Buddhism puts the taste back into Christianity. But this service can be rendered in the opposite direction too: "Those who think that Buddhism contains the answer to all their problems, fail to see the strength of their own tradition. While Buddhist pundits were hairsplitting grasping desire into many dozens of variety, Western thinkers were analysing the political consequences of grasping desire. The foremost was St Augustine [...]" (*OS* 41). Furthermore, apart from the instruction on the political implications of desire that Augustine can give his Buddhist colleagues, he shows his strength by calling to our minds the fact that distorted desires do not point the way to eliminating desire, but to the need for elevating them (*OS* 47). For Versfeld, instead of this debate leading eventually to the elimination of one of the parties, rather the reconstructed discussion serves to enhance the searching effort: since "[e]very man is naturally in the truth – a Zenist would say that he is a Buddha; a Christian that he is in the image of God" (OS 87) – the mutual contradictions remind us of the provisional character of both, and should encourage continual discussion by which we are led back to this nonpropositional truth in which we live.[20]

---

[20] The complex interplay between traditions should deter the reader from reaching unjust conclusions, such as reducing Versfeld to his appropriation of oriental thought – as was done by the anonymous reviewer of *Our Selves* in "Mirror of Enlightenment," *The Cape Times*, 12 May 1979. In his review of *Our Selves*, Hennie Rossouw is more precise by saying that Versfeld

Let it immediately be added that philosophy has its voice to add to this chorus. Having transcended the strictures of the materialism–idealism debate, contemporary philosophy finds the unity between humans and their world, and as a result can help us to better understand oriental thought (*OS* 90). Particularly remarkable is the role attributed to philosophy with regard to Aquinas: his proofs of the existence of God "must be given an existential interpretation" (*OS* 159) and from the context of Versfeld's argument one should understand this as an existential, phenomenological interpretation. The fact that Versfeld undertakes this existentialisation of Aquinas by means of the Catholic philosophy of John Henry Newman is of secondary importance.

The spirit of this confrontation of different traditions seems to me perfectly captured in the phrase, "[...] to go back to the perennial philosophy", in which the latter is immediately defined in terms of the meaningful relatedness of people to a world (*OS* 90) – in other words, as a means of leading one back to what precedes philosophy. Versfeld's way of doing this consists of leading his reader and his dialogical partners back from spectator perspectives (and especially from the modernist absolutisation of the spectator perspective) to the perspective, or rather the fact, of being a participator in a world, in other words to our true selves.[21] It is only from participation in existence that one can find one's own humanity and world *meaningful* (*OS* 168). By contrast, philosophy that starts from doubt withdraws the thinker from the personal, social and natural world that makes that thinker into a person (*OS* 105); by recognising the practical situatedness and the meaningfulness of one's situation, one can think about things that matter. Hence, the superiority of Aquinas over Descartes (*OS* 158), or Newman over Russell (*OS* 161). Hence also the importance of Aquinas's assertion that the human being has intellect and hands (*OS* 108, 111, 135, 159). The combination of intellect and hands amounts, for Versfeld, to practical reason or prudence (*OS* 107, 169) – in other words, reason as physically, historically, socially and environmentally situated and which seems to be the root of anything that could

---

doesn't plead for a "spiritual emigration" out of the Western tradition and rather seeks to affirm one's embeddedness in that heritage by means of oriental wisdom (see "Versfeld – filosoof met eie boodskap," in *Die Burger*, 12 July 1979). But this holds, of course, only for those standing in the Western tradition.

[21] I have underscored the position of a certain influence of phenomenology on Versfeld, not only because the notion of "leading back" (reduction as *re-ducere*) is a central notion operating in phenomenology, but also because reduction is charged with coping with the relation between the self as spectator and the self as participator. See Rudolf Bernet, "La réduction phénoménologique et la double vie du sujet," in *La vie du sujet. Recherches sur l'interprétation de Husserl dans la phénoménologie* (Paris: PUF, 1994), 5–36.

be called rational or reasonable for Versfeld.²² Hence the importance of the life that supports an argument: who one is, or rather, what kind of life one has, matters at least as much as what one's opinion is. In fact, philosophy is for Versfeld first of all a way of life, as has been affirmed with force by Pierre Hadot, and one could rightfully claim that the message of *Our Selves* is the call for the art of coming home.²³

But by working towards the confluence of these traditions and carefully choosing which aspects to highlight and which parts to make echo with others, has Versfeld not in fact created his own theory of human existence and made it the universal code of entry into meaningful human existence?

4.2. Detachment – Throwing both thorns away

Versfeld answers the objection above explicitly:

> It may, of course, be retorted that in this chapter I have been theorising myself, and simply putting up an alternative construction. I could reply in the words of a Buddhist that Buddhism was using a thorn to take out a thorn, after which one throws both away. [...] [W]hat I have tried to do is to point to a moral fact rather than explain it. It remains a mystery to me. If I have called your attention to yourselves you can forget about me. (*OS* 88)

If the sociopolitical evils of the modern world and the philosophical expressions that supported it, implicitly or not, represent the first thorn, then all the traditions that Versfeld deploys, and certainly his own work, represent a second thorn, one that is destined to be discarded with the first one … but not without being used first. And not without the conviction (or the assumption, *OS* 157) that by doing so, something of decisive importance is laid bare. But have we not seen from the beginning that this something decisive, this mystery, is "our concrete individual being historically situated in the world" (*OS* 157)? Has this concrete existence

---

22   While avoiding for current purposes extensive comparisons between Versfeld and other philosophers, one can hardly omit noting the striking similarity between the centrality of a metaphysics in which all categories of being are reduced from a phenomenological reinterpretation of Aristotle's notion of *phronesis* (prudence) as in Heidegger, and Versfeld's existentialisation of Aquinas – with the help of Newman –to place practical reason as the source of all intelligence.

23   As Hennie Rossouw pointed out in his discussion of *Our Selves* in "Die kuns van die lewe is om tuis te kom," 18–19.

not been expounded as the most primitive form of having? Why then speak of detachment and not rather of attachment?

To be sure, these questions lead us to the apparent paradox that "the only attachment is detachment" (*OS* 47). As "intellect and hands", human beings penetrate their surrounding environment and establish ties of relevance with that which they are not (*OS* 102), and it is exactly by appropriating a world in this manner that one becomes a person (*OS* 105). Accordingly, attachment is epistemologically and practically given (*OS* 48, 108). This seems to me to be ultimately the significance of Versfeld's ceaseless insistence that the basis of acting in the world is the fact that the world is already in us (e.g., *OS* 28, 32, 73, 79, 103, 129). Reformulated, that an environment has meaning to someone is what makes it possible to act. Therefore, the speaking about detachment is a "spiritual counsel" (*OS* 48) not to become so obsessed by the people and things with whom we interact that we lose sight of how we are meaningfully woven into our environment of people, things and nature. Detachment, therefore, doesn't aim to withdraw from the world or dissolve into a bland state of apathy, but rather to reassume the meaning that constitutes us as persons by "relaxing into what we are" (*OS* 21). It is a major persuasion of *Our Selves*, and probably of all Versfeld's work, that what we are, is given to us, proceding from divine generosity and coming to us as the procession of the creatures created by God (*OS* 48, 50, 109). If detachment is relaxing into the flow of time initiated by this creative process, then finding the true self means acting "directly out of what we are" (*OS* 85). That is why "the saint's detachment is really a higher form of attachment" (*OS* 48) and therefore ethics has everything to do with creativity and not that much with rules, in Versfeld's mind. In other words, moral judgement is for him less the application of principles or ideals and rather a matter of spontaneity – and on this, Christian, oriental and contemporary existentialist thinkers would concur (cf. *OS* 86). One could say that the ethics of detachment is an ethics of love, because "love is creatively spontaneous" (*FT* 92).

But I have announced the theme of detachment by saying that it forms part of Versfeld's way of working. By describing what detachment entails for one's life, I have not lost my thread, but prepared the context from which detachment as a manner of philosophising draws its meaning. We can observe in a number of ways how Versfeld attempts to detach himself from his writing even when writing. The interference of different traditions of thought could be considered the first of these, or it might be that elements from them are woven together in a supportive manner to form the "second thorn", but this can be done only at the expense of whatever claim to exclusivity any of them might have. The value of

Versfeld's trade is submitted to a similar relativisation: detached dishwashing is in final consideration more valuable than expressing one's ego by writing a tome of philosophy. This means that philosophy is reduced to recalling or pointing to truth, instead of containing it: "If I have called your attention to yourselves you can forget about me" (*OS* 88). Humility, which is the basis of the cardinal virtues, is therefore certainly more than the style of presentation of one's writing or action – it is the act of detachment by which one affirms that one belongs to a world that is given, not self-made (*OS* 104f.).

Versfeld seems to drive the detachment of his philosophising to a climax in the last chapter of *Our Selves*, when he digresses on the nature of philosophy (*OS* 165f.). He discards the pretence of philosophy to discover new truths, and pushes aside the claim of a certain philosophical tendency to master its own hold on reason by methodological doubt in favour of drawing from naivety. In this sense philosophy thrives on a sort of stupidity (*OS* 10). Furthermore, instead of serious work or even serious creation, the first virtue of the metaphysician is now said to be play, understood as "conflict creatively controlled by a containing order" (*OS* 166). One can hardly miss how far Versfeld is down the road of detachment, when he – who insisted that philosophy starts with anthropology and adamantly affirmed the anthropomorphic nature of our knowledge – asserts that the human being is not only insignificant (*OS* 26f.) and unknowable, but funny, and so promotes humour to the heart of philosophical seriousness. Kierkegaard is singled out as a thinker who "had the humorous sense of incongruity and the comic necessary for a metaphysician" (*OS* 166).

Readers of Versfeld's work of the 1980s might interpret his exquisite sense of humour as the licence of a retired professor who is fed up with the discipline of academic writing. Perhaps this is not devoid of truth. But it would at least be equally plausible to see this turn of style as progress in his detachment. "Detaching yourself from things is a good old advice", the Catholic philosopher writes in an essay on "Mucking Out" and continues: "If you chuck the Bible into the wastepaper basket, it proves perhaps that you have learned its most intimate lesson." [24]

---

[24] See "Opruim" in *NA* 2nd ed. 30.

5. Questioning from where we are

But if Versfeld confronts us with ourselves and the world in which we live, he can do so only by confronting us with himself. In this chapter I have attempted to show how he does this by highlighting a number of the most striking themes that run through this selection of essays and by interpreting their interconnection. A proper evaluation of the book can be undertaken only by considering it in all its complex and intricate detail – a pleasure to which I hasten to invite the reader. Thus, in conclusion, I shall merely suggest a number of questions – ensuing from the previous discussion – that might enhance the reader's attention when reading the book and contemplating its contents.

Decisive for any reception of Versfeld's thought is the extent to which one considers his diagnosis of modernity convincing. The decay of the mediaeval unity, started by the nominalist revolution and developed fully in modernity, tends to be represented as a lens for reading contemporary sociopolitical evils, as the historical manifestation of the political implications of an Augustinian diagnosis of distorted desires. Versfeld surely suffers from no shortage of examples to make the case for an ailing Western world, and when he goes so far as to consider Hitler to be "an inevitable phenomenon of a utilitarian rationalising society and a product of the Enlightenment" (*OS* 66), one has to acknowledge that he is in good company (think especially of the critical theorists of the Frankfurt School). Yet, one could wonder if more recognition of the other fruits of modernity is not due in his philosophy of history. I think not only of the virtues of existentialist phenomenology (because he sings its praises in *Our Selves*), but more importantly of the humanist cultural politics of the Enlightenment, which (apart from whatever valid criticism one might want to formulate against it) should at least be credited for creating the intellectual climate and institutional support in which translations of and commentaries on the Upanishads, Lao Tzu and Chuang-tzu, and the Buddhist masters (on which Versfeld's thought flourishes) could be made. Such modern tendencies of thought are, additionally, responsible for creating the means by which to edit and distribute these and other texts, without which Versfeld's work would simply be impossible.

Conspicuous in Versfeld's encompassing outline of modern decay is the absence of the profusion of the arts. Surely one can trace modernist characteristics in the different forms of artistic invention of the modern era, but I find it difficult to see the music of Bach, for instance, as a symptom of decay of anything. Or should one rather understand Versfeld to maintain that some modern sociopolitical tendencies are harmful, as motivated or testified to by modern philosophers, but that other typical modern phenomena are either good or at least harmless? But if this is the case, one will have to embark on a very tough search in Versfeld's text for the sources of such nonmediaeval (and non-Buddhist, non-Taoist, etc.) sources of well-being in modernity itself. Furthermore, if the decay of the mediaeval unity explains Hobbes and Descartes, what explains Kierkegaard and Nietzsche?[25] Or is it implied that modern culture is to be understood to carry some good despite itself, analogously to the deformed desires of which Versfeld says that they should not be uprooted but elevated, since they contain some good (*OS* 45, 47)?

Contrasting a philosophy that starts in doubt with one that seeks to excavate and explicate meaning is not unacceptable (think, for example, of Versfeld's contemporary, Paul Ricoeur, who drew a similar distinction between interpretation as an exercise of suspicion and interpretation as recollection of meaning). But would one not risk succumbing to plain naivety if one were to practise a philosophy of the explication of meaning without confronting the preformed meaning steadily with different varieties of doubt or suspicion? Now, since one can certainly not attribute such a basic naivety to Versfeld, is one then to conclude that the kind of suspicion generally required by our times, can be delivered with the help not of Marx, Freud, Nietzsche and company, but with other means such as an elaboration on Augustine's philosophy of desire? (That such a cultural criticism through alternative means is realisable, is amply illustrated in Versfeld's feminist critique of modern Christian culture in *OS* chapter 5.) But still, this Augustinian critique does seem to have left the tissue of meaning weaved by the real self's being in the world in a state of uncompromised innocence. There is, for instance, according to Versfeld, "often more wisdom in our bodies formed by the eternal Tao than in our minds" (*OS* 70). In other words, for Versfeld the true self is not a predator, but is truly innocent, and yet, at the same time, the true self is also the singular, historically formed and situated self. Subsequently, this line of interrogation ultimately leads to the heart of the thesis of *Our Selves*, since the reader will have to decide with what justice Versfeld can suppose that the true self to which Versfeld attempts to lead his readers (and

---

[25] In my introduction to the reedition of *Oor gode en afgode* (now Chapter 3, §5) I have shown that in Versfeld's very first development of his criticism of modernity, Nietzsche is exempt from criticism and co-opted as a diagnostic partner. This reading of Nietzsche is repeated with only a slight deviation in *Our Selves*. See again Van Tongeren's examination of Versfeld's relation to Nietzsche in Chapter 4. While he subjects Kierkegaard to a harsher reading, Versfeld elevates him in *Our Selves* at least to the position of quite a good modernist philosopher.

himself) back and which is characterised by the exercise of balanced desires, is the same as the particular historically situated being of every individual. One could also ask if it is not imaginable that the ego could sometimes act as the first defence against the mysterious forces at work in the inscrutable depths in which the singular, historical self is constituted. The answer to these questions will decisively influence one's idea of the desirability and success of Versfeld's project.

These reflections on modernity inevitably direct one to ponder the notion of the world in which we live, or as Versfeld would say, the place where we are. Now, I understood well that he has insisted that this world is neither the sum of things around us, nor merely the sum of mental pictures that we have of it, but the incarnate living in a sphere of relevance. Yet, this notion of the world cannot be thought without consideration for the things that happen to surround a specific person. Therefore, whereas one might easily go along with Versfeld's criticism of contemporary capitalism and consumerist society, it is less obvious to see where his philosophy of the true self would lead those people whose daily lives are shaped by the way in which they are inescapably embedded in this historical context. This matter becomes painful when one ponders what it could mean to find your true self by relaxing into what you are, for people living under conditions of social injustice, where what one is, is constituted by structural injustice. It might be a drawback of all his recuperation of classical and mediaeval authors, that none of them wrote from or for the life in the big modern city and hence their wisdom – as rich in instruction as it might be – doesn't occupy itself with the intricacies of having to live in such an environment. Consequently, the teaching of the true self can remain intact, and the complicated question regarding practically living in the modern world is swept under the rug of a cultural criticism of modern society. Or should the reader rather accept that the nature of advice for true living is such that it cannot be prescribed, and that *Our Selves* is an invocation to an ethic of prudence and spontaneity for which every agent has to take individual responsibility?

But the question concerning "where we are" also has an intellectual side: if one concedes to Versfeld's claim (as regards mediaeval Christianity) that one cannot tear oneself from the spiritual tradition in which one is historically rooted – should it then not be admitted that three or four centuries of modern history suffice to form a tradition of its own, one from which it might be equally injurious to tear oneself? And if one lives in plural traditions, would it not be necessary to reflect on the relative importance, significance, desirability and influence of these respective traditions? One would also have to contemplate, when reading *Our Selves*, what the status is of traditions that are not named here. Are they omitted simply because Versfeld didn't have time to work on all of them, or is it that they make no significant contribution in calling us to who we are? Something should at least be made explicit about this – a demand that has over the last three decades of South African history only gained in importance. And then one could also ask questions about the traditions that Versfeld draws on with as much enthusiasm as creativity. One case in point: I certainly don't deny a philosopher the right to select from other thinkers what to take on and what not to, but if one considers the kind of repeated criticism to which a political thinker like Hobbes is exposed, one cannot but be astounded that Versfeld, for whom the very political import of his philosophy of our two selves is structured by an Augustinian continuity between ethics and politics (*OS* 41), never even mentions that Augustine's justification of violent opposition against the Donatists constitutes "the key witness for the theological justification for forcible conversions, the Inquisition and the holy war, against deviants of all kinds".[26] The reader will have to decide if the charge of a lack of even-handedness against Versfeld's use of historical sources is valid, and if so, what the significance thereof is for his central arguments.

A last set of interesting questions with which to explore *Our Selves* concerns exactly the relation between ethics and politics. I simply accept Versfeld's insistence on the role that interpersonal relations play in weaving a social and even political fabric. However, it is something quite different to deduce that the "great injustices are the cumulative expression of the injustices done in particular personal relationships" (*OS* 107). I cite this statement because it says a lot about a tendency in *Our Selves* to reduce political action to ethical action. The consequence of doing this is that a very heavy load of decision-making, also with a view to political justice, is placed on the *individual* (cf. *OS* 106f.). This fits awkwardly with his insistence on the primordial *sociality* of people. But then, it cannot be denied that this shift gives vigour to individual responsibility in the repressive context of apartheid in South Africa, which could perhaps be said to have necessitated a shift in the balance from political to ethical initiative. One will have to decide to what extent his ethicopolitical convictions in *Our Selves* took shape in response to these particular historical circumstances and whether such convictions could be considered appropriate for this situation and for ours. Furthermore, even when considering the importance of individual responsibility, one has to contemplate if the desiring ego wouldn't under certain circumstances fare at least equally well in obstructing injustice as a mindset of detachment.

---

[26] See Hans Küng's discussion of this in his chapter on Augustine in *Great Christian Thinkers* (London: SCM Press, 1994); citation, 82.

If these questions succeed in plunging the reader in the lively flow of a life of reflection of which *Our Selves* is a midway account, they have served their purpose. A midway account is indeed what *Our Selves* is – not only because, as has been indicated in the chapter's introduction, this selection of essays documents something of the life and evolution of their author, but also because this selection of essays represents an episode of the continual effort of the author to go back from his own grasping ego to his true self. Pointing out the developing tensions and unsettled issues in *Our Selves* doesn't amount to rejecting it; rather, by entering into a vigorous contemplation of these essays, the reader will be questioned, and challenged, by the development of a singular human being's efforts to find his real self, to find *nirvana* in his particular *samsara*. Besides, the reader that looks to philosophy for a soup that has no strange aftertaste, will die of hunger.

CHAPTER 6

VERSFELD'S DIALOGUE WITH EASTERN THOUGHT

By J. S. Krüger

1. Introduction

The encounter of Marthinus (Martin) Versfeld (1909–1995) with Eastern thought is a fascinating thread in the tapestry of his life and work. Brought up in the Dutch Reformed Church, Versfeld joined the Roman Catholic Church a number of years after his exposure to Aquinas and Christian mystics during his doctoral studies at the University of Glasgow. As a result, Catholic thought, represented particularly by Augustine and Thomas Aquinas, became the lifelong mainstay of his thinking. He completed his doctoral thesis on Descartes, which was subsequently published as *An Essay on the Metaphysics of Descartes* (1940). This figure would remain the lifelong negative reference point of Versfeld's thinking. The third side of the triangle of his work was his interest in Eastern thought, which also commenced at a fairly early stage of his life and continued to its end. A number of articles dealing with his philosophy[1] refer to this interest,

---

[1] W.A. de Klerk, "Marthinus Versfeld: mens en denker"; W.A. de Klerk, "Marthinus Versfeld: die man en sy denke"; Rossouw, "Die kuns van die lewe is om tuis te kom"; Wolff, "Sanctus Marthinus Laudator Philosophicus"; Wolff, "Selfkennis, verstandigheid en inkarnasie: 'n Interpretasie van Martin Versfeld se *Oor gode en afgode*"; Wolff, "Grasping the Truth from Where We Are"; and Wolff, "*Poeisis*. Oor maaksels en hul wêreld na aanleiding van Versfeld se *Pots and Poetry*."

but as far as I could establish, this aspect of his thinking has not been investigated in detail before.

How far did he journey, how deeply did he penetrate the religious landscape of the East? Who were his guides and companions? Was he a casual tourist or visitor, or did he find a second home there? Versfeld does not offer any significant autobiographical pointers in this regard, so I shall trace his development as it unfolded in his publications (both more academic and more popular, in both English and Afrikaans) in the chronological order of their appearance, and that will determine the format of this chapter. I am interested in the following aspects:

(a) The measure of his direct contact with Eastern thought, by which I mean acquaintance with primary texts (perhaps in the original languages) and/or exposure to any living traditions.
(b) The extent to which his encounters with at least some oriental religions are embedded in a well-informed understanding of their historical contexts and developments.
(c) An explicit theoretical model in his writing concerning the relationship between Western Christian thought and Eastern thought. To what extent do his encounters express an explicit comparative methodology and hermeneutic? To what extent does his writing accommodate both Western and Eastern religions in one comprehensive, inclusive theoretical context?
(d) The possible structural similarities between his own thinking and Eastern models, regardless of his own intentional articulation of such relationship.

Starting with (a), Versfeld does not appear to have had any direct linguistic access to Mandarin (the literary language of Taoism, his Chinese field of interest), Sanskrit or Pali (the two classical languages of Indian religions, including Buddhism, his particular religio-philosophical interest in that subcontinent). This is noted, but will not be held as a serious criticism of his dialogue with Taoism and Buddhism, taking into account that he was a pioneering figure in the twentieth-century South African context. On the other hand, for the sake of a realistic appraisal of his work, it needs to be said that he made no serious contribution to the study of Chinese or Indian religions as such in a linguistic, historical or philosophical sense. To put this in proper historical perspective, bear in mind the contributions made to the study of Sanskrit by, for example, William Jones long before, beginning in the end of the eighteenth century, and Wilhelm Schlegel in the early decades of the nineteenth century. In this analysis, I shall limit myself largely to his encounter with Indian religion in the form of Buddhism, not least because I am not a specialist in Taoism with the linguistic requisites to give an expert opinion on that religion. However, his references to Taoism will be carefully noted.

Versfeld's writing is usually of an entertaining, relaxed, essayistic type. That is not regarded as a handicap to intellectual, academic or religious work, but appreciated as part and parcel of the entire package of his thought.

2. Groundbreaking early works

1. The foundations of Versfeld's mature thinking were laid in two works appearing during his thirties, in the decade spanning the beginning of the Second World War (1939), and the beginning of the system of apartheid as government policy in South Africa (1948). The first work was his doctoral thesis on Descartes, written in English: *An Essay on the Metaphysics of Descartes* (1940); the second, a book of protest and warning, written in Afrikaans: *Oor gode en afgode* (*On Gods and Idols*) (1948). Both books are led by a sense of crisis: the first aspired to a break with Descartes and the birth of "a new kind of man",[2] the second, to a break with nationalism and apartheid; both marked the outlines of Versfeld's future development.

The thesis does not yield anything of relevance concerning Eastern religions. It is a critique of Descartes, blaming the French philosopher's subjectivism and egocentrism for the error of psychologism in modern philosophy. The course of Versfeld's thinking was by this point fixed, but there is no evidence of an awareness of and interest in Eastern religions. An interesting question is what difference it might have made if Versfeld had been conversant with, for example, a third (Eastern) possibility, such as early Buddhism's critique of both the construction of views of what lies outside the limits of human cognition (an equivalent of which was Aquinas's five proofs for the existence of God), as well as of the fixation on the "ego" (which is what Descartes's position boils down to). Likewise, one may wonder what difference an early confrontation with the epistemological critique of a Nāgārjuna would have made to Versfeld's adherence at this stage to two alternatives: theistic religion of the Augustinian-Thomistic type, and what followed in the wake of Descartes. But such speculation is futile; such a meeting would have been outside the bounds of what was available to the young scholar in 1940.

---

[2] Versfeld, *An Essay on the Metaphysics of Descartes*, 148.

2. Eight years later (in *Oor gode en afgode*) the Eastern side of the triangle is slightly more evident, but still in rudimentary form. Neither an inclusive religio-historical framework, nor an explicit comparative religious hermeneutic, nor a theory inclusive of all religions is as yet discernible. By comparison, his endorsement of Platonism-Aristotelianism and his intellectual and existential commitment to Augustinian-Thomistic thinking has taken clear shape in his Christian philosophy. His response to Descartes has taken off.

In Versfeld's view, Aquinas presents "the best, perhaps the perfect solution" (*GA* 3) to the problem of the relationship of Greek philosophy and Christian faith. Those who took wrong turns are the ones turning away from that model, and they include Luther (with his contradistinction of faith and reason) and Kant (as follower of Luther). Eternal God (*GA* 149) as "Primary Existent" (*GA* 97) is the axiomatic point of departure, and Christian faith is "a life of loving commitment to a Person" (*GA* 55). Thomas's supranaturalistic realism is aligned with Plato's notion of a "reality beyond reality" (*GA* 65). Contrary to the Renaissance, which viewed the human person as merely a "natural being" "without any transcendental context" (*GA* 84), Christianity views the world as God's creation (*GA* 57). Some religious truths, including the real existence of God, can be proven by reason, analogically (*GA* 35); others, such as the Incarnation and the Trinity, cannot, although they are compatible with reason (*GA* 5ff.). Overall, Versfeld presents his view as "metaphysics" in the sense of a "Christian philosophy", a "Christian science" (*GA* 138).

That is the context of his critique of nationalism and apartheid. Remember, it was 1948, when the Nationalist Party came to power in South Africa. To Versfeld, "only a super-natural morality can make of this earth an inhabitable home" (*GA* 101). With the destruction of Plato's and Thomas's connection of metaphysics, morality and politics were involved several evils, including the split in the Church with the Reformation (*GA* 40ff.); the disintegration of mediaeval society into separate nation states (*GA* 40); the rejection of religious sanction for morality by Descartes (*GA* 101ff.); the split in the individual human person of body and mind by that same philosopher (*GA* 41); the split between individuals by yet the same founder of modernity (they can now only be united mechanically, *GA* 63); the split between church and state with Rousseau (*GA* 67ff.); and the split of humanity into separate races and nations (*GA* 97). In this modern dispensation (read: South Africa in 1948), race could become "the final reality" (*GA* 97), and some races could be seen and treated as "inferior" (*GA* 94, 97). Versfeld's position is clear: the crises of modern culture derive from the disintegration of mediaeval Christian culture, "the loss of universality of catholicity" (*GA* 137) – the context leaves no doubt that this is a loss of Christian universality and catholicity. There is no "uniting metaphysic" any more (*GA* 137).

References to Eastern metaphysical resources are not entirely lacking in this book, but they play no constitutive role. Versfeld lists the Upanishads along with St Augustine, Julian of Norwich, Jacob Boehme and St John of the Cross to illustrate the point that religious experience is unique, and different from science and art (*GA* 25ff.) – but makes nothing of it. And the early *Brihadarayaka* and *Svetasvatara Upanishads* and the phrase *tat tvam asi* (*GA* 26f.) may be valid as examples of religious knowledge and mystical experience, but mentioning them *en passant* (with neither primary nor secondary references) serves no real purpose; as far as content goes, these examples do not appear to be, at face value, reconcilable with Versfeld's version of Christian belief. He offers no reflection on the significance of those ancient Indian sources.

Hardly more elaborate are his references to Buddhism (*GA* 145ff.) in his treatment of the Christian notion of history. Here the claim that to Buddhism, the temporality of things and physical bodies are simply "illusions" ("*illusie*"; "*droombeelde*"), is incorrect. And the emphasis of early Buddhism on impermanence (*anicca*) as a fundamental truth of things opens a promising perspective on a metaphysic of history and a dialogue with Christianity, but Versfeld lets this opportunity slip away unnoticed. He also makes a fleeting, at best seriously unclarified and at worst seriously wrong, reference to Buddhist "Nothingness" ("*Nietigheid*"), contemplation of which is said to be the aim of "the good man" (*GA* 148).

Such isolated references do not occur in any developed metareligious hermeneutic or synoptic philosophy of religion. For example, the ancient Buddhist notion of impermanence could be extrapolated to a philosophy of history, implying the finitude of all human systems of meaning, including Christianity. But Versfeld does not touch on such a possibility, and leaves no space for any challenge to Christianity. In this book he remains bound to Christian universality and catholicity; his promising notion of "a uniting metaphysics" (*GA* 137) is not extended to include non-Christian systems of ultimate meaning. Humanity is indeed seen as "one indivisible whole" (*GA* 138), but this does not seem to apply to the field of religion and metaphysics. As an apologetic book, it is directed at modernity, not any other religion. There is no real inter-religious encounter.

In his opposition to apartheid, Versfeld trod a path that was followed by many Christian critics of that system, such as his slightly younger contemporary, Beyers Naudé (1915–2004). Such critics opposed apartheid by falling back on strongly entrenched versions of Christian orthodoxy, and in Versfeld's case, of Augustinian-Thomistic thought. His book positions Christianity against all forms of separateness in modern society, but does not address the root assumption: the ontological separateness of God and world in the orthodox Christian belief system – erased in neither the Incarnation nor mystical experience. He does not investigate the possible authoritarian implication of such a two-level ontology, both politically and religiously. In the Indian systems that he mentions, precisely that separateness of natural and supernatural is denied. This I find a key aspect, *the* key aspect, of the encounter investigated in this chapter.

So far Versfeld did not allow for an eye to eye meeting of Christianity and Eastern thought as equals, working together towards a wider horizon including – and radically relativising, and thereby saving – both discourses. Is Indian religious thought here a toothless tiger, merely paraded? Let us not rush to conclusions. Those were early days and such ideas were novel in the South African context. Even being a Catholic in 1948 was an act of defiance for an Afrikaans-speaking South African, and required some courage. Would he accept the challenge, would he be prepared to engage in serious conversation? The fair conclusion to draw is that at the time, Versfeld had a mild interest in, but no thorough acquaintance with, any Eastern religion.

3. Midcareer

3. In *The Perennial Order* (1954), putting forward his philosophy in systematic form, Versfeld emerges confidently as established Roman Catholic philosopher (*nihil obstat, imprimatur*). He deals with a variety of topics: God, the human state, science, morality, history, law, art. In terms of our present interest in Eastern thought, this book marks no advance beyond *Oor gode en afgode*. Building on Thomas's proofs, the phrase "God [...] the absolute selfsubsistent Being who is the source and ground of everything that is" (*PO* 245) reveals the bedrock, the *norma normans*, of his thinking. From this follows the endorsement of the derived but real character of the empirical world (e.g., *PO* 23). The book as a whole flows from the point of departure that the world is historical, God eternal. In terms of this most basic point of departure, he, not surprisingly, disqualifies Indian thinking. Quoting the *Svetasvatara Upanishad* via Berdyaeff, he affirms that Hinduism establishes an antithesis between history and eternity (*PO* 58).

Buddhism fares no better: for it, "the world of time is the world of illusion, and material bodies are simply phantoms which haunt the unenlightened mind, caught up in the sorrow of birth and death" (*PO* 151). A number of relevant issues receive no attention, including the differences within "Hinduism" in this regard, for example, between the Advaita and Dvaita schools (the latter being much closer to Versfeld's Christian position); the differences between "Hinduism" and "Buddhism"; the Buddhist critique of a substantialist notion of God; and the potential points of growth of a rapprochement between a Buddhist emphasis on continuity and the value of the empirically unique (cf. Zen), and Versfeld's own emphasis on history and empirical existence. Especially the last is of interest: the gradual increase of an existential focus in Versfeld's work (qualifying his enduring allegiance to Thomism) announces itself, and may have been fertile ground for his growing interest in Zen over years. On the other hand, a link with Versfeld's equally enduring rootedness in Augustinian thought is obvious.

Given the scope of *The Perennial Order*, I fully grant that it may be unrealistic to have expected a more nuanced view of these religious complexes. Moreover, Versfeld refers to them from a Christian perspective; provides no evidence of finding or building a second home there, having made a first-hand study of them; outlines no methodology for dealing comparatively with them in relation to Christianity; and does not envisage a large-scale synthesis, perhaps amounting to a demolishing of both the first and the second homes on an absolute horizon of mystical silence. In significant respects, this book is a continuation of *Oor gode en afgode*. Yet, were the seeds for a truly integrated perennial philosophy sown?

4. Looking back on his own philosophical development in 1960, with the publication of "Descartes and Me" (*Sum* 13–24), Versfeld again pledges his well-established allegiance to Augustine and Thomas and decries Descartes and like-minded philosophers such as Comte. However, in passing he also makes a noteworthy comment: "I am always prepared to go back to Aristotle or Aquinas or Confucius or Samkara [...]. Incidentally, there seem to be good reasons why we should devote some time to Eastern philosophers" (*Sum* 21). He adds the methodologically telling point that such historical truth "must be able to make sense of and to integrate our contemporary experience, and the historical processes which have given rise to it" (*Sum* 21). Both comments mark an advance, compared to his position in 1948 and 1954, and are useful in themselves, as far as they go. But he does not demonstrate having gone back to Confucius or Samkara (did he perhaps do that over previous years, without writing about it?). He does not elaborate on the "good reasons" for devoting time to Eastern philosophers.

And he does not argue how thinkers such as Confucius and Samkara could be integrated with the Western-Christian historical processes and the contemporary experience of that religio-cultural complex. He provides useful programmatic guidelines, but no real evidence of executing them.

5. Again he confesses his orthodox Christian belief that at least "a God exists" in *The Mirror of Philosophers* (*MP* 21), without venturing into the agora of inter-religious encounter to test this. In the substance of his thinking there is no change, yet his sentiment that "the notions of mystery, contemplation and metaphysics go together" (*Sum* 22), coupled with the notions referred to above, are promising as far as a true *pax fidei* (Cusanus) is concerned. But the bridge has not been constructed or crossed.

6. Two years later, in *Rondom die Middeleeue* (*On the Middle Ages*) (1962), Versfeld proceeds to provide his Afrikaans readers sympathetic insight into the mediaeval spirit, which is part of their own history. In itself this was a most commendable undertaking. His readers could easily have forgotten that majestic chapter in their cultural and religious tradition. Indeed, this book, all the more impressive because of its charming presentation, draws a convincing picture of, among other themes as can now be expected, Augustine and Thomas and the latter's intentions with his proofs for the existence of God. By now, age 53, Versfeld made up his mind, found his peace. This book is not the first time his readers follow him into the Middle Ages and the normative Augustine and Thomas. Yet there is no in-depth dialogue with Eastern thought. We find only one swipe at an unspecified "Chinese Buddhist writing" expanding on the "Tao", but the reader finds no sufficient ground to either agree or disagree with Versfeld's claim that there "cannot be a more thorough anti-scientific manifest" (*RM* 94f.).

Of more importance is the opportunity missed in that book to engage the Thomistic proofs for the existence of God via analogy (*RM* 59–92) with the alternative routes traversed by Taoism and Buddhism. This is where the Western and Eastern religious continents meet, where the real essentials are at stake. Our present question does not concern the merit or not of Aquinas's and Versfeld's arguments as such, but whether his arguments here were informed by a certain knowledge of the Taoist and Buddhist positions. This cannot really be proven either way, but one may suspect that if these two Asian religions had been fairly well known to Versfeld, it is conceivable that he would have discussed the relationship between Aquinas's proofs that God exists, and those versions of emptiness conceived in the East beyond analogical bridges. Conspicuous in this context is also the apparent lack of awareness of the Buddhist notion of causality (*paccaya*) in Versfeld's elaborate discussion of causality (*RM* 77ff.). Thomas argues that the all-pervasive phenomenon of change ultimately, logically, necessitates the notion of an unchanging but all-changing Being ("called 'God' by all"); Buddhism rests with the acceptance of a pan-conditional impermanence of all things, issuing not in substantiality (including divine substantiality), but in radical non-substantiality. If Versfeld had known of this fundamental difference, he would have tackled it; of that we can be quite certain.

We are here not dealing with innocuous, nice-to-know-and-show peripherals, but with the most central issues in the encounter of Christianity (as a matter of fact, any theism) with those Asian models. I am all too aware of the dangers of drawing conclusions from silence, whether by design or lack of information. Could Versfeld have been aware of this direct, seemingly irreconcilable encounter, but not prepared to deal with it for whatever psychological or strategic reason? Or could the full strength of the wind from the East not have touched him yet? I suspend judgement, but suspect the second. The most likely conclusion is that at the time he was not cognisant of it. I fully endorse Versfeld's high regard for the Christian Middle Ages, and specifically for Augustine and Aquinas, and his own passion for ultimacy, but must point out the lack of serious encounter with Eastern religions at this stage of his life. It could have enriched his Christian thinking.

7. I now turn to a key paper that Versfeld presented at the Eighth Congress for the Advancement of Philosophy in South Africa in 1965, entitled "Talking Metaphysics".[3] He was 56 years old, well advanced and established in his publishing career and at the height of his powers; some interest on Versfeld's part in Eastern religions had surfaced some twenty years earlier. In this paper he championed metaphysics; it could indeed be read as a programmatic statement, containing his view of the vital ingredients and concomitants of a viable programme of metaphysics. He expresses the typical concern of metaphysics, namely the "desire for and pursuit of the whole" ("Talking" 12), behind and beyond all special disciplines. By definition, such desire and pursuit would include all serious religious thought, West and East (and more). Yet, at this crucial point Versfeld remarkably stops short of what could have been a groundbreaking step in the highest academic body of South African philosophical thought fifty years ago.

---

[3] Marthinus Versfeld, "Talking Metaphysics," in M. Versfeld and R. Meyer, *On Metaphysics* (Pretoria: Unisa, 1966).

His argument as a whole in the paper is steeped in the symbiosis of Western thought with its founding father Socrates, as well as of Platonism-Aristotelianism, and the Christian faith, resulting in the Christian syntheses of Augustine and Thomas. He also does not mince his words concerning the dangerous deviations of Descartes and what followed with Kant, Comte, Hegel and analytical philosophy. Care should be taken not to make too much of an *argumentum e silentio*, yet the fact that Versfeld does not make a single reference to any Eastern religion precisely in this context is telling. Was it an implicit admission of a lack of sufficient knowledge? A failure of nerve, perhaps on an assumption that such references would not seem relevant or be palatable to his audience of Western-trained professional philosophers? Perhaps, but could it also have been indicative that, after all, Eastern thinking was of secondary importance and that, ultimately, Eastern thinking did not play a central, constitutive role in his own metaphysical model? Or did he simply not have enough time to deal with that? This omission would have to be evaluated in the context of his corpus as a whole.

The above lacuna becomes obvious in his references in this paper to the basic metaphysical questions of the ultimate origin of the world and the human being. These themes as such are not expressly dealt with in detail, yet the Platonic and the orthodox Christian teaching as finally formulated by Thomas, are assumed, without admitting any Eastern challenge. The Platonic view that truth has to do with Being is normative. That is a most respectable position to take, but in our present context it is noteworthy that dialogue and comparative analysis involving, for example, Vedantic monism, or Taoist or Buddhist notions of Emptiness as the ultimate horizon and source of all things beyond Being, play no role.

Epistemologically, Versfeld adopts a "nescient" position, presenting that stance as in line with Plato ("Talking" 8ff., 17ff.). True metaphysics is the opening of horizons rather than the provision of final solutions ("Talking" 19ff.), demonstrating "an essential capacity for relativising itself", "rooted in its own contingency", resting in "humility"; whereas Descartes moved from doubt to certainty, Augustine moved from scepticism to questioning. Versfeld obviously turns away from any variant of authoritarian truth. Here an obvious structural link with Taoism and Buddhism appears, yet Versfeld gives no hint as to whether Eastern religions are silently present, and if so, how – as constitutive elements, or perhaps reinforcing influences, or mere interesting coincidences?

This teasing silence can be heard elsewhere in his paper, where sub-themes are dealt with which occur in Eastern as much as in Western metaphysics, in Confucian Mencius as much as in Christian Augustine – such as that metaphysics is essentially connected to emotion (e.g., love, a moral passion for the good), and that it has a social dimension; that it is about human relationships, a just society, politics, in which truth and justice are intimately connected, and imperialism of any kind is ruled out. And here, I suspect, lies the reason for his omission of Eastern thought: he had his hands full with the South African social crisis of the time. The country was in a state of emergency as part of the aftermath of the Sharpeville shootings in 1960. Versfeld, an outspoken critic of apartheid, indirectly but clearly for philosophers who had ears to hear, addressed that moral and political crisis. That is why he makes a strong point of the importance of the historical dimension of metaphysics, much more so, he says ("Talking" 14), than understood by Plato. Metaphysical awareness and existence take place in time and history, in a certain society, a certain century, a certain milieu ("Talking" 14ff., 19). That is the point he wished to make, as cautiously as prudence at the time prescribed. Here he had a political agenda, not a religio-comparative one, and the inter-religious dimension was not central to his argument.

8. In the same year, in *Wat is kontemporêr? Vier opstelle oor ons tyd* (*What Is Contemporary? Four Essays on Our Time*) (1966), Versfeld consistently continues along the road taken in his youth, with the Christian patristics and mediaeval philosopher-theologians as normative guiding lights against the backdrop of European classics and Scripture. As always, modernity since the seventeenth century is his main adversary. The essence of his argument is that to be truly contemporary, "a thinker should experience the mystery of the Divine Presence".[4] That was also the year that his lecture "Talking Metaphysics", analysed above, was published. These four essays confirm the conclusion that at the time Versfeld did not have a profound knowledge of Eastern religions. Perhaps one may suspect that had he been well acquainted with Buddhism, he might have made something of the interesting parallel between this religion and Hume's views concerning a permanent personal identity,[5] but I do not wish to make much of it.

More significant is the appearance of Zen in his writings. Again a hunch that cannot be definitely confirmed: could he have made an acquaintance with an introduction of Zen to a Western audience in popular literature at the time, such as the books by Alan Watts? Zen, mostly isolated from the wider Buddhist setting of which it was one manifestation, became quite a buzzword in the West at the time. In any event, Versfeld makes no references to any sources here (in *OS* 85 he refers to Watts). But perhaps Watts was not a major source of information and

---

[4]   Versfeld, *Wat is kontemporêr?* 35.
[5]   Versfeld, *Wat is kontemporêr?* 28.

inspiration, for Versfeld seems to associate the practice of Zen with "withdrawal from the world" (*OS* 30) (which was hardly the view of Watts). Versfeld also refers to Zen as a "flight from time" (*OS* 34), shared with "sorcerers and drug-users" (*OS* 34). That is all. Whatever the other merits of this book may be, it does not excel in the conversation between Christianity and Eastern religions.

9. In *Klip en klei* (1968), a volume of entertaining essays on various topics, the reader finds many insightful observations. One of these is a loving sketch of Versfeld's father (*KK* 44f.), which gives an insight into the circumstances behind Versfeld's turning away from the Dutch Reformed religion of his youth and his turn to Catholicism – a move lovingly understood by his father. The reader also comes across a fleeting, strangely ambiguous reference to "the Zen tea ceremony" (*KK* 38). Of more significance is the lack of congruence with the Buddhist ethos apparent in this book as far as the treatment of animals is concerned. He enthusiastically endorses hunting and the consumption of meat, one of his arguments being that "the death of an animal and the death of a human being are totally different" (*KK* 59), and finds that "much of the fuss about blood-sport is morally unhealthy" (*KK* 59). With these statements, he in fact stands considerably closer to the views of his archadversary Descartes than to the typically Buddhist view of the interconnectedness of all life and the maxims of non-violence and nonkilling that flow from that ontology. The salient point in the context of this chapter is not the issue of vegetarianism per se (I am not advocating that here, not at all), but the fact that Versfeld obviously did not seriously engage with Buddhist thinking in this connection. Apart from explicit references, one does not sense a closeness of thought and sentiment with Buddhism. For example, neither of the two parts of the observation that "the only immortal nation is the Church of God which is the body of God" (*KK* 106f.) is compatible with the essential pattern of Buddhist thought, which would not allow for the idea of an eternal *civitas Dei*.

10. One year later, in *Beweging uitwaarts* (*Movement Outwards*, co-authored with W.A. de Klerk and J.J. Degenaar in 1969), Versfeld contributes three essays. In one of them (dealing with "morality and moralism", *BU* 67–88), an unexpected step is taken, compared to his book from the previous year. Could it be because he now wrote for a different audience? Or did something he read, or some personal contact, trigger a newly found interest? Or did a seed, present yet slumbering over the years, suddenly start to sprout? Not only does the chapter start with a Zen poem ("the oldest Zen poem", he says, and presumably taken from Watts, going on what he would say in *OS* 85), but we find, for the first time, a reference to central Buddhist issues, in this case, the teaching of *anattā* (*BU* 71ff.), albeit not in a convincing sense. What Buddhism does, he says, is destroy the constructed *ego* of our own making with which we usually identify ourselves. That is correct. But then he seems to see the Buddhist view as part of what he terms "Indian" thought (*BU* 71), which is said to identify the self with the ground of being (*BU* 71), which is not correct as far as Buddhism is concerned. The watershed between Buddhism and the type of monism commencing in the Upanishadic age and culminating in Advaita Vedanta is not recognised. He also conflates Buddhist "atheism" with the Christian *via negativa*, assuming that the Buddha merely "did not want to speak about God" (*BU* 73). What Versfeld glosses over is that even in the most apophatic forms of Christian mysticism the personal being and existence of God are not in doubt, whereas in the message of the Buddha that notion is utterly emptied and transcended.

We also find a useful reference (but again without a source) to a "technique" developed by "Zen Buddhists" to break down the conceptual barriers we erect (*BU* 82), and a few other nice brief quotes from Buddhism (*BU* 87). Overall, the enlisting of Buddhism, particularly Zen Buddhism, in a critique of moralism is very much in order. Also, the willingness to enter into dialogue with that religion can only be applauded. But there is no denying that those were early days. No references to sources are provided. I am not pointing this out for fussy, technical, formalistic reasons, but simply because it would have helped us to understand the extent and quality of his guides and the context of his thinking. It cannot be said that this lack is simply a consequence of the communication style adopted here; quotations from Western sources in this particular book are sometimes paragraphs long. The overall conclusion must be that neither his rendering of Buddhism nor his integration of Buddhism and Christianity breaks significant ground. As far as Taoism is concerned, we read only that "Thomas and the Taoists had much in common" (*BU* 87) insofar as both view love as undercutting the intellect. This is a promising bud.

First steps in a "movement outwards" in a religio-philosophical sense had been taken. South Africa was in the grip of closed thinking, politically as well as religiously. The philosopher, now sixty years old, to his credit pointed towards a wider horizon.

4. Mature thought

11. Versfeld started his seventh decade with a celebration of Plato (*Plato. Die Simposium of die drinkparty*, 1970), an enduring mainstay throughout his life. This translation of the *Symposium* and the light-hearted introduction to it are classic Versfeld, with his firm anchorage in Christianity and his loyal indebtedness to Plato, expressed in his unique literary way – but there is not the least glance sideways at Eastern thought. It is popularisation of a classical document at its best, yet without any use of the original Greek text of any consultation of secondary literature to contextualise his work in the large, continuing debate with Plato. This is relevant in our present context, because this lack of citation also marks all his dealings with Eastern texts.

12. Four years later, a similar book appeared, this time not a translation but an introduction to Plato's *Republic*, intended for a young Afrikaans academic readership: *'n Handleiding tot die Republiek van Plato* (1974). We meet an excellent lecturer in this text. Not unexpectedly, this book too links Plato with the Roman Catholic tradition: Plato's mystical notion of the contemplation of eternal Being is reminiscent of what has become part of the European tradition, and is echoed by Augustine.[6] But this time there are a few references to other works on Plato and a few casual glances to the East: similar to Platonic morality, we read, Zen spontaneity requires discipline;[7] comparable to Plato's appreciation of the impact of art on politics, is that of Confucius;[8] and similar to Plato's notion of education for society, Confucius emphasises education for social unselfishness, sympathy and authority.[9] Such asides are interesting, but lack any strongly argued structural significance.

13. Between the above two Afrikaans works on Platonic thinking appeared a more systematic work in English (*Persons*, 1972); the substance of some of these chapters had appeared previously in Afrikaans. The central thought of the book is that knowledge of persons has priority over knowledge of things. The first chapter of this book ("The Socratic Spirit") is his inaugural lecture at the University of Cape Town of 1971 (*Persons* 1–15). It would seem to be of singular

---

[6] Versfeld, *'n Handleiding*, 66, 80ff.
[7] Versfeld, *'n Handleiding*, 30.
[8] Versfeld, *'n Handleiding*, 45, 112.
[9] Versfeld, *'n Handleiding*, 61.

significance, because "in an inaugural lecture a man should declare himself" (*Persons* 1). Exactly five years have now elapsed since his other programmatic statement ("Talking Metaphysics", 1966). Has anything significant happened in this period? Perhaps. It causes no surprise that he chooses Socrates as the topic at this illustrious occasion, and handles the Greek well. Then follow the usual crown witnesses: Plato, Jesus, Augustine, Thomas and the usual rascals, starting with Descartes. But now, compared to five years before, Zen makes a happy, relaxed entry onto the stage (*Persons* 2). And mention is made of the fact that Socrates, like Jesus and the Buddha, wrote nothing (*Persons* 3f.). The reference to Zen still does not contribute to the substance of the argument, but to its style: the "supreme feat" of laughing at oneself is lauded. I sense that in his essayistic, aphoristic style of communication Versfeld felt an affinity with the seeming simplicity of Zen (not unlike that of Socrates) and its quotability. The thinking was all very much and essentially about the West ("our tradition", *Persons* 5), but perhaps something new was afoot.

This surmise is confirmed by what might be interpreted as a new, mild ambivalence about God in this book. Versfeld still accepts Augustine's classical understanding of God and does not doubt His eternity (e.g., *Persons* 71, 121), but now we again read that Buddhism is "wise" "because it refuses to talk about God" (*Persons* 86). Versfeld is concerned with sinful people's idolatrous conceptual constructs of God, but this does not make a serious dent in his acceptance of the being of God as such; the constructed God is a false God. However, refusing to talk about God is one thing, nihilating such talk altogether and at most accepting it as a penultimate step in a process towards radical nihilation is another. What we find here is a virtual enlistment of Buddhism in the service of Christian apophaticism, but not a square confrontation with the full force of the radical dissolution of such a concept emerging in, for example, the *Tevijja Sutta* in Theravāda Buddhism or the *Mūlamādhyamika-kārikas* of Nāgārjuna in Mahāyāna.

It is as if Versfeld hovers on the brink of a bridge over a chasm. He displays an intuitive affinity with certain aspects of Buddhism, but not a clear grasp of the historical continuities and discontinuities among various Eastern religions, specifically Buddhism, Hinduism, Taoism and Confucianism (cf. *Persons* 97f.). We find some exploratory, suggestive matching and mixing in the service of his well-established Augustinian-Thomistic model, but not a thorough theoretical dialogue that risks everything in the fire of an encounter with India and China (e.g., *Persons* 85f.). We find an encomium on Augustine and the Catholic faith (*Persons* 126ff.). That is quite in order, but it cannot be said to be argued in the process of an in-depth confrontation with Eastern patterns of thinking. Notions such as the changeability and constructed nature of ideas and interpretative schemes make their appearance (*Persons* 69f., 191f.), but are not carried through in ways that would have passed the test of, for example, classical Buddhism. At this stage Versfeld does not exhibit a coherent macrohistorical picture of religions West and East, a developed comparative hermeneutic or a systematic macro theory encompassing the various religions and philosophical models he mentions from time to time.

14. In 1978 Versfeld produced a short essay, "Wyn en wysheid" ("Wine and Wisdom"), in which we enjoy the ageing Versfeld at his youthful best, playing beyond the constrictions of abstract thinking. It is a celebration of the wisdom of appreciating wine, of finding the miraculous in the everyday, not only in the bread and wine of the Christian Eucharist but equally present in the Zen tea ceremony and ancient Taoists' peaceful use of their mouths for the business of eating. Versfeld pokes fun at abstract thinking, and by implication – presumably, ultimately and rightly so – at any attempt to construct a final inclusive philosophy or theology of religion. Here at least he was not interested in that.

15. However, the following year, he demonstrated his enduring interest in establishing a *pax fidei* at a more theoretical level. In a slender book called *Our Selves* (1979), published seven years after *Persons*, Versfeld – now seventy years old – presents the most comprehensive systematic presentation of his oeuvre thus far as far as his encounter with Eastern thought is concerned. These ideas had evidently simmered for several years.[10] In *Our Selves*, Versfeld engages with Buddhism, Taoism and to a lesser extent Hinduism – to an extent unprecedented in his own work and in South African academic work up till then. He does this without compromising his longstanding loyalty to revered figures and his unwavering censure of others in the Greek-Christian Western tradition – the first starting with Socrates, the latter with late mediaeval nominalism. Versfeld enters into some debate with Eastern systems, more so than before.

But overall he does not work from within a well-developed linguistic-historical frame of reference, and some of his understanding of Indian and Chinese thought is suspect. For example, we find a two-page analysis of Rāmānuja, Ramakrishna, Patanjali and even the *Tibetan Book of the Dead* (*OS* 17ff.); also present are references to the five Buddhist *khandhas* and the Buddhist insight

---

[10] Cf. Wolff, "Grasping the truth from where we are."

into impermanence and non-substance (*OS* 3ff.). But alongside that occurs the fatal identifications of "the real self" in Buddhism with *Brahman* (*OS* 5ff., 15ff.), of *Atman* with *Buddha nature* (*OS* 20), and of "union with God" with "Nirvana" (*OS* 21). He treats "Indian thought" (*OS* 9f.) as all of one kind, and that is said to be the same as Paul's teaching (*OS* 15). In encounters like this, the acknowledgement of differences is as important as the acknowledgement of possible convergences, and in this respect no real advance has been made compared to his position ten years earlier (cf. *BU* 71). The problem is compounded by the fact that Versfeld does not provide any information on the sources he draws on for his information, which would have helped his reader to gauge the extent and depth of his reading. His sense that "the contemporary fugue into the Oriental" (*OS* 40) may tempt people to forget the strength of their own tradition is valid, but that insight does not diminish the need for careful comparative analysis if "the Oriental" is introduced in a meeting of faiths. His method adds up to short-circuiting eclecticism rather than true synthesis. Yet, he ventured onto a path as yet untrodden in South African academic discourse in both philosophy and theology, and at a time when an independent subject of religious studies (comparative religion) was non-existent at South African universities.

As for Taoism, we find cursory quotations from Chuang-tzu (*OS* 34), but also quite extensive use of the *yang* and *yin* model to explain two types of historical epochs (*OS* 42, 52ff.). The match between the strong Western-Christian presence, with all its Latin quotations, and the much weaker presence of Eastern thought is unbalanced as far as scholarship and insight are concerned. Nevertheless, for the first time, Versfeld deploys Eastern thought (here, especially Taoism) in a context critical of Western thought: Taoism throws light on the present "dominative phase of our Christianity", the masculine urge to dominate, individualism, industrialism, moralistic religion, the self-oppression of spontaneity, and the "explosive *Yang* mixture of Puritanism and Cartesian rationalism" (*OS* 57, 66ff.). Indeed, the *yang* phase of Western Christian culture is over, but then Christianity has reserves of *yin* (*OS* 68), and there is no reason to "sell our birth-right for Oriental ideas" (*OS* 69). Praise is bestowed on Zen and Taoism, but the brakes are also applied: we should not "get rid of our past" (*OS* 68); we may find "many correctives in Eastern thought" (*OS* 68), yet it would be wiser if "Eastern ideas served to remind us of things that have been forgotten or have gone stale in our own tradition" (*OS* 69). He remains with the twoness of East and West, and does not attempt a larger historical or theoretical synthesis or consider the possibility of one shared, common religious space. Rather, Eastern religions are absorbed in the terms of one, more dominating one.

In *Our Selves*, Versfeld's commitment to Aquinas, including the great mediaeval theologian's analogical proofs for the existence of God, remains solid (*OS* 146ff.). Yet he also goes along with the existential slant of John Henry Newman (incidentally, like Versfeld, a convert to Roman Catholicism), which does not remotely imply doubting the real being of God. In the last chapter of *Our Selves*, at this most critical point of his meeting with Buddhism and Taoism, Versfeld does not take their respective emphases on ontological emptiness into consideration. Or, is it conceivable that his endorsement of Newman's "softer" version somehow might have taken place under the influence of Buddhism and Taoism (apart from his reading of Western existentialism)? Is that why he now emphasises the belief in God as a matter of assent, rather than of strict rational proof? I do not draw any firm conclusion here, except that Versfeld was not prepared to openly come to terms with what he might have seen as the subversive, devastating theological consequences of these two systems of religious thought. In the end, he opts effectively to reduce them to inspirational reminders of spontaneity and simplicity, found in Christianity anyway. The final verdict in Versfeld's investigation of Eastern thought has now probably been delivered in grand style: traditional, orthodox Christian theism remains intact.

Thomas's formulation of *cognitum est in cognoscente per modum cognoscentis* (the known is "known in the knower in the way of the knower"), favoured by Versfeld and often recurring in his writings, usually contra the epistemology of Kant, again makes its appearance in *Our Selves* (*OS* 159). Versfeld uses this expression to emphasise the realistic implication of Thomistic thinking, particularly concerning the existence God, which at the same time allows for a subjective element in that knowing. Whatever the merits of Versfeld's position vis-à-vis Thomas, Kant and Newman may be, he made no real allowance for the epistemological critique of Buddhism. He claims to reveal all such thinking to be constructions, projections – like a staircase built up into the sky leading to a non-existent palace (*Tevijja Sutta*). In other contexts, Versfeld is aware of similar critiques in Western quarters, such as those of Marx and Nietzsche, but does not draw conclusions that would overturn Thomistic thinking. Structurally, Versfeld conducts Christian apologetics; he engages with Eastern thought on the fringe of Catholic Christianity. I do not mean that as criticism, merely as fact.

16. Three years later a selection of essays appeared in Afrikaans (*Tyd en dae*, 1982) shedding no new light on his balancing act of Western-Christian and Eastern thought. In the footsteps of his beloved Augustine, Versfeld cataphatically refers to God "the Present" (*TD* 93), Lao Tzu and Chuang-tzu merely marginally embellishing his attack on the idol of the modern time machine (*TD* 85f.).

17. In *Food for Thought* (1983, I use the 1991 edition) we read Versfeld at his best, and his most mischievous, continuing the thread spun in his 1978 essay, "Wyn en wysheid". This is also the best possible illustration of the implications of his analogical thinking: the ordinary as bridge to the miraculous. This nimble-witted book does much to commend itself, above all showing a love for nature and life. The book is liberally spiced with quotes from and quick references to Taoism and Zen. And quotes from the *Taittiriya* and *Maitri Upanishads* confirm the point that "ultimate reality" is "food" (*FT* 18f.; 43ff.). This is stirred in with the Catholic Mass, during which "we eat and drink the Truth", without adding that in the Mass the consumption of Truth is restricted to the flesh and blood of one Man. To Versfeld's credit, in his thinking it appears that from the Incarnation a secondary effect radiates outwards, including the sharpening of a pencil, the building of a house and the making of soup. Again this brings him in the vicinity of Zen, in which every leaf on every tree, every frog plopping into the water reveals eternity – yet without any implication of an analogous relationship with an ontologically Other level of Being. Versfeld never, as far as I can tell, directly addresses the problem of the exclusivity of the Incarnation in Christ.

He makes a delightful comparison of his own thinking with the culinary art, "concocting" it like soup (*FT* 13), playfully admitting that "my mind is a rag-bag, bits occasionally cohering to form some sort of unity" (*FT* 13), and wisely confessing that it is "difficult to assimilate properly the cuisine of one other country, say Chinese or Japanese" (*FT* 13); ultimately, "the soup your mother made" (*FT* 13) is always to be chosen. Read this as a confession of the important difference in his evaluation of Christian theology-philosophy on which he has been nourished on the one hand, and Eastern thinking, the taste of which he also likes in small helpings, on the other. Again his relative lack of knowledge of historical context shows, for example, as he (like many Westerners) somehow sees "Buddhism" and "Zen" as different entities (*FT* 19). Compared to his position on vegetarianism fifteen years earlier (1968), nothing has changed. Christian man has been carnivorous man, meat is processed plants, the difference between animal and cabbage is smaller than the difference between animal and human, and vegetarianism is not clearly distinct from sentimentalism (*KK* 46ff.).

The issue here is not the eating of meat or not as such, but Versfeld's lack of thorough engagement with the philosophical underpinnings of, say, the Buddhist injunction not to kill, mixed with his suggestion that consuming meat is essential to Christianity.

18. *Die neukery met die appelboom* (*The Nuisance with the Apple Tree*) (1985) adds nothing new to Versfeld's previous work, apart from a welcome ecological twist.

19. The same verdict applies to *Pots and Poetry* (1985). Taking all into account, Versfeld (now seventy-six years old) has reached a plateau in his writing, parallel with the incline of his thinking over decades. With a certain but light touch, he moves with ease and confidence among the figures who have over decades, increasingly become the furniture in his spiritual home, now all dusted again with love. His emphasis on the earthing of philosophy and theology in the context of redefining the human being's position in nature is to be appreciated, as is his sustained critique of apartheid ("The Rape of District Six").

Pots and Poetry is Versfeld's most integrative book. We find a critical comment on the restriction of interest, in Western philosophy, to Western philosophy (*PP* 62). He shows the way forward by example in a fine comparative chapter on Plato and Plotinus (and Taoism) (*PP* 69–84). He delivers at times lengthy quotes from the Upanishads, modern Hinduism, Zen, Confucius, Lao Tzu and Chuang-tzu (the latter from the translation of fellow Catholic Thomas Merton). Versfeld is now clearly at ease with the Chinese thinkers. Taoism has crystallised as his favourite Eastern partner, and he can refer to Lao Tzu, "the unknown Old Man", as "present to me like a brother" (*PP* 59). This occurs in a clear affirmation of "a new world-wide wisdom and holiness that is not confined to the few canonised European Baroque saints who are, if we hold any such conversation at all, all that most of us know" (*PP* 55). Yet, Augustine remains the one whom "I owe what I have been saying almost entirely to" (*PP* 49). The ghost of eclecticism has not been exorcised, and his knowledge of Eastern religions is not comprehensive. We find an honest self-revelation such as "I am not capable of sorting out Hinduism from Buddhism" (*PP* 63), and he still tends towards a facile, unclarified conflation of apophatic theism and Nirvana (*PP* 58). Yet, he was sure of the direction to take.

Stylistically, Versfeld here demonstrates his forte: the quick wit, the brilliant put-down, for example, in his treatment of Hegel (*PP* 77). He pays a price for that, of course. The real test for intercultural, inter-epochal, inter-religious encounter in our time is the ability to patiently construct higher, more inclusive syntheses of what may appear to be irreconcilable opposites. The challenge for today is the connection of a Plato, a Thomas, a Hegel and (to mention one name from the East) a Fa-tsang in one theoretically articulated frame of thought, giving proper regard to each figure. It is one thing to ridicule Hegel, another to construct a similarly impressive synthesis of seeming opposites, appropriate to one's epoch. Versfeld, a pioneering figure, does not quite achieve that, may not be interested in that.

Overall, this is vintage Versfeld. The breadth of his interests and the depth of his commitments are clear. This is communicative writing with a broad public in mind, with the inevitable price to pay.

20. With *Die lewensweg van Lao-Tse* (*The Path of Life of Lao Tzu*) (1988),[11] Versfeld clearly felt emboldened enough to venture deeply into new territory: translating an ancient text. It was an Afrikaans translation of the classic Taoist text, the *Tao te ching*, in a series on "Poetry from distant lands". As Versfeld admits apologetically in the introduction, he has no knowledge of Mandarin whatsoever, so the translation must have been based on existing translations in other European languages, none of which is disclosed by author or title. Whether the work has literary merit in its own right is not for me to judge, and is irrelevant in our present context. What matters is the extent to which it was true to the letter and spirit of the original, and whether it succeeded in conveying that intention in the new context of the receiver language. Any translation based on another (undisclosed) translation (or translations) of an ancient epoch in a different culture is deeply suspect. This would particularly be the case with ancient Mandarin, with its notoriously or pleasingly (depending on one's perspective) multivalent and ambiguous nature, far more so than is the case with Sanskrit, a cousin of Latin and Greek. Versfeld provides no explanatory notes to help bridge the vast gap between that ancient language and thinking, and what the readers are accustomed to. He does not reveal his hand, does not help his reader, but places the latter in the position of sceptic detective or credulous recipient.

One instance of at the very least a misleading translation occurs in sections 73, 77, 79 and 81. He does not translate *tiān* as "heaven" (which is usually the case), but as "God", without any further clarification or motivation. That is a fatal shortcut. By now, the reader is fully aware of Versfeld's endorsement of the Augustinian-Thomistic concept of "God". To what extent is he uncritically, unwittingly, projecting that into this text? "God" is not a univocal word by far. In a serious bridge-building exercise between cultures and religions, a lot of hermeneutical work, worthy of being made explicit, goes into the translation of

---

[11] Marthinus Versfeld, *Die lewensweg van Lao-Tse* (Cape Town: Perskor, 1988).

any donor text. That was not the case here. By way of comparison, Heidegger also had a longstanding interest in Taoism, but did not indulge in wading into that religion in his writings, in all likelihood because of academic reserve: he could not work from the original language itself. In my view this publication of Versfeld was an error of judgement, although I grant that it could have helped to make "Taoism" more of a household word in the provincial South African cultural context of the eighties, and that is to be appreciated.

21. In 1990, at age eighty-one, Versfeld published his last book. In keeping with his remarkably consistent writing over decades, it was a return to his first and true love, Christian philosophy: *St Augustine's Confessions and City of God* (1990). The East features, but as semi attached to his true spiritual home. A true theoretical integration, doing justice to the tendential drift of both religious continents, is not achieved. Versfeld's intention can be applauded, but the execution, the fitting and joining, did not quite succeed. Thus we read that Augustine has much in common with Gotama and the *Upanishads*: all three "seek to eradicate ego" (*ACCG* 57). True, but he seems to identify the ways in which this is done. Can Augustine's "story of persons made meaningful by a Person" (*ACCG* 81) so easily be conflated with the *Atman* of the Upanishads (*ACCG* 57)? Or Augustine's *tranquilitas* with Buddhist Nirvana (*ACCG* 114)? Overall, the creative spark of difference does not ignite. Versfeld breaks no new ground in comparison to his earlier work. One throwaway formulation captures what his strategy over decades boils down to: "The revelation of Christ can include Chuang-tzu" (*ACCG* 99). That is of course one way of structuring a dialogue with Eastern thought, and I feel no need to criticise him for that. However, it is clear that the exploration of a space beyond all religious institutions and theological systems, including those of Christianity, would have been a next step. Versfeld did not penetrate to the *anattā* nature of all things, including constructs about God, due to the constraints of the *anicca* nature of all things, including brief human lives of 86 years.

5. Conclusion

Versfeld was a contemplative thinker, the relationship with God being his lifelong central concern. In the course of his career, he succeeded in forging integrations of seemingly disparate schools of thought around that interest that served him well, both psychologically and intellectually. After his conversion to Catholicism,

Augustinianism and Thomism merged seamlessly to form the basic pattern of his religious thinking. He also unified philosophy and theology in his model of Christian philosophy. And he celebrated an integration of Greek thinking, in the form of Platonism, with Christian thought. Remarkably, Plotinus and Christian Neoplatonism remained in the background shadows. I mention that, because a stronger association with that accent in Christianity might have facilitated his attempts to come to terms with Eastern religio-philosophical thinking. Within Christianity, he was, taking all into account, not a particularly ecumenical spirit. For example, he does not seem to have made an attempt to engage with Reformed theology and mysticism (say, a Calvin, or a Bavinck – both very much part of his own personal and cultural context) extensively and *in bonam partem* at any stage of his life. This may be attributable to the fact that his was a dramatic conversion, a turning away from that institution in utter disillusionment and the embracing of another with exclusive commitment.

Apart from his switch from irreligion to Catholicism, Versfeld never changed his mind substantially. Nevertheless, over decades, he increasingly strove to harmonise his understanding of Christianity with Eastern thinking, mainly in the forms of the Upanishads, Buddhism and Taoism, with Confucianism on the fringe. Fascinating albeit brief interchanges with those religions abound in his writings, but essentially they remain excursions, external to his Christian structure. Overall, his strategy of weaving selected threads of the East into the basic, normative configuration of Trinity, Incarnation, Creation and so on turns out to be comparable to the theological approaches of, among others, Catholic scholars Thomas Merton and Bede Griffiths – but closer to Merton than to Griffiths. That is an understandable procedure, and I do not wish to fault it as such. However, the question does announce itself whether there may not be a further step beyond the ones taken by Versfeld. In this regard, Versfeld did not achieve by far the same degree of theoretical harmonisation as was the case in the fields of his interest mentioned above. Also, he did not clearly explicate his hermeneutical procedures in this undertaking.

A first factor inhibiting such creative synthesis was probably that Versfeld did not study any one of the Eastern systems at root level, by which I mean the basic texts in their original languages, or serious involvement in those religions as living traditions. He knew Latin and Greek, but no Sanskrit, Pali or Mandarin. I do not wish to make a measure of linguistic competency the only or final test. It would indeed be possible to understand and internalise the intentional structure of a religion from secondary literary sources and serious personal engagement with that religion. However, it seems to me that an intellectual programme of appropriation and informed critique would require a degree of historical-critical understanding of such an investigated religion: a sufficient knowledge of the historical context in which it arose, its development over time, its various branches and the differences between them. Versfeld does not provide evidence of having made such a study. However, here too I would add a qualification: intellectual, academic competence is not to be confused with existential understanding. It cannot be said that Versfeld made a serious study of these religions in the strict "academic" sense, but that he was personally intensely interested in them and appreciated their depth and beauty up to a point is beyond doubt. Yet it cannot be denied that he sometimes cut corners impressionistically rather than undertake painstaking analyses, and that his conclusions were not always accurate and his probes not always deep. Indeed, he tended to opt for the popular simplification rather than a wrestling whatever the cost or outcome. This resulted from time to time in the facile identifications and subsumptions under Christianity pointed out in paragraphs above.

In the dialogue of West and East, Versfeld was a pioneer in his own country, with an affinity for especially Taoism and Zen. His resolute, pro-cosmic life, his affirmation of the concrete ordinary things of everyday life, his pithy style of self-expression and his humour all drift naturally towards the synthesis of Buddhism and Taoism as it took shape in philosophies such as Hua-yen, inspiring Zen. However, he did not manage to harmonise that theoretically with his Christian Catholicism: the concept of God in the theism of Augustine and Thomas, and emptiness as ultimate horizon in Taoism and Buddhism, remain unreconciled. Versfeld did not produce a creative, original framework; he did not break new ground, relativising all religions to a point of final breakdown and thereby saving all of them, yet as penultimate vehicles of salvation, not more. That is in my estimation the ultimate shortcoming of his work. He did much to promote inter-religious encounter, but did not venture into a dimension of radical metareligious critique and transreligious mysticism. Yet I pay my sincere respect to this student of Socrates, Lao Tzu, Chuang-tzu and Augustine, whose company is impossible not to enjoy and whose contribution is not difficult to appreciate.

CHAPTER 7

POIESIS – ON THE VOICE OF POETS, PHILOSOPHERS AND OTHER POTTERS

There is almost no commentary on Versfeld that does not mention his special use of language. I am certainly no exception. In Chapter 2, §3, for instance, I comment on the rich stylistic and argumentative variety in his writing. There I argue that this is not mere decoration, but is to be understood as continuous with the metaphysical and cultural-critical views that he conveys. But giving an account of the *philosophical* meaning of his use of language is only part of the story, as could be seen in another strand of reception of his work. It is a well-known fact that he was well received by important figures of the South African *literary* world.[1]

---

[1] In divergent ways this could be derived from Dennis Walder, *Athol Fugard* (London: Macmillan, 1984), 21; André Brink, "In Praise of All that Is Fleeting and Eternal," introduction to Marthinus Versfeld, *Pots and Poetry and other Essays* (2nd edition) (Pretoria: Protea, 2009), 7–16; Breyten Breytenbach, *Dog Heart. A Memoir* (London: Faber & Faber, 1999), 44–51; Remona Voges, "Antjie Krog, gemeenskaplikheid en die behoefte aan interverbondenheid in Mede-wete (2014)," *LitNet Akademies* 16, no. 1 (2019), https://www.litnet.co.za/wp-content/uploads/2019/06/LitNet_Akademies_16-1_Voges_145-165.pdf [last access 12 February 2020]; Marlene van Niekerk, "Die etende Afrikaner. Aantekeninge vir 'n klein tipologie," in *Van Volksmoeder tot Fokofpolisiekar. Kritiese opstelle oor Afrikaanse herinneringsplekke*, ed. A.M. Grundlingh and S. Huigen (Stellenbosch: SUN Press, 2008), 75–92; and perhaps the note on Jeremy Cronin in "Johann Lodewyk Marais. Marthinus Versfeld (3)," http://versindaba.co.za/tag/marthinus-versfeld/ [last consulted 3 March 2020].

Some of his essays were also reprinted in anthologies of literature; cf. "Die pampoen" ["The Pumpkin"], in *Borde borde boordevol. Verhale en essays oor kos*, ed. Hennie Aucamp (Cape Town: Tafelberg, 1998), 157–159; and "Oor huise" ["On Homes"], in *Vertellers: die groot Afrikaanse verhaalboek*, ed. M. Scholz (Cape Town: Tafelberg, 1990), 23–41; "Die pampoen" ["The Pumpkin"], in *Vertellers 2: Die tweede groot verhaalboek*, ed. M. Scholtz (Cape Town: Tafelberg, 1991), 404–406.

Furthermore, the esteem for Versfeld in literary circles is witnessed by the incident that occasioned the present chapter. When Protea published a reissue of Versfeld's *Pots and Poetry*, the editors of *Tydskrif vir Letterkunde (Journal for Literature)* approached me to write a review article thereof. That was fifteen years after the philosopher's death and a quarter of a century after the original publication of *Pots and Poetry*.

This was a good opportunity to reflect on the relation between philosophy and literature in Versfeld's thought. The aim of this chapter is to comment on his understanding of "poetry" as it is found in the book, where one gathers from the title that it cannot be detached from his understanding of pots. Explaining this link will also require that I clarify the relation between writing poetry and writing philosophy as Versfeld understood it. In all, I hope to shed some light on the appeal that Versfeld's thought and writing have exercised on people with a vocation for poetry, literature and the arts.

1. On writing

The decision to reissue Martin Versfeld's work[2] not only honours the author, but is an exceptional occurrence in the South African intellectual world. That such an event is considered to be remarkable enough to be celebrated by reflecting on it in an academic journal is perfectly in order. However, there is something unusual about the fact that the *Tydskrif vir Letterkunde* requested me to comment on the reissuing of Versfeld's *Pots and Poetry*.[3] Versfeld was not a man of letters, and his philosophical texts contain fairly little commentary on literature. Literature as a theme also enjoys relatively little attention in his work. A quick glance at the names of the chapters and at the contents of his book will reveal that *Pots and Poetry* is not concerned with the theory of poetry. In fact, almost as if in disdain of the title, the author appears to be more interested in stones and their rights, the relationship between Western and Eastern thinking, criticism of society or naughty jokes than in poetry. In view of this, one could be excused for suspecting

---

[2] Finally this project by Protea publishers stopped at a handful of reissues.
[3] Where two page numbers are separated by a forward slash, they refer to the first and second editions of *Pots and Poetry*, respectively. For reasons I am unable to explain, there are minor differences between the two editions: see, for example, *PP* 30f. / *PP* 2nd ed. 56f. However, the differences that I found made no real difference to the content.

that the *Tydskrif* had erred in requesting this review of *Pots and Poetry*, and all the more from me – also rather a philosopher than a man of letters. However, this suspicion could be removed by investigating Versfeld's reason for using the words *poetry* in conjunction with *pots* in the title, and the multiple implications that can be developed from this connection.

It may strike the reader that Versfeld starts his book with a few autobiographical comments about himself as a philosopher,[4] and it might be helpful to approach the content by carefully considering the author's own description of the nature of his practice.[5] Two references are sufficient for the current purposes. In his inaugural speech at the University of Cape Town (1971), Versfeld revealed the following:

> I must confess at once that I do not know what philosophy is. This sometimes embarrasses me before the innocence of students, but not before those who have come to realise that the things by which we live are the things about which we know least. We do not know what life is, or what knowing is, or what truth and goodness are. Or if we do know we can't say it [...]. (*SS* 1)

In my opinion, this statement is the heart of Versfeld's (somewhat idealised) view of his own work at that time, but it also presents us with an uncertain starting point: if philosophy is, as it were, nothing more than a constant discussion of what eventually turns out to be ineffable ignorance, one can understand why "philosophising" is often used in common parlance as a euphemism for "talking nonsense". And if philosophising is nothing more than pompous drivel, one could wonder whether such a philosophical discourse will succeed in doing anything better than presenting poetry as mere doggerel ("*verdigsels*").

However, a second statement made by Versfeld about the task of a philosopher takes us in another direction and also helps us better to understand the first statement:

> [...] the philosopher shares with the poet an *absorption* in the *articulation* of existence, expressing itself in the unique *voice* by which a tree and stone and blade of grass proclaims itself to be this and to be lovable. (*MP* 13, my italics)

---

[4]   On this point, see also Chapter 2, §2.
[5]   See Rossouw, "Die kuns van die lewe is om tuis te kom", or Chapters 2 and 9 of this book for an overview of Versfeld's philosophy.

If Versfeld's opinion of the philosopher and the poet is correct, it would mean that philosophising and the writing of poetry both stem from the same experience of reality: an experience that acknowledges something that deserves to be called the *voice* of everyday things like trees, stones or grass, as well as the *lovableness* of such things. In other words, the philosopher and the poet do not merely write, but respond to an initiative that precedes and provokes their writing. Furthermore, both philosophy and poetry *articulate* things to which one is sometimes so close that it is as if one were *absorbed* by the experience – so close that it is impossible to take an impartial distance from an object, with the result that one cannot know much about it (as expressed in the first quotation). It therefore cannot be expected that this absorption in the things of the world can articulate itself exhaustively, and if it makes no sense to expect of a poem to sing its theme comprehensively, it would also make no sense to expect a philosopher to fully capture in words "the things by which we live".

These two quotations from Versfeld's earlier works orientate us towards the type of philosophising that should be expected from the author and also guide us to the threshold of *Pots and Poetry*. Do not expect Versfeld to present a treatise on poetics! Rather, prepare yourself for a conversation aimed at highlighting the exceptional aspect of commonplace, everyday things – as clearly explained on the first page of *Pots and Poetry*.[6] The motif that is present throughout this collection of essays is his attempt to find and reflect on this absorbing and loving everyday connection with reality.

2. Connectedness

The collection titled *Pots and Poetry* is comprised of nine stand-alone essays of which at least two ("Time and Speed and the Quality of Life" and "Plato and Confucius") were previously published in journals, and to which Protea had added three essays from *Sum. Selected Works/'n Keur uit sy werke* (1991) for the reissue. The original issue had been published in 1985 and the essays from *Sum* were all written afterwards. A quick review of the divergent themes dealt with in

---

[6] Versfeld's examination of the relationship between philosophy and poetry started at an early stage. Already in chapter 1 of *Oor gode en afgode* he uses poetry to illustrate the non-rational, non-irrational reasonableness of practical reasoning. A further discussion of this follows below.

the book does not seem to produce a single obvious theme. Chapter 1 deals with pots and poetry; the following three essays could be characterised as sociocultural critiques;[7] chapters 5, 6 and 7 contain a contribution to the co-ordination of Western and Eastern themes and ways of thinking; and the original collection concluded with a reflection on the inevitable sociopolitical implication of writing and a plea for naughty jokes. The additional chapters in the Protea reissue include discussions of ecology, the university and the thoughts of some early members of the Mountain Club of South Africa.[8] Would it be possible to identify coherence in such a hotchpotch? I am convinced that it is not only possible, but that the coherence simultaneously reveals the central theme of the collection, which is closely linked with the author's way of working. To support this assertion, we have to consider another clarification given by Versfeld concerning the nature of his philosophical work – this time from *Pots and Poetry*:

> [...] connecting in my thinking has a priority over analysis. I am impressed with the relation of all things to each other, that is, with the fact of communication. I have my moments when I can see the universe as a vast and divine festivity, and catch faint echoes of what St Augustine called the *carmen universitatis*, that is, the singing that should accompany a fiesta. What I have to say about pots and poetry arises from this. (*PP* 3–4 / *PP* 2nd ed. 22–23)

On the first page of the book the author confesses that, besides the previously mentioned qualifications, the kind of thinking performed in his book was inspired by the *connection* between things. The appropriate way of writing about them is therefore one that *connects* things.[9] However, working in such a way is possible only if one has refused to play a particular game: if a decision in favour of prioritising an analytical way of thinking is taken from the start, this means

---

[7]   A somewhat later publication of one of these essays, "Our Rapist Society" (*PP* 29–40 / *PP* 2nd ed. 55–70) was reviewed by Neil Viljoen, "Shakespeare's *The Tempest* and Martin Versfeld's 'Comments on the Rapist Society,'" *English Academy Review* 5, no. 5 (1988): 116–137.

[8]   The new edition of *Pots and Poetry* includes a foreword by André Brink, which is basically an English version of the foreword he had written for the reissue of *Die neukery met die appelboom*. Therefore my critical evaluation of the foreword also applies here – see Wolff, "Die neukery met verval en herstel in Versfeld se storie van die appelboom," *Koers* 74, no. 3 (2009): 539–542, here 541.

[9]   Reminiscing about Versfeld as his professor in philosophy, Jeremy Cronin highlighted this idea of connection and integration in his teaching – see Jeremy Cronin, "Interview with Helena Sheehan", recorded on 17 April 2001 at the University of Cape Town. http://helenasheehan.ie/interview-with-jeremy-cronin/ [last access 12 February 2020].

that a particular genetic defect of modernity is *de facto* reactualised and the ability to hear the song or poem of the universe (the *carmen universi*) is adversely affected. Versfeld's justification for placing connection before analysis – which is expressed in different ways throughout his work[10] – is based on the conviction that a whole series of pathologies of the modern world are the result of a wrong way of thinking, and if we change the way we think, we may be able to change our quality of life (on the significance of quality of life or well-being, cf. Chapter 3, §4). The choice that we encounter throughout *Pots and Poetry* is the choice between thinking as analysis and control, or as surrendering to the song of the universe (exactly what this is will be discussed at a later stage).

The first option is summarised in *Die neukery met die appelboom* (*The Trouble with the Apple Tree*):[11] "During the 17th century the Western mind became very

---

[10] It is strange that the idea of an analogy, which is at the centre of Versfeld's thinking and is not only at the core of the concept of connectedness in *Pots and Poetry*, but is even practically executed (see, for instance, the analogy between Divine *poiesis* and human poetry), is not explicitly mentioned in *Pots and Poetry*.

[11] *Die neukery met die appelboom* is close in spirit and content to *Pots and Poetry*. An excursion on the former is therefore warranted.

This short volume was written for a wide audience and large parts can be read for the sheer enjoyment of its conversational style. However, it would be wrong to assume that the author is merely chatting: the entire book was informed by Versfeld's philosophical work of the preceding fifty years (as is evident from the resurgence of his favourite themes), and the playfulness with which he deals with them is simply another expression of the passion with which he writes about these themes in all his other works. Versfeld's ideas of decline provide the background to these essays. Indeed, the dawn of the Renaissance and modernity represent a disintegration of the unitary nature of life in the Middle Ages (*NA* 2nd ed. 19, 43; cf. Chapter 3, §5). Descartes's rationalism and the accompanying desire to use science to control both the environment and humankind attest to the maladies of our time. The name Newton comes to denote the progressive realisation of Descartes's dream for science. The association between Newtonian physics (cf. the anecdote about his experience with a falling apple) and human alienation from the natural environment (cf. Adam and Eve's original sin involving the "apple tree" and their expulsion from Paradise) creates the tension from which the book's title was derived. This "trouble" or "botheration" with the apple tree refers to the tension between a diagnosis of his era and the cure for which Versfeld pleads.

Versfeld's diagnosis or cultural criticism emanates from the scenario of decline that underpins this book (and all his works): modern rationalism disrupts the unity of body and soul, subjects our lifeworld to a scientistic reduction, alienates humankind from the environment, and provides people with modern technologies that enable them to control and exploit nature. It therefore becomes exceedingly difficult to be at home in such an objectified world. This unhomeliness results in a compulsion to be constantly on the move (not only by moving away from your local place, but also by moving away from your true self), to become subservient to abstract time, and to develop an inflated, domineering ego, which results in your having a negative effect on others (this diagnosis has been explored in Chapter 5, above).

analytical. Descartes's world is a disintegration of multiple substances. *Things fall apart*" (*NA* 2nd ed. 19).[12] In a similar characterisation of Western thought, the desire to control, inherent in its analytical thinking, is pointed out: "criterion of truth becomes pragmatic: the workability of concepts and their serviceability for prediction and control" (*PP* 16 / *PP* 2nd ed. 39).[13] And when thinking becomes obsessed with control, its powers are exerted on people and the environment, eventually with catastrophic results. This diagnosis of modernity is encountered throughout *Pots and Poetry*, but is concentrated in the three social critique chapters (chapters 2 to 4).

In opposition to this violence of modern Western culture, Versfeld endeavours to connect with his world in a different way. He does this by attempting to give renewed credibility to specific moments in the Christian and Eastern traditions of thought. Two things – represented by the "psalm of the universe" and the "dance of Shiva" – should be highlighted in this regard: (1) the connectedness of everything that exists, in the way that individual notes are connected in a melody (see *PP* 49, 87 / *PP* 2nd ed. 82, 130) or single movements are connected in a dance, and (2) the rejection of the greedy and domineering will. Every denial of the connectedness of things represents a transgression against their rightful

---

[12] Such an ego leads to the warped idea of the possession and exploitation of others (cf. "Wat is myne?" ["What is Mine?"], *NA* 2nd ed. 49ff). In three places (*NA* 2nd ed. 23, 37 and 37), Versfeld criticises forced removals, by which people who are not truly at home in the world deprived others of the possibility of being at home.

However, Versfeld also provides the medicine: think metaphysically (his views in this regard are briefly described in "Tyd, lewe en dood" ["Time, Life and Death"], *NA* 2nd ed. 39ff.); be aware of the temporary nature of your own existence; think analogically rather than analytically about reality; acknowledge the unity of body and soul; and learn to be at home in the "here" by developing an understanding of your place in the world. God remains the anchor of this metaphysics. Versfeld offers no argument to support the acceptance of the idea of God, but his plea is constructed in such a way that agreement with his diagnosis ultimately implies a certain degree of consent to a (rather vague) idea of God. Harmonising with Versfeld's earliest work, his deepest conviction is that we should recognise the miraculous in the secular (*NA* 2nd ed. 34, 38, 47, 70). Such recognition makes one at home in the world, but it also means withdrawal from the ruinous mechanistic world (*NA* 2nd ed. 33–34). As a philosopher, Versfeld implicitly attempts to do the same: he declines participation in the careerist form of academic activity (*NA* 2nd ed. 34), but does take on the role of the "philosopher as vulture", feeding on the ruins of a disintegrated society (*NA* 2nd ed. 67ff.).

[12] For Versfeld, the disintegration of the (mediaeval) unity was the guiding diagnostic category for social and political pathologies form the early stages (cf. Chapter 3 on *Oor gode en afgode*) and right up to his last work (as just demonstrated in *NA*).

[13] Also see: "We seldom question this assumption, nor ask ourselves how many of the ills that we wish to control have been caused by the desire to control" (*PP* 41 / *PP* 2nd ed. 72).

place in the whole and a step towards a meaningless world; every concession made to the domineering will is an affirmation of an individual, cannibalistic rapacity. According to Versfeld's diagnosis, the central problem in Western society, or in any society shaped by Western influences, is the intellectual and practical withdrawal of the individual from the meaning-giving connection into which individuals are embedded and the obstinate perseverance in that isolated existence. By contrast, Versfeld offers no alternative programme for the rehabilitation of people or a new social project, but rather describes the connections existing between people.[14]

Against this background it becomes clear that the two forms of thinking that Versfeld contrasts on the first pages of his book – analysis-driven thought and connection-driven thought – are not, in the first place, two ways of being clever, each with its forms of institutional embeddedness. Here we have two forms of being that stem from two fundamental possibilities for existence for the same person (*PP* 40 / *PP* 2nd ed. 70).

3. Creativity, love, generosity

The first insight gained from Versfeld's alternative approach to life is that humans exist in no other way than in response to an enormous gift: "Man, then, is absolutely gratuitous, a gift to himself. His self-possession, his property in himself is relative and dependent […]. But his most common delusion is that he has absolute property in himself" (*PP* 24 / *PP* 2nd ed. 49). If we have seen earlier (§1) that, for Versfeld, philosophy, like poetry, has always been a response to the world in which we are engaged, it is because the essential initiative that leads to our being human has always been situated outside of us. In the language borrowed by Versfeld from the Judaeo-Christian tradition, human beings are "[themselves] spoken by the creative Word through whose reverberations we can hear nature speak" (*PP* 25 / *PP* 2nd ed. 51). This is an implicit reinterpretation by Versfeld of Aristotle's definition of human beings as living beings who possess language:

---

[14] Marlene van Niekerk certainly understood this point correctly when – making use (with approbation) of *Pots and Poetry*, particularly the first chapter – she wrote her culture- and literary-critical essay on "The eating Afrikaner", in agreement with Versfeld's spirit of connection-making. Cf. Van Niekerk, "Die etende Afrikaner. Aantekeninge vir 'n klein tipologie," in *Van Volksmoeder tot Fokofpolisiekar. Kritiese opstelle oor Afrikaanse herinneringsplekke*, ed. Albert Grundlingh and Siegfried Huigen (Stellenbosch: SUN Press, 2008), 75–92.

the conceptual pairs *carmen universi-poetry* and *Word-reverberation* present the bearer of language as a being who responds to and is a continuation of the origin of life. A third pair of concepts is hidden within a third form of language usage:

> God must find the denial of his existence very funny indeed. His laughter is the pouring forth of creatures into the Void so that they may echo his Word. Creation is funny and that is why copulation is funny, and why the best jokes are about sex. They spring from our participation in God's creativity. (*PP* 92 / *PP* 2nd ed. 137)

Here, Versfeld's intention is to speak a true word in jest.

Human creativity, of which poetry and philosophising on the meaning of connectedness are two forms, owes its emergence to the original generosity, which is mentioned throughout *Pots and Poetry*. As is evident from the passages quoted above, Versfeld regards this generosity as synonymous with creativity. Whoever talks about creativity is talking about the beginning of things, and therefore about time. Versfeld views creativity as the possibility of a new beginning and a new course. The thing that creativity and generosity have in common is that they are both unexpected – each opens a door to a new future (*PP* 40 / *PP* 2nd ed. 70).

A third key term (which is relatively infrequently used in *Pots and Poetry*) fits in this context, namely love. Like generosity, love is the origin of all things and the power through which they come into existence: "Everything that is has the dignity of being loved by God, which it expresses precisely in being what it is" (*PP* 21 / *PP* 2nd ed. 45), and if love is spontaneously creative (*FT* 92), we can understand why he regards love as being "anarchist" (*PP* 23 / *PP* 2nd ed. 48).[15]

Versfeld's ambitious project in chapters 5 to 7 of *Pots and Poetry* is to show that this original orientation of human existence can be heard in the harmonious resonance between Christian and Eastern wisdom. Here, *Pots and Poetry* offers an extension of a project of which chapters 1 and 2 of *Our Selves* most likely present a more sophisticated version, and which had its roots as far back as in *Oor gode en afgode* (see *GA* 25ff.).

---

[15] Hence the title of Marlene van Niekerk's review of *Sum*: "Martin Versfeld. Anargis van die liefde" ["Martin Versfeld. Anarchist of Love"], *Die Suid-Afrikaan* (April/May, 1992): 70 and 77. The mutual relationship between the three key terms can clearly be seen in the following: "God is sheer generosity, and there is no reason for creating nor compulsion to generate in God. Creation is a joyous outburst of sheer generosity. The universe has no being but the love of God. If the being of creatures is time, it is also love. [Love] is the being of things: the hardness and weight of stones, the greening tree, the rising sun, the breaking wave: whatever makes things relevant to each other" (*PP* 50 / *PP* 2nd ed. 82–83).

4. Poiesis

Since Versfeld is concerned, in *Pots and Poetry*, with the complex and amazing connection between things and is determined to do them justice, the collection contains a wealth of themes. I would like to take time to focus on the two themes announced in the title of the book – more specifically on the second, poetry – because this is the concern of the present chapter. At the same time I will share my answer to the question: how does Versfeld's book relate to poets and writers?

It is well known that in the Western cultural and intellectual history, the Greek verb *poiein* – to make – developed into two very different views on the *poiemata* – the things made – and on the processes by which they are respectively made, which is *poiesis*. In my opinion, the fact that Versfeld attempts to bridge this violent divide between artefact and art (poetry, in this case), and to view and contemplate the products of human cultural life-activities together, is a major merit of his work. The "and" in *Pots and Poetry* represents these efforts, while the two forms of *poiemata* are represented by pots and poetry respectively.

As asserted in §3, "Creativity, Love and Generosity", the source from which one can truly live – that which you have to acknowledge in order to be your true self – is the super- and pre-human generosity of which the cosmic song is the key metaphor. This original orientation can also be expressed as poetry: "[...] the world is the *poiesis* of God, chanted with every sunrise and echoed by poets who perform the rites of wonder at the rising of the sun" (*PP* 2nd ed. 152). Anyone who does not acknowledge this origin (regardless of whether it is articulated in Christian, Eastern or any other discourse), in other words, who believes that to be a "self-made man" and therefore chooses the degenerated self, is, according to Versfeld, not able to create (*PP* 58 / *PP* 2nd ed. 94, 152). This creative or poetic origin of the true self, including the necessary criticism against the ego which denies this origin, is not only the principle behind *poetry*, but in a parallel way also the principle behind *pots*. If we can cook a tasty stew, it is because we have already been served with a delicious world. From the pot, which represents the oldest and most common and durable aspects of human culture, the creation of a human world fans out so that art and science, social interaction and landscape formation (agriculture), industry and politics become mutually involved (see especially chapter 1 of *Pots and Poetry*). As widely as the connections of creative activities can ripple outwards from the cooking pot, just as widely can the scope of the misdeeds of the greedy ego become evident in human actions: from the formula-like recipes in glossy magazines that smother the poetic nature of the art of cooking (*PP* 3 / *PP* 2nd ed. 22), to the pressure cooker (*PP* 10 / *PP* 2nd ed. 31), which is symptomatic of a society in which "saving time" (so that more can be done) becomes more important than "making time" (for other people), to "cannibalism" (see *PP* 30 / *PP* 2nd ed. 56), which reigns supreme in a society in which the struggle for survival has become the ultimate law (themes that Versfeld developed in more detail in *Food for Thought*). All of this results in the world becoming anthropomorphised in accordance with the functionalist and domineering prescriptions of the greedy ego. According to Versfeld, C. Louis Leipoldt has shown us that the original generosity does indeed make it possible for us to write poetry and cook, thus echoing the original creativity:

> [...] the poetry of Leipoldt celebrates this [Cape agricultural] landscape and these people, and is by no means to be separated from his interest in food. His books on cooking celebrate the poetry of the kitchen. *Poiesis* means "making", and we make pies as well as poems. Thus his poem "Oktobermaand" and his *Cape Cookery* fulfil each other, and his poetry enables you to taste the landscape. (*PP* 7 / *PP* 2nd ed. 27)

For Versfeld, being poetic – be it as a poet, cook, philosopher or whatever – means first and foremost that you have to be a particular kind of person (*PP* 87 / *PP* 2nd ed. 130). This type of person is able to acknowledge the connectedness of all things and can appreciate their uniqueness, or love them: "A poet is a man [*sic*] who can take off his hat to a brick in honour of the original *Poiesis*" (*PP* 25 / *PP* 2nd ed. 51) and "all poems are love poems, since poetry is about real things and whatever is real is related to other things" (*PP* 50 / *PP* 2nd ed. 83). The poet's love of things is expressed in beautiful, accurate and exact language (*PP* 93 / *PP* 2nd ed. 138). The real things about which the poet becomes lyrical are the ordinary–extraordinary things (cf. *PP* 1 and 88 / *PP* 2nd ed. 19 and 132), and in this respect the poet and the philosopher are kindred spirits.

This idea of the poet does not in any way reflect the romantic adoration of the artist as the secular messenger of the gods; whatever Versfeld considers to be characteristic of poets is, in principle, equally characteristic of any other person. All writing has a social dimension and, ultimately, political implications. The same applies to all human activities (*PP* 85f. / *PP* 2nd ed. 128f.). Versfeld's belief that a poet must have some degree of unsoundness of mind (*PP* 93 / *PP* 2nd ed. 138) comes close to the idea of the insanity of artists, but this unsoundness, rather than capturing a secularised idea of inspiration, is in fact a revolt against a dominant form of rationality. It is an alternative form of reasonableness that he had sought since his early neo-Thomist days. Already in *Oor gode en afgode* (*GA*

14f and cf. Chapter 3, §6.1), poetry served as an example of an alternative form of reasonableness: the art of writing poetry is an activity that cannot be regarded as rational, but it is easy to acknowledge that it does not contradict, but rather supports, an intelligent approach to life. As such, poetry is an expression of practical reason. This seems to be the current of thought that underlies Versfeld's claim that poetic activity has political implications: poets specialise in awarding each thing its rightful place in such a way that each element, regardless of how insignificant it seems, contributes to the consonance of the whole (*PP* 85 / *PP* 2nd ed. 129). In this sense, poets can be regarded as the true lawmakers (*PP* 88 / *PP* 2nd ed. 130): they control (at least their perspective on) the practical reason that awards a place to each member in a way that does justice to each one. This idea seems even more acceptable when the broad meaning of poetry – the practical reason that ripples out from the pot – is taken into consideration. It is for this reason that *Pots and Poetry* continuously returns to culture-critical themes.

Although I shall not here discuss these themes in detail, it is important to point out that various sociopolitical outrages constitute the dark background to the merriment of *Pots and Poetry*; to some extent *Pots and Poetry* also responds to this. It is, in my opinion, one of the main shortcomings of *Pots and Poetry* and, indeed of Versfeld's work in general, that it does not provide a truly credible and respectful place for human suffering. Versfeld pays only scant attention to the question of how it is possible for the *carmen universi* to be silenced by the cacophonous chords of military bands. How it is possible to echo the psalm of the universe or dance with Shiva if the rhythm of your life is determined by violent labour relations or political injustice, is a dilemma to which Versfeld does not readily pay attention. In certain cases, Versfeld's philosophy of history simply has to be judged to be unacceptable, for instance, when one thinks about the atrocities of the political history of the past century and then read: "History is the time that cooks created men and women until they are ripe and fully leavened" (*PP* 9 / *PP* 2nd ed. 30). Something that may, for some, make sense on the level of personal psychology could, on a larger scale, be an unacceptable political theodicy.

5. Silence

Even if the meaning of poetry resides ultimately in using words to express appreciation for the connectedness of things, one should nevertheless remember that a naughty joke can sometimes fare better than a poem – and such jokes can be poetic (*PP* 93 / *PP* 2nd ed. 138). The complicated song of the poem could be silenced by an ordinary witty remark, which sometimes does more justice to things. Furthermore, the laughter evoked by a good joke silences all language and may show up as laughable some of the most courageous efforts to use language in a meaningful way.

Should one then conclude that ultimately the philosopher has outperformed the poet with regard to the use of language? No, because – as I have indicated in the first quotation, above, in which he talks about philosophy – many years spent thinking eventually leads to the amazing acknowledgement that we do not really have a clear idea of what we have been doing. For that reason Versfeld at least attempted to replace an academic philosophical language with a more playful colloquial language.[16]

What then about the theologians? Ultimately they do not escape this "negative" fate either. About God Versfeld writes:

> The only "proof" of his presence is his absence. He is too near to be seen and too real to be credible. No propositional truth can attain to him because he is its source. If it is true, it is because it is sufficiently true to Him to obliterate itself. (*PP* 58 / *PP* 2nd ed. 93–94)

It is in this silence that Versfeld wants us to arrive home. It is not the silence of dejected surrender or fatalism; neither is it a silence that finally silences the poet, the philosopher or the theologian. It is a silence from which we can once again hear the world and respond to it – "being still and keeping quiet are not the same" (*PP* 53 / *PP* 2nd ed. 87). Perhaps the greatest life skill a poet and a philosopher can develop is the ability to write silently.

---

[16] However, one does not have to believe him when Versfeld claims that he bade farewell to the *higher unintelligibilities* (as he derogatively referred to his previous philosophising, cf. *PP* 1). The large number of French, German and Latin technical terms that are used – without translations – throughout the book, and the number of references he makes to philosophers, apparently assuming that his readers will be familiar with their work, contradict this supposed farewell.

CHAPTER 8

REVERBERATIONS

In the previous chapter I examined the wide sense in which Versfeld uses the word "poetry". At the same time, Versfeld's forms of expression (examined in Chapter 2) and his ideas found echoes among a wide range of novelists and poets.[1] Indeed, the literary reception of Versfeld is of equal importance to the philosophical reception. This congenital match is witnessed by the poems by which Marlene van Niekerk and Antjie Krog preferred to articulate their responses to Versfeld.[2]

By Marlene van Niekerk

Johnny in the mountain park instagram*

From *Johnny's Anthropocene Blues*

This rock has all a hostage
needs: fresh air, solid
footing, grass, the thrill
of being touched by slicks
of moss and nodding
ferns. She hides her lithium
like the jewel in that Box
of the World, painted by
Courbet though he preferred
to do the central cleft in oils.

---

[1] See again the references at the beginning of Chapter 7.
[2] The title of this chapter is my choice – EW.

We keep her in a fenced
reserve while we exploit
the cliffs outside. We drill
into the tops when lower
reaches prove abstruse. Once
that fund's exhausted,
we'll start exploring here.
Meanwhile, for the world
to see, we care for mountains
in our custody.

On a day like this,
with noctilucent cirrus
and gorges rife with petrichor,
do yourself a favour,
and take your little Zeiss field
glass with which to scan
her face. Soon you'll find
an aquarelle, wet on wet,
the bleeding greys and blues
on red. You won't hold
back the tears, your eyes
shall bathe the limbs
of our lady erstwhile risen
from the magma swells.
If you watch and wait,
your lenses misting over,
you'll feel the bond emerging
between the keeper
and the kept

Her approach is irrevocable,
you might mistake it for the dusk,
a dimming way down in your gut,
a deep unfastening of locks.

You won't forget the moment
she first put her hands in yours,
and surrendered to your better
judgement. It's pure chemistry,
please note, it started way back
with the Bang.

Henceforth you can have
your way with her, anytime
you want. Re-charge your
batteries, suppress
your bi-polar.

This here is the two of us, please
like and forward to your friends.

L'envoi

It's known, I am told, as
Stockholm syndrome, applicable
to urban rooks, to herons
and the small red fox. They
all eat from our hands.
As of now, I have proof,
it also holds for rocks.

*Written in response to the address given by Versfeld at Maclear's Beacon, Table Mountain, 24 February 1991. *Pots and Poetry and other Essays* 171–172.

I have the sense that nature is a Heraclitean fire in which man is the phoenix. Let us be mindful of the fuel, for the rocks, too, have their immortality of which we are the keepers. We have to redeem nature from the death that we have brought and are bringing upon it. Unless we work to preserve each other, seeing only the humanity, the image, in each of us, we shall lose the mountains and the sea. The rights of man and the rights of rocks are inseparable.

By Antjie Krog

Sunday lunch

everyone's home
I cook   the world as food
is a humanised world
to cook is an act of courtesy

the kitchen steams in golden batter
of laughter wine and spices
the umbilical cord between us and the world
is the casserole – Grandma Dot's casserole

in the oven – stuffed with rosemary
and garlic ingots the joint sizzles
every burning bush is a holy bush but
he who presides over leg of lamb is a priest

I boil rice as if I'm caring for little children
with a grain of nutmeg I praise creation
scrubbed carrots begin to glow from within
in butter and ginger they find a true

voice   beans plunge into white pepper and fennel
a salad spoon reveals a flash of currants softly
clicking jewels of naked olive cherry tomato and
almond   the deepest precision of pumpkin arrives

at the table   the eaten-of-abundance-world
is a beloved world   a meal that overflows
with warmheartedness's blessed
sounds   yes, feeding people is a moral deed

a resurrection. my exuberant family sits down to eat –
suddenly brittle in their enoughness   their un-
scathed selves   our all-still-togetherness. we praise
easy generosity as the great sufficient Guarantee.

The takers of the earth take hands.

(after Martin Versfeld)

the founding principle of generosity

the waxy
cufflink of the
orchid the bit-
ter sneeze of quinine
in sacred bark
the peacock's eye-
splashing wifi a-
rea are useful
for survival thence
the concept:
survival of the
fittest

but the earth does not appear
to be one huge conglomeration
of competing
egos

nothing
tears us away
from its

eyeflood

to feed someone

> *The world as food is the world humanised.*
> Martin Versfeld

the sandwich and tea in my hands
are the making of breath in the world
each one who comes to my front door asking
for food   dissolves an estrangement:

as the knife carefully spreads the butter right
to the crust the triangle of sandwich has already
unconstricted me   a body kneels between hunger
and abyss   an eaten world is a beloved world

butter is the approachable face of bread
bread attends to the slices of creamy smooth avocado
tomatoes singing beneath the grinding salt and pepper
ribbons of crunchy spinach, a twist of bitter rocket

spikes of orange peel   a drop of balsamic
and the true baritone of cheese
hear how the solid centre of the bread resounds
   – presented this way the sandwich becomes a psalter

to wrap food in heartness is a moral act
the sandwich filling that spills with a soft sigh into
a cupped hand   the mug of rooibos-buchu tea – all this
records the spreading aroma of a related adverb: goodwill

the umbilical cord between you and me and the world
is the sandwich – bread and butter spread embodied light
butter reveals the ruddy bread   tomato
the clear-breathing onion   eating on the pavement

from hunger perhaps you long for a drink   yet some part
of you also seized by the flavour of deeply attached earth
:resurrection begins with the bread and the butter
and the man at the open door's mouth of a shared world

convivium

1.
why do my knuckles linger so tenderly on your cheek? why
do I hurry when I hear you're hungry or frightened or suicidal if
the firmament is exploding like a thing hurled in fury?

what sense does your downy summer cheek make
if gravity grinds ice frigates to skyscrapers of dust if
collisions leave behind ruins and new viciously flaring kernels?

why should I care that your cheek hollows fill with tears if
we stand surrounded by helium lightning   startling sunwinds that
devour moons   tear apart finer-spun stars   shatter surfaces?

oh abandoned wells empty of all but darkness
oh holes filled with nothing where only violence holds sway

what use is the luminescence of your cheekbones against
gravitational whirlpools where supernovas collapse with
such force that not even miniscule splashes of light escape?

what use my caress in the breath-earthed night if a centre-
less universe opens space in the nonexistent for dark
matter to overpower a few broken beads of light?

oh holes where only empty violence holds sway
oh abandoned wells filled with darkened nothingnesses

2.
but spiral wands exist you say
the lovely feathery slender spiral arms of our galaxy exist

in a dreamy ballet you say   of haze and orbit
and the slowly pulsing lifespan of stars   oxygen

and quasars nebula wombs and the immense light
at the outer reaches of the visible universe you say

the Milky Way's humming   peaceful silver-purifying orbits exist
the love of moons   tides   light paths and eternal equilibrium   all this

exists you say: is it not precisely the stars as profusion of piercings
on still summer evenings that hold us in outreaching orbits?

whenever we turn to each other in fallow surrender
we do it under a roaring baldachin of stars

3. Symmetry (*HH212**)
at first you do not see the disk-shaped cloud's accreting might
   firing gas swirls in opposite directions –
      both of them pulsing shimmering creamy rays towards
         semi-benign collisions lightly bumping
            urging each other on to visibility: look back at how
               within her cleaving elbows, the star now threads symmetrically
                  on either side a pristine incandescent vertebra of light.
                  on either side a pristine incandescent vertebra of light.
               within her cleaving elbows, the star now threads symmetrically
            urging each other on to visibility: look back at how
         semi-benign collisions lightly bumping
      both of them pulsing shimmering creamy rays towards
   firing gas swirls in opposite directions –
at first you do not see the disk-shaped cloud's accreting might

4.
my body echoes with pockmarked Mercury
– the airlessness and embedded iron core

my body weathers Venus's sunwind   the inferno
of it   the orangeconsuming azure blue sulphur
of slow precise turning to the other side

my wrist holds the Earth aloft – our water planet
chastened blue throbbing under light fingerprints of vapour

my body ploughs duststorms from Mars – ochre
icesilting   sulphurstained desert planet   and starts
to measure the two frost-trapped blondbearded little moons

it is my body that takes the enormity of Jupiter
in tow: the virulent speed   the circling

raging red abscess   the cluster of moons   along creamy paths
of smoky serpentine patterns and metal hues
she can fit three-quarters of the solar system inside her body

only through my body can I love Saturn's freezing beauty –
the still yellow light   the caressing imprisonment of rings

the spaces between the rings   the heartpebble smoothness
the exuberant greatness of perfect form   the lovely
tilt of the body – you are so light Saturn   you can float on water

my body stares through its fingers at the pearl eye of Uranus
fallen on her side   fallen one   methane-heavy palate

my body sinks with the stormy blue darkness of Neptune
mumbling marrowing under gas oceans   autistic   morose
frozen through with deposits of wind   torpid   obscene

5.
the universe is differently unstopped, you say   than just through
a fight for survival   look how celestially throated this morning
is the spread of light on the Mooiberge   the lyrical counting of hours
the heartbreakliturgy in the ear of autumn   you crouch amazed

within it   for blessed are we
that this thin bony inherited mortal body
tuneforks such abundance

*The birth of a twin star was discovered by the Berlin astronomer Hans Zinnecker. HH 212 is pumped out symmetrically by an invisible proto-star near the Horsehead Nebula in the Orion constellation. The poem was written in collaboration with Zinnecker as part of a project of the Calouste Gulbenkian Foundation.

CONCLUSIONS

CHAPTER 9

SANCTUS MARTHINUS LAUDATOR PHILOSOPHICUS – OR, SITTING AT THE GURU'S FEET

IN WHICH I RELY ON EXPERIENCES GAINED THROUGH READING THE WORKS OF THE SAINTLY MARTIN VERSFELD IN ORDER TO INTRODUCE THE READERS TO THE MULTIPLE ASSOCIATIONS EVOKED BY HIS SOCRATIC LIFE[1]

I started reading Versfeld's work around the time of his death[2] and I will take advantage of the momentum granted by the folly of youth to comment on it. However, I do so hesitantly, while my thoughts involuntarily go to another man from Africa. Doctor Luke relates that Philip once met an emasculated Ethiopian statesman who, in addition to this problem, also struggled to understand the text he was reading[3] – as a result of his disabilities, in time and in an amazing way, he became the father of all of us who suffer from impotence in understanding.

Having invoked saints, I need to clarify the title of my chapter. The reader might find it strange that I refer to Versfeld as a saint. It would be very difficult to imagine him as an ascetic, although he did speak kindly about the hermits (*NA* 19) who did not fit into the great Roman political system, but knew how to live from the land and by God's love and how to share this grace through hospitality with others. Something of this is reflected in Versfeld's love for his

---

[1] Has litteras expono ad gratiam agendam meo dilectissimo professori Jano Scholtemeijeri qui me introduxit in amorem Marthini Versfeldis et rerum classicarum.
[2] Intended as an oblique reference to the first chapter of Jan Terlouw's *Koning van Katoren*.
[3] Cf. Acts 8: 26–40.

house in the Kouga. However, he was no puritan. A puritan is someone who wears his fig leaf over his mouth (*PP* 93) and those readers who know how many children Uncle Martin had will share my suspicion that his fig leaf must have, at some point, landed in a stew. He enjoyed cooking, you see.

No, Versfeld was a saint in the degree to which he viewed his work as a calling and made it a song of praise to God. His saintliness can be seen in his common sense (*RM* 44 and *ACCG* 10), in the way he prepared vegetables for the pot, in the way he built his house, the amazement with which he looked at speckled things, and in the way he blew his nose. In brief, his saintliness can be ascribed to the fact that he was simply himself. Saintliness is a biographic adjective. The saint is a *doctus tempore suo*, educated in the training school of his own circumstances, and since life is larger than logic (*MP* 18), nothing is more important to him than to be himself before all else, and to be at home within himself, as he himself provides the perspective from which he looks at and writes about the world.

When he states that his own contingent life precedes his philosophy, that philosophy is based on a person's specific existence (*MP* 20), he does not view it as a mere theoretical finding. This can be seen in the autobiographic line that is evident throughout his work: I would like to start by introducing myself. I am a professor of philosophy (*PP* 1). I live in the Cape and I identify with the cultural tradition of the people who came here to establish a refreshment station for the crews of passing ships (*FT* 9). This is the soil from which I grew (*KK* 13). I was absent for a time, while I studied in Scotland, in the English world, where I hoped to expand my initial presumptuous rationalism (*MP* 16). Master Bowman's integration of faith and reason (*Sum* 14–15; *MP* 16–17) caught me unawares and nowadays I work in a room where the shelves contain works by Augustine and Aquinas, and also the Upanishads. I have built myself a little house in the Kouga (*KK* 7–25) and sleep on a mattress that my grandfather had made for my father in the 1880s. But let me tell you about the delicious stew I cooked.[4] I have to confess that I do have a pressure cooker in my kitchen and that I regularly use it (*FT* 94), etcetera. In his commentary on Augustine's *Confessions* (*ACCG* 9), Versfeld states that to write an autobiography is to talk about yourself, by situating yourself in a specific time and place. In this specific time in history, and at this specific time in the world, I am not alone – my world is filled with constant references to other people (*PP* 6; *TD* 110) who have their own biographies; I interact with other people who share history with me. A genuine autobiography is not a story about a solitary *homo incurvatus in se*, the ego, detached from others, who narcissistically

---

[4] This is found throughout *Food for Thought*.

admires himself. It is *our* story, told from my perspective; without others, I do not exist.[5] Because I am a *zoon politikon*, a social and political animal, I have an autobiography to relate, a life that provides me with things that I can contemplate. Philosophers who are not themselves in this world, who cannot be at home among others, cannot be saintly.

For this reason one should expect Versfeld to frequently address his readers directly. His philosophy is not directed at humankind, but he speaks to you, my esteemed readers, because you are the only mode of existence of humanity (*MP* 4). We should be continuously involved in conversations about our world, because it is through dialogue that we help each other to give birth to better perspectives on the truth. It should not be surprising that Versfeld's inaugural address at the University of Cape Town (cf. *SS* or *Persons*, chapter 1) deals with the Socratic spirit, the spirit of dialogic obstetrics. This spirit took possession of Versfeld and it is right to see him, in his description of the original university, as an inspired guru seated on a tree trunk while conversing with his students (*TD* 109, which alludes to the *Sitz im Leben* from which the Upanishads derived their name).

At the same time, he states that the purpose of this conversation is not to exchange information. The philosopher's search is a search for wisdom. Socrates had learnt from his mother (and we could all benefit from constantly ruminating on our mothers' wisdom) that the midwife not only facilitates the process of creation, but also knows how to deal with people who are ill or have died; she is familiar with both the beginning and the end of life. As people who seek wisdom, we are also seeking the Truth about the beginning and ultimate end of things – the alpha and the omega (*MP* 10), the big *Therefore* to the *Why?* behind everything. That is wisdom. Note that Versfeld is really after Truth with a capital T. However, he does not pretend to have already obtained wisdom – the philosopher is a lover of wisdom. The professional philosopher is a professional amateur. The prerequisite for philosophical thinking is not to be uninvolved with and detached from the world about which one wants to think, but rather embrace and love that world. Someone who loves, Versfeld says, wants to conform to the loved one; the one who loves always feels somewhat unworthy and inadequate towards what is loved and therefore aspires to overcome that shortcoming. Therefore, he comments: "No one is a good lover who has no capacity for adventure, and adventure rests on the faith that one will get somewhere. It is not so much a

---

[5] "We are saturated with others to our innermost recesses and exist, so to speak, in the mirrors which reflect us. We think therefore I am, and all thinking is 'political.' *Sumus ergo cogito*" (*SS* 3).

matter of getting the truth, as of being got by truth, and repressing the unworthy fear that one may be had by it." (*MP* 8–9) That which we love, the purpose of wisdom's search, is the relationship between us, the world and our fellow humans.

Since I have here again touched on the topic of our nature as social beings, I would like to say something about the role played by the community in the love of wisdom, which will further elucidate Versfeld's view of philosophy. As mentioned earlier, the life of every person takes place within a community. We depend on the community for the meaning of our activities. Consider the following example: if I should ask a scientist to explain to me why objects fall towards the earth, he/she would offer a scientific explanation. However, if I should ask: "Why would anyone ask such a question?" or "Why would you think that the way in which your question is answered is reasonable?", the scientist would not be able to give me a scientific answer. The reasonable nature of science is the result of how science is embedded in a community. It is only when we get to know ourselves as a community that we can answer the question "Why is it reasonable to practise science?" ("Talking" 10–11) On one particular page (*GA* 8), Versfeld is ahead of both Kuhn and Gadamer when he offers the insight that our frame of thought develops within a community, and that our tradition of understanding enables us to understand the world. The community also helps us to understand what is reasonable, in other words equitable: "Pasteur's conviction that fermentation is caused by microscopic organisms was a truly reasonable conviction; in my case it is a belief" (*GA* 9). However, no one will object if we share Versfeld's belief – he is reasonable, even though he is not a scientist. The point here is that scientific findings cannot be justified scientifically – they are reasonable due to the social existence of people, which precedes science; science can be understood as an activity of a human community (see also *MP* 20). This explains my earlier statement that life is larger than logic.

We could also look at this issue from another angle: physics makes judgements about matter. This statement is not a judgement about matter, therefore, it is not a judgement based on physics. Physics thus does not make judgements about physics judgements, but simply provides information on the basis of which this could be done ("Talking" 15–16). (This of course also applies to the other sciences.) What makes this interesting is the fact that such judgements about scientific judgements are historical events. However, history could also not be the final underlying reason for, or explanation of, that set of events that we recognise as scientific judgements. The historical judgement as such is a historical event and it is still necessary to answer the question: "Why history?" Neither science nor history can make judgements about themselves. Because science deals with the truth about things and history makes statements about the truth of events, we now have to look for a way of thinking that makes judgements about the truth of the truth, which could, in other words, be the consciousness of science and history. This way of thinking that can scrutinise itself is called metaphysics ("Talking" 17). Any attempt to define metaphysics from outside of metaphysics, or to discard it from the outside as a valid form of knowledge, can – as Versfeld claims – be compared to singing in Gregorian chant a proof that music does not exist ("Talking" 7).

The question that now arises is whether I should not apply the earlier grounding of the reasonableness of science to metaphysics, for does life not also precede metaphysics? Versfeld would not agree, and this is exactly the point he wishes to make: this self-reflexive reasoning already *is* the living reasoning of a specific, self-observing, living human being. It would be impossible to move further away from the Absolute Spirit. Versfeld's metaphysics is thought by a man with a name, a life story and an address – a man who stands grinning at a specific spot in his kitchen while chewing a knobbly carrot.

Two things mentioned in the previous paragraph deserve further attention. The first is Versfeld's fundamental conviction that the Socratic words of wisdom ("Talking" 17; *MP* 19; *Persons* 2; *Sum* 15, and many more), "know yourself" and "I know that I know nothing", constitute the basis of all knowledge. However, this basis of ignorant self-knowledge is not an undoubtable foundation. Descartes's *cogito*, which is the pacemaker of the modern heartbeat, represents an attempt to use self-knowledge – the knowledge *that* I exist – to remove all uncertainty; it is the starting block for explaining all mysteries. By contrast, Augustine's *si fallor sum*[6] (which is usually related to *cogito*) speaks the same language as Socrates: it discards scepticism, but welcomes the mystery that is reason ("Talking" 18–19) – *factus eram mihi ipse magna questio*.[7] The person posing the question *is* the question:

> The mysteriousness of reason itself was the fundamental fact with which reason had to cope, a wonder at our confrontation with the *abyssus humanae naturae*, which is at the root of our physical investigations themselves, and thus lies at the root of that very science by the false idolisation of which we so often endeavour to destroy the mystery of

---

[6] This is the argument according to which one cannot doubt the fact that one thinks you are – even if I am mistaken, I exist.
[7] I became an enormous enigma to myself.

the human nature of the scientist himself. (*MP* 20; see also *FT* 89 and *Sum* 22 in particular)

It is this vast unknown, ignorance, nescience (or what should one call it?) inside me that opens me up to outward questions. Mystery and reason are inextricably bound together (*MP* 20). Compelled by the mystery of our being, we do everything in our power to think through the big *Why?*, and a truly comprehensive philosophy always takes us back to the mystery that the things cannot be thought comprehensively by our reason (*RM* 47). The ultimate *Therefore*, the reason for the *Why?* beyond which we can ask no questions, is God. God is his own self-sufficient reason.[8] This is the answer provided by Thomas, who reminds us that, despite all the volumes of his *Summae*, we cannot grasp God through reason.

The saint of Aquino brings us to the second thing that I still needed to explain: the knobbly carrot. The idea that metaphysics is the pastime of people with an interest in concepts that are abstract and beyond time is incorrect. Rather, the metaphysicist attempts to rely on general concepts to make contact with concrete, specific things (*MP* 12), and in this regard we will benefit from rereading Marcel – the man who spent his time keeping a diary of the metaphysical.[9] The first question asked by metaphysics – "Why is there something and not rather just nothing?" – stems from the basis of remarkable tangible things. Thomas's proofs of the existence of God are *a posteriori* (*RM* 63): they are based on his amazement about the existence of particular things in the world. In common language one could say that if there were no knobbly carrots and no grinning elderly men, Thomas's proofs of God's existence would not fly. It is not surprising that Thomas, who had to remove a crescent-shaped section from his dining table to accommodate the particular shape of his stomach, was one of Versfeld's favourite interlocutors. Descartes's God is *clare et distincte*, Versfeld's is *hic et nunc*, close at hand.

If the metaphysical is tangible and close at hand only in specific instances, in the here and now, we can understand why Versfeld is so happy to apply to himself the criticism of Callicles when he remarked to Socrates: "You constantly talk about food and drink and doctors and nonsense: I do not speak of those

---

[8] Versfeld explains how he had arrived at this conclusion: "I was thus led, by my wish to defend reason, and by ways which I need not dwell on here, to affirm the existence of God, who was his own sufficient reason, whose being was his own intelligibility, and in whose mystery alone was the foundation of our rationality to be found. In short, no mystery then no clarity, no God then no reason. Thus alone could I have that confidence in my reason, the loss of which Socrates deplored as the greatest of evils" (*MP* 21).

[9] Cf. Gabriel Marcel's *Journal Métaphysique* (Paris: Gallimard, 1927).

things".¹⁰ His constant return to Whitehead's remark that "it requires a great mind to take an interest in the obvious"¹¹ is by no means superficial. Even when Versfeld writes practical suggestions for mountaineers, he does not replace his comfortable slippers with hiking shoes; we recognise his voice when he advises prospective climbers to pack the following: "[...] a writing pad, a pencil, and a book of poetry is also recommended. May be you are overcome by a sudden romantic incident – or decide to make your will".¹² This association of poetry with one's presence in nature, and with life and death, is not coincidental. His descriptions of plants, workspaces, stones, brinjals, pencils, lavatories, hats, Christmas trees and cinnamon clearly reflect the poet's keen powers of observation. The philosopher who wants to get beyond the exactness of the scientist's metricating, domineering approach to the world needs to learn another type of exactness from the poet:

> Wisdom is the capacity to see things in their totality, where by "totality" we mean not a vague togetherness but the concrete fullness which challenges the mind with the opulence of its meaning. Hence the philosopher shares with the poet an absorption in the articulation of existence, expressing itself in the unique voice by which each tree and stone and blade of grass proclaims itself to be this and to be lovable. (*MP* 13 and also see *TD* 106; *PP* 4, 93; *KK* 17–18; *GA* 15–23, and many more)

Versfeld is a poet – in the sense of the Greek word *poiesis*, which refers to the making or creating of things¹³ – and his philosophy is a song of praise to the One who started all the creating, the One who sings the *carmen universi*. (For this reason Versfeld's essays should be read aloud, preferably with a mouthful of food.) Like the philosophy of Augustine, his philosophical *narratio* is simultaneously *laudatio*,¹⁴ because of his love for the superfluous mottledness of the world. The world is so much more than just a closed system of essential functions to which dreadful decorations have been added *ad nauseam*. Unlike Sartre, God did not puke on the orchids¹⁵ – He laughed while *ex nihilo*, from nothing, He playfully

---

10   For example, *PP* 1; and *SS* 6.
11   For example, *PP* 1.
12   Versfeld and De Klerk, *Die berge van die Boland*, 164.
13   Another of Versfeld's favourite references. See *PP* 93, and many more.
14   As in Augustine, see *Sum* 112.
15   Versfeld detested Sartre's (the reference is to the latter's *La nausée*) loathing for the unnecessary detail spawned by what Sartre considered a functional reality. Sartre's view is as far removed from Versfeld's emphasis on the here and now as Hegel's idealism.

and joyfully created a world filled with voluptuous, colourful things.[16] Everything is redundant, superfluous – it doesn't have to be there, yet it is, and therefore we are free to accept it as a gift. People too, are of course totally redundant (*FT* 93). This is the basis of our love for one another, which is, in turn, the exact place where we find God (*FT* 21).

The human being was also created from nothing and we exist thanks to God, in whose image we were created. Versfeld's understanding of the human being as *imago Dei* is Thomistic: because of the *analogia entis* – the idea that our characteristics are analogous with the ways in which God exists – we are able to know something about God, know Him in a way that reminds us that in many languages of antiquity "to know" also had a sexual meaning. I have already mentioned that just like love, wisdom is an act of intimate creativity. It therefore makes sense that God, who is Wisdom and Love, accommodates us by presenting Himself as a gift to us at a specific time and place in history. Probably Versfeld's favourite biblical text was from Luke's Gospel, where it is told that Jesus was born in an open cave and placed in a manger at the time when Caesar Augustus reigned over the Roman Empire and Cirenius was the governor of Syria, etc.[17] God's punctual incarnation here and now in Bethlehem is the climax of His reaching out to humankind. He arrives on time because Jahwe is who He is[18] – He meets us in history, because love means making time for someone (*TD* 112, *FT* 95). Thomas's *quod Deus est, quod Deus est aeternus, quod Deus est sua aeternitas*[19] is the title of the *carmen universi*, God's love song sung for us.[20]

Versfeld regards Augustine's ability to reconcile the biblical concept of a God of history with Greek thought as one of his rare insights.[21] As is so often the case, Versfeld walks the same road as Augustine – and therefore also runs into the same problems. The major question that arises from this view is how

---

[16] Cf. *FT* 90, *BU* 121 with reference to Proverbs 8:27–31; *PP* 92, and others.
[17] Cf. Luke 2:1–2; *KK* 19, and others.
[18] Cf. Exodus 3:14, referred to in *Sum* 104; also see *KK* 21.
[19] That God is, that God is eternal, that God is His own eternity (*SS* 6, and many others).
[20] In this paragraph I have included almost all the elements of what Versfeld regarded as the core of the Christian faith, or at any rate as he saw it in 1954: "What is that belief? That a God, whose essence is to be, created, that is, gave being to, a Universe, which had no shred of being before the creative act, and that when nature had defected from Him, He restored and more than restored it, by taking upon Himself the nature of a man with all its fleshly and local accidents" (*PO* 240).
[21] See, for example, *Sum* 88: "[...] however much Augustine may owe to Greek and, especially, to Platonic philosophy, he is spiritually a Semite. The God of Augustine is the God of the Old and New Testaments, who is the God of history."

one can somehow arrive at an understanding of the specific suffering of people in the here and now. This is such a prominent problem in our century, perhaps more than ever before, since the dark twentieth century is a barbaric period. It is therefore disappointing that Versfeld often ignores it – just when we would expect him to deal with it. Here I would like to mention a few examples: I am still searching for his interpretation of Augustine's heavy-handed dealing with the Donatist. If a giant meteorite had collided with Earth and wiped out all the dinosaurs, was the *carmen universi*'s percussion not too loud? And if Lisbon is destroyed by an earthquake, I have to confess that my master totally missed the point when he remarked that "[e]veryone has the world that he is and deserves. If it appears ghastly, the ghastliness was injected by us" (*TD* 110; similarly *PP* 5). This comment is particularly lamentable against the background of South African political history.

However, I do not want to create the impression that he was ignorant regarding what was happening around him in the country – in fact, his essays are peppered with references to the sociopolitical burning points of the time.[22] Apart from the general criticism of apartheid (1972 – *Sum* 68), nation and race (1968 – *KK* 8), racial classification (1971 – *SS* 4) and capitalism (1971 – *SS* 8), he levelled specific criticism at the Separate Amenities Act (1962 – *RM* 104) and the District Six affair (1985 – *NA* 23), for example. Having thus far spoken about Versfeld with so much appreciation, I now have to give him the benefit of the doubt. There is, in any case, no doubt that he was thoroughly aware of the problem.[23]

What does this tell us? I could speculate that Versfeld might have been so grateful for his own life that he would have regarded it as dishonest to, in a manner of speaking, climb out of his own life to talk about things that were not part of that life. Besides, philosophy cannot be expected to provide answers to all questions, and he would have commended me for getting cornered in this mystery of the human situation as *flentes et gementes in hac lacrimarum*

---

[22] Readers who are not familiar with South African sociopolitical history may want to consult, as background to the points that follow: Deborah Posel, "The apartheid project, 1948–1970," in Robert Ross, Anne Kelk Mager, and Bill Nasson (eds.), *The Cambridge history of South Africa. Volume 2: 1885–1994* (Cambridge: Cambridge University Press, 2011), 319–368; Keith Hart and Vishnu Padayachee, "A history of South African capitalism in national and global perspective," *Transformation: Critical Perspectives on Southern Africa* 81/82 (2013): 55–85; and Leonard Thompson, *A history of South Africa*, revised fourth edition, by Lynn Berat (New Haven and London: Yale University Press, 2014).

[23] For example, *FT* 10. I will leave it to someone else to undertake a thorough study of this topic.

valle,[24] weeping and moaning in this vale of tears. Obviously the mystery of my own being, the world and God will always lead to new questions. Thoughtful, ongoing conversations with others about these things constitute a form of therapy ("Talking" 12). This belief, which Versfeld adopted from one of Plato's dialogues, resonates with the activities of the Truth and Reconciliation Commission.

Moreover, Versfeld makes at least two interesting suggestions for how to deal with this problem. First, he encourages us to be constantly amazed by the beauty that surrounds us, because God created the Tao to be beautiful. This happy but sometimes tragic approach to life coincides with flow of the Tao, which cannot be encompassed, because it is created anew by God every moment (*FT* 11–12). The second suggestion was influenced by Augustine (*Sum* 111–112) and is based on the understanding that people who are free to act in any way they want to are the ones who, through the sins they commit, release the powers of evil into the world. The fruit of sin is death – actual death, such as the death lamented in Psalm 88. This Psalm is important because the Jewish poet, who did not believe in the immortality of the soul, described with poetic precision the horror of death. In this regard, Versfeld continues:

> The Bible does not present us with a philosophy of immortality, but with a religion of resurrection. We cannot appreciate the central position of the preaching of the resurrection by the apostles, nor the thrilling joy of the Easter liturgy, unless we see it against this black background of sin and death. (*Sum* 112)

This asks for a corresponding way of life in which one bears one's cross because, as Versfeld believes, this is the only way in which to make sense of history and of your own life story, here and now.[25] However, when talking about the cross, it is necessary to include another remark made by the same man: "I was once moved to say that the Redemption is excruciatingly funny" (*PP* 92). The *crux* of the matter is that true religion has to admit to its strangeness. For now, however, I will not discuss the mystery of this paradox any further.

---

[24] Quoted in *NA* 17.
[25] "[B]earing one's cross, which is Christ's cross, is the only way to make sense of history, and of one's own history, and transforming what is perhaps the humdrum necessity of here and now into an eternal moment significant for the future of mankind" (*Sum* 119).

Dear reader, forgive me for not being able to say everything about God here, but I do hope that the foretaste will arouse your interest. The last aspect, and perhaps the most prominent of Versfeld's views on reality, at which I will here take a closer look, is the removal of the division between transcendence and immanence through incarnation.[26] This theme repeatedly appears in a kaleidoscope of different forms: the secular is the miraculous (*FT* 89); the ordinary is the extraordinary (*PP* 1); paradise is the place where you are at home, and the pearly gate is your own garden gate (*NA* 23); God is present in the performance of our everyday tasks (*FT* 20); slicing bread is a prayer (*ACCG* 9); your spiritual life is your normal life, your lifestyle (*ACCG* 10); it is impossible to see where nature ends and grace begins (*GA* 32); a unity exists between rationality and mysticism (following Socrates, *SS* 4, and following Aquinas, *RM* 44); when you talk to God, you are talking to the world (*KK* 8); you are a priest when you roast a leg of mutton, and you have to kneel when you light the fire (*TD* 109); and so forth. The unity that exists between these apparent opposites asks the lovers of wisdom to follow a suitable approach to their journeys of discovery in life, to refrain from searching for their ideal self somewhere else, to simply be themselves and to love themselves exactly where they are, because philosophy is "knowledge *in via*".[27] Spiritual life does not consist of withdrawal from the world, but rather that you have to embrace it and dwell in it, because it is only when you are at home within yourself that you can offer hospitality to others (*ACCG* 10 and *KK* 8). In brief, make sure that you love and then do whatever you like. You don't get to know a tree by learning off by heart its definition, but by tasting its fruit.

It is not surprising that Versfeld savours the fact that the Latin word for wisdom, *sapientia*, is derived from the word *sapere*, meaning to taste (*PP* 7). If Augustine was the *doctor charitatis*, Versfeld was the *doctor gastronomicae*. Food and related things provide the core around which we can gather to partake in his philosophy – the students of this guru seated on a tree trunk sit around a friendly fire on which a tasty stew is simmering. And even if the guru is not simply a Thomist in his thinking, he will still proclaim himself to be a Thomist cook. All good cooks are Thomists:

---

[26] I have questioned this interpretation in Chapter 3, §6.3 and I have given a revised interpretation. Versfeld also summarises the two aspects of Christian metaphysics as (1) an understanding of God, the highest Actuality, which He is, and (2) the incarnation as the prime example of how God moved closer to humankind in history (*RM* 48).

[27] "Talking" 9, i.e., gathered only during and through the course of a search.

> In assembling his ingredients he brings together the variety of the sensible world, and combines them in a manner which respects the principle of identity. This is mutton: let it remain mutton; these were olives: *fiant olivae*. Cooking is creation and I do not believe that God made a hash of the world.[28]

It is also Thomas who points out that, rather than being a type of knowledge, religious observation is a type of tasting, or a kind of loving (*GA* 28). Therefore the philosopher, the poet and the cook all practise the same things. Plato's *Symposion* is a song of praise to love.

Just like the poet and the philosopher/theologian, the cook is also ideally situated to observe and participate in the interaction between people and the world. People and the world create each other (*TD* 110–111, and others): the world makes it possible for us to exist and we are what we eat (*der Mensch ist was er isst*, as Feuerbach said), because we are dependent on our environment for our spiritual-physical existence; our lives are shaped by that which is at our disposal. However, we also eat our world using our senses and our mouths; with our teeth and hands we change the environment in a way that demonstrates the things that are important to us: vineyards, farmlands covered with maize, grain silos, power stations, canning factories, roads, shops and eventually weapons factories – everything planned to provide food.

The fire under the pot is therefore the beginning of science and technology. The trouble really started when technology appeared on the scene, because, Versfeld argues, technology represents an attempt to gain control over things by objectifying and measuring them so that they can be known and their importance can be calculated. The idea of metrication in a cookbook would be, to Versfeld, as ridiculous as having to get to know his wife by studying an anatomy textbook.

The problem with technology is that it can be compared to when you are plagued by a mouse and end up with your fingers clamped between the teeth of the mousetrap. This problem was identified many years ago by Chuang-tzu, who concluded that the person who attempts to dominate things ends up being dominated by them (*TD* 114–115; *PP* 10, where the poet is quoted). Love is the opposite of domination. Love takes time, but technology is in too much of a hurry to have time to love, because for it time is money. This is the origin of the view of nature held by popular Darwinism (*FT* 91–92): nature is engaged in a battle to eliminate unnecessary abundance and generosity to ensure the survival of

---

[28] *MP* 4. The principle of identity is guaranteed by God, who is who He is. A broader exposition of this topic will have to follow at another time.

the strongest egos, measured against optimal functioning and usefulness. If I can succeed in mimicking this battle in my kitchen, I will be a technological winner, and I will be an even greater achiever if I can succeed in taking in the correct number of kilojoules and the right vitamins, and using other mechanisms that drive success and facilitate functioning.

But if I take time to stir my soup, I will recognise the vegetables in the pot for what they are: a never-ending dance of abundant things. Their Creator is unpredictable, because love is spontaneously creative (*FT* 92). Once we understand this, we will enjoy our food in a way that celebrates the fact that God did not regard it as robbery[29] when he became bread and wine. When we think about food, we will inevitably arrive at questions relevant for life and death, especially if we think too long, and the question about whether the centrality of the *abyssus humanae naturae* in Versfeld's thinking is the source of his appetite remains unanswered. The philosopher is a vulture.[30] He understood that the body of a philosopher is important and I will not be convinced that he had to learn this from Thomas, even though Versfeld was a smaller philosopher.

It is, of course, with our bodies that we are present to each other. To receive someone's body is to receive the whole person. Hospitality is the home of Versfeld's ethics as his home is the centre of both his inward and outward interactions. People can only be hospitable if they have a home into which they have already received themselves with hospitality. Self-love is the precondition for neighbourly love (*ACCG* 9; *NA* 23; *KK* 7–9). The house, your home, is the place from where you study the world, from where you go out to work and rummage around in the world. However, like the seven dwarfs, one always has to return home, undertake a venture into the "interior", see what one has in one's workroom (who knows what you might find there?) and attempt to clear up some of the chaos (*NA* 16; *KK* 47).

Versfeld's style is evidence of such a situation in life. His philosophy is a journey to discover the world, which starts with a *venture into the interior*.[31] Having arrived there, he then receives guests from every distant corner of the written universe: from the wise men of the Upanishads to Plato, from Lao Tzu to Augustine, Aquinas and Descartes, Newman and Leipoldt (Sartre and Hobbes are sent to the kitchen, where they may have tinned food, and Hegel is free to go and externalise his ideas about food in the outside lavatory). Everyone is made

---

[29] Cf. Philippians 2:6
[30] *NA* 46–49. This theme opens Chapter 10 (below).
[31] *MP* 2 and the title of chapter 3 of *MP*, which was borrowed from the title of a book written by Laurens van der Post.

to feel thoroughly welcome at his symposium. He enjoys talking about their previous meetings and generously gives them all the credit due to them – Versfeld had a very thick Bible, indeed. It is not always easy (and perhaps intentionally so) to distinguish Versfeld's opinion from that of, for example, Aquinas (which explains why he typified his thinking as Gothic and analogous). Elsewhere, however, I get the feeling that Versfeld treats his interlocutors as though he himself were a little boy who is eating only the icing and leaving the cake. Have you ever heard him comment on Augustine's essay on fasting? And Aquinas would have a hard time trying to recognise his *Summa contra Gentiles* as a guide for converting heathens by teaching them to clean carrots properly (*FT* 20), and if Feuerbach says *der Mensch ist was er isst*, we have to join Versfeld in picking off the icing sugar if we want to share his understanding. If I were to accuse him of setting his sails to the wind, he would probably remind me that the wind blows wherever it wants to blow.

For this reason, Versfeld also cannot be dogmatic or construct systems (*MP* 2–3) (the wind does not blow systematically; the closest he gets to this is *The Perennial Order*), but he rather relies on reflection, with which he tries to open the doors to the truth (*MP* 6). He admits that he gives priority to relating things to one another, allowing them to talk to each other, rather than to undo them through analysis.[32] This stems from his steadfast loyalty to concrete detail – he describes how his father had taught him to sharpen a pencil (*KK* 40–41) with the same care with which the sharpening is to be carried out.

Sometimes his claim that his texts are clear[33] has to be taken at some places with a pinch of salt. However, he has to be obscure and somewhat incoherent – he is, after all, attempting to render reality.[34] The way he generally writes his essays without subsections or clear units, and repeatedly, through the years, attempts to articulate some or other amazing issue, is evidence of his approach to reality – which has to be repeatedly viewed from different limited, non-final perspectives, because reality is not final. It is a reality in which he stands at the centre, since it is his life; what he says about *The Mirror of Philosophers* applies to all his work: "I want to present a book which is philosophical precisely in being autobiographical, and somewhat disjointed because I am a human being, interested in being, and

---

[32] "[…] connecting in my thinking has priority over analysis. I am impressed with the relation of all things to each other, that is, with the fact of communication" (*FT* 3–4).

[33] Those for which he likes to take credit, at least. See *PP* 1, and others.

[34] I have to admit that although his essays are generally easy to understand, they are sometimes complicated by obscure references and allusions. A person who is not familiar with Hopkins's "Pied Beauty" would, for instance, miss something in "Cooking the marvellous" (*FT* 89–93).

somewhat involved in my own. Only thus can I hope to achieve an objective unity of presentation" (*MP* 2).

But did I not start with Versfeld's life? At present,[35] when we would have been celebrating his ninetieth birthday, I would like to give him, speaking from the other side, from God's City, an opportunity to invite us to come closer:

> I realise that I'm getting on in years. The day will come when I will have to leave everything behind and depart from the room of the world. To prepare for this, one should get rid of a few things now. To detach yourself from things is sound, old advice. If you do not do this, they may leave of their own, which could be hurtful. If you also throw the Bible in the basket with the rest, it could prove that you have learnt its most intimate lesson. Should you arrive at the gates of heaven clutching your Bible in both hands, you may not be able to ring the bell. We approach the new life with open hands. (*NA* 17)

What Versfeld says about the Bible is of course equally valid for his own work and, dear reader, if you have not done it yet, I would like to ask you to do the same with my essay.

---

[35] Referring, of course, to the date of first publication of this chapter: 1999.

CHAPTER 10

WHAT IS LIVING AND WHAT IS DEAD OF THE PHILOSOPHY OF MARTIN VERSFELD?

– OR, THE PHILOSOPHER READ BY A VULTURE

> "The Philosopher as Vulture"
> (title of an essay, *NA* 2nd ed. 67–71)

It may seem curious to choose as heading for this last chapter a book title from idealist philosophy that Versfeld so energetically critiqued – namely, Benedetto Croce's *What Is Living and What is Dead of the Philosophy of Hegel*.[1] However, it makes sense if one presents it as a kind of counterpart to Versfeld's first philosophical text, his MA thesis, which was on Croce.[2] In any case, the title fits quite well with what I intend with this last chapter: a somewhat messy task captured in the subtitle. Again, for the author who prided himself in mindful cooking, it must have taken some courage to liken a philosopher to a scavenger. But indeed, like vultures that arrive after the event to quarrel over bits and pieces of rotten remainders, so one of the tasks of philosophers is to do the same with whatever the accidents of history leave behind for them.

In this post scriptum, which is also a post-mortem, I will not dish up a lavish five-course meal. I will fully assume the role of the vulture by pecking at a number

---

[1] This is the title of the translation: Benedetto Croce, *What Is Living and What is Dead of the Philosophy of Hegel*, trans. Douglas Ainslie (London: Macmillan, 1915).
[2] I have not been able to obtain this thesis and cannot confirm that a copy of it still exists. One should also note Versfeld's remark: "I did an MA thesis on Croce, of whose thought I remember nothing at all" (*Sum* 13).

of issues that those reflecting on Versfeld's thought will have to digest. They are all mutually related and all touch in one way or another the core of his work.

1. Augustine: Ventriloquism or interpretation as independent thought?

A curious tension which Versfeld willingly assumed is between affirming the "perennial order"[3] – as he dared to call it earlier on – and a sensitivity for contingency which is captured in his insistence on time, history and biography. But even this tension was subject to change. In Chapter 3 we saw that the critique of early modern rationalism, his allegiance with a few important authors, the importance of history, political critique, certain theological themes, the anthropological mystery, and the call to a cultivate one's generous self are quite stable features. But the changes in this general framework are as revealing of what the name "Versfeld" should evoke. This point reaches to the heart of his work – let me illustrate it in his reading of Augustine and in his aesthetics/ethics of generosity.

When Versfeld wrote his last book, *St Augustine's Confessions and City of God*, he often reformulated and even copied arguments from two earlier texts, *A Guide to the City of God*[4] and *Rondom die Middeleeue* (*On the Middle Ages*).[5] This makes it possible to trace a shift in Versfeld's general appraisal of Augustine. If he initially hailed Augustine as a major foundational author of Western civilisation, whose writings provide valuable stimulation for the present-day reader (cf. *RM* chapter 1), Versfeld later opines that "If the fault of Western Christianity has been an excess of philosophising and theologising, Augustine is certainly a guilty party" (*ACCG* 25). And Augustine made a substantial contribution to "exclusivist Catholicity" through his "biblical literalism" (*ACCG* 100). Still, he would redeem

---

[3] But see his comment in *MP* 85.
[4] This book is still cited as an authoritative reference by Christoph Horn in "Augustinus, De Civitate Dei (ca. 413–427)," in *Geschichte des politischen Denkens. Ein Handbuch*, ed. Manfred Brocker (Frankfurt-am-Main: Suhrkamp, 2012, 4th edition), 62–77, here 77.
[5] The 116 pages of *ACCG* are divided into thirty short chapters (plus an "Introduction"). Of these, chapters I and II correspond largely with the first chapter of *RM* and chapters VI–XXVIII (except X and XVII) cover essentially *GCG* chapter II to the first half of chapter VIII. In short, if I see correctly, the Introduction and chapters IV, V, X, XVII, XIX and XX (about 28 pages) of *ACCG* are new.

Augustine by transforming him into a mystic. Mystics, according to Versfeld, are people who have experiences of the Truth and although the Truth is unspeakable, they respond to these experiences by "erecting thousands of verbal signposts", pointing us to "the centre". If Augustine was talkative – as mystics tend to be (*ACCG* 25) – then it was because his mystic, transrational experience quickened his reason and, one should add, his tongue (*ACCG* 25).

Already in the early commentaries, Versfeld discussed the Augustinian idea of a trinitarian universe (cf. *GCG* 22–24; *PO* 242; *Persons* 104), a central tenet of which is the idea of the world as held together by God's love. But in a new insertion in *ACCG* (55–57), Versfeld calls on Chuang-tzu to shed different light on this creative power: "Chuang-Tzu holds: To organise is to destroy. Just as all beliefs must be unbelieved, so all organisations must be disorganised. This is the function of the mystics, and that is why they are disliked by politicians, positivists, planners and ecclesiastics" (*ACCG* 55). The Eastern sage wins out against Versfeld's most beloved theologican and ecclesiastic![6] Furthermore, the reference to Chuang-tzu is quite typical for the new reading of Augustine. Without abandoning his own Christian orientation, whatever domineering view it may have had[7] is replaced by curiosity about the possible exchanges between intellectual and religious traditions.[8] Curiously, while the later Versfeld is no less "materialist" than the earlier Versfeld (cf. *PP* 2), one does not find in *St Augustine's Confessions and City of God* Versfeld's earlier indication of where to look for salvation for the weaknesses of Augustine's historical thinking: "Modern Augustinianism still has a great work to do in exploring [its] empirical bearing. An Augustinianism which has learnt from Marx has a future" (*GCG* 70).

On the level of cultural critique, a shift is evident too. Is Augustine's life story not the quintessential conversion from a life of frivolous bodily pleasures to Christian austerity? One may get this impression from Versfeld's rendering in *Rondom die Middeleeue* (and indeed from Augustine's *Confessions* itself!). But in *St Augustine's Confessions and City of God*, Versfeld shifts the emphasis in Augustine's autobiography, and thereby gives this conversion story a delightful cultural-critical twist:

---

[6] And one can gauge the dimension of this victory by recalling a passage from *The Mirror of Philosophers* where Versfeld enlists Augustine to critique the devastation of individual and social disorder (cf. *MP* 291–293).
[7] The strongest formulation thereof is perhaps *MP* 98–99. However, I am not convinced that this passage can be upheld in the light of Versfeld's own philosophy at the time.
[8] The limits of this openness in Versfeld's published work have been outlined very precisely by Kobus Krüger in Chapter 6 of this book.

> But let us get all this in perspective. Augustine was neither a fool nor a rake. He had become a responsible and very able professor in the arts, he had firm friendships with highly placed people, and he had formed a stable connection with a woman who bore him a son, Adeodatus (Godgiven) for whom he had the deepest affection, and he could attract young people to him in love and respect. Let us be clear about this. Augustine's conversion was not a conversion from lurid vice. By ordinary worldly academic standards he had done very well, and perhaps the real significance of his conversion is that it was a conversion from the ordinary decencies of which we are all rather proud. His conversion was from the city of this world, in which we are all striving to make ourselves comfortable. In fact he had done well enough to feel confident that he could cut a figure in Rome, so he joined the brain drain. (*ACCG* 20)

This rereading of Augustine is a second attempt to out-augustinianise Augustine. And the change of perspective is not trivial. Instead of presenting Augustine as the exemplar of abnegation, Versfeld reframes the issue as that of a critical stance towards the status quo. Augustine's story of conversion is then not an initiation into a life of conventional middle-class conservatism, but becomes a challenge, in the first place, to those who benefit from bourgeois life, a challenge to someone like Versfeld himself or his peers – or to the kind of person who would likely read his book!

The meanders in his own reception of the Church Father illustrates his conviction that awareness of a tradition is not to be confused with historical determinism.[9] But at the same time, the reader has to remain careful about this reception which, although erudite and considered, strives at independent thought rather than objective exegesis. Ventriloquism may well be a philosophical art. In matters of receiving Augustine, there is then not just one Versfeld and this should predispose his readers to find this plurality elsewhere too.[10] And thus the perennial order was slowly shifting.

---

[9] "Tradition is an enduring technique/technology [*tegniek*] of renewal" (*Wat is kontemporêr?* 1) he writes, and in a slightly reworked version of the same passage: "To do something new, and to help to renew the tradition by which we live is an essential manifestation of the creative spirit" (*Persons* 66).

[10] A weak point of my 1999 article (now Chapter 9 of this book) was not to have taken this fully into account.

2. Plurality

At numerous places in this book we have come across the remarkable fact that this author, who knew himself to be rooted in a tradition, welcomed insights from foreign traditions. Not only did he have an open mind on this matter, but he actively studied and promoted the study of other forms of wisdom. One should not underestimate the significance of these facts. And yet, one cannot sidestep the question: what about the absence of African philosophy in his work? Both his insistence on the locality of philosophy and his critique of imperial and apartheid politics point to the need to engage with the modes of thinking of this continent.

This absence has to be stated and regretted. Yet, the matter is a bit more complex. Written, published and distributed literature in which the authors present the content as "African philosophy" emerged slowly after the Second World War. By the mid 1960s, interesting debates seriously questioned the philosophical claim of these first works, while relaunching the case for philosophy of, or in, Africa in different ways. In the 1970s, and even into the 1980s, African scholars were still debating the existence of African philosophy.[11] Now let us recall that Versfeld retired in 1972. If one then bears in mind the speed at which academic publications and trends spread in an era before the internet, one has to be careful not to exaggerate the practical overlap between the writings of early African philosophers and that of Versfeld.

The critical question thus has to be reformulated: how much should one expect of the philosopher in the years after his retirement? Or, before that time, what knowledge could one have expected of him to have of Africanist intellectual work in a broader sense? In this way one could decide "whether the content of [his] philosophy squares with the historical existence of that philosophy" (*MP* 83). And then there remains a host of questions that can be generated in comparing his philosophy with themes from African philosophy, for instance, the significance of tradition, the situatedness of thought, place, embodiment, and cultural and political critique.

---

[11] Earlier overviews are quite telling – see for instance Tshiamalenga Ntumba, "Die Philosophie in der aktuellen Situation Afrikas," *Zeitschrift für Philosophische Forschung* 33, no. 3 (1979): 428–433; or V.Y. Mudimbe, *The Invention of Africa. Gnosis, Philosophy and the Order of Knowledge* (Bloomington: Indianapolis University Press, 1988), chapter 5.

3. Something or nothing?

In his more metaphysical moments, Versfeld defined philosophy by the question: why is there something rather than nothing? (*PO* 17; 20; *MP* 13, 20).[12] Through long, carefully constructed argumentation, he could arrive at dealing with this most general and abstract of questions, by attention to the minute, contingent detail of one's own incarnate being. And the way in which he does so enables him to turn this body, with its extensions of clothes, houses, landscapes, people and histories, into a point of orientation for understanding contemporary culture and politics. It is not a detached metaphysics, but one that strives to be thorough and encompassing.

But what obliges us to start with *that* question? Consider Cléophas Nketo Lumba's question: why is there nothing, rather than something?[13] This inversion is not really intended as an alternative approach to metaphysics. It aims to recentre the question of the reason why things are as they are. The question does not aspire to metaphysical generality. However, it has a major claim to critical force. The "nothing" in his question is what the title of his book captures as "the hunger [*faim*] without end [*fin*] in Africa". The extreme hardships that people suffer in a world where something could be done about it, serve no end, have no aim, and are thus arbitrary. And because there is ultimately no sufficient reason for this situation, this question contains critical force: there is no justification for the nothing that prevails, where there should be something.

I will not play the arbiter here. Two views, two approaches, many similarities. But in the end, a major difference to how we understand the task of philosophy.

---

[12] Cf. Leibniz's classical formulation: "now we must rise to *metaphysics,* by making use of the *great principle,* […] that *nothing takes place without sufficient reason* […]. Assuming this principle, the first question we have the right to ask will be, *why is there something rather than nothing?* Furthermore, assuming that things must exist, we must be able to give a reason for *why they must exist in this way,* and not otherwise". Gottfried Wilhelm Leibniz, "Principles of Nature and Grace, Based on Reason" (1714), in *Philosophical Essays*, ed. and trans. Roger Ariew and Daniel Garber (Indianapolis and Cambridge: Hackett Publishing Company, 1989), 206–213, citation 209–210.

[13] Cléophas Nketo Lumba, *La faim sans fin en Afrique* (Paris: L'Harmattan, 2015).

4. Close to the earth?

If one thing has to be singled out by which Versfeld impressed his contemporaries, it was his celebration of the mundane. Often it is called with a curious Afrikaans adjective, *aards*, literally "earthly" or "earthy", but not in the English sense.[14] It evokes being down-to-earth, being modest, appreciating the simple things, being practical, grounded. Associated with it are generosity, gratitude, hospitality. Blasé, lofty, arrogant, lavish, trendy, abstract, complicated, greedy or uncongenial people are not *aards*. In agreement with this appraisal, Kantinka Heyns and Chris Barnard entitled their documentary: *Martin Versfeld. Man van klip en klei* (*Martin Versfeld. Man of Stone and Clay*). This title indeed takes over a book title of the philosopher: *Klip en klei* (*Stone and Clay*) – probably the publication by which this "earthy" reputation was generated for the first time. And fair enough, since the 1970s numerous texts confirm this impression: *Food for Thought, Pots and Poetry* and *Die neukery met die appelboom* containing the most obvious examples.

But may I ask, on what is this posture or "feeling" or "sense"[15] found in his work based? To do justice to the complexities involved in this question, my thousand-page response would start with a reconstruction of the intricate detail of Versfeld's early metaphysics, and then compare it term-by-term with his later aesthetics and ethics, just as carefully unravelled. However, I can anticipate the outcome of such a fascinating study in less than a thousand words. To do so, let us turn to an earlier, more austere book, *The Perennial Order*.[16] Pardon the abundant citations, but I need to exhibit the evidence.

In an attempt to capture the central tenet of mediaeval Catholic culture, Versfeld describes it as "an age whose genius was the integration of all things in God, and whose prepossession was with the concept of unity" (*PO* 205).[17] Nevertheless,

---

[14] Cf. *PO* 4: "[…] philosophers, like poets, must stick to the earth".
[15] I cite this term on purpose, from *PO* 211, 212.
[16] The illustrative points are harvested from chapter 14, "Medieval Catholic Culture" (*PO* 205–223), but they can easily be found elsewhere in the book and in Versfeld's writings from the 1950s and 1960s.
[17] Cf. "This conception of the unity of truth and indeed the unity of culture rests on the conception of the unity of being. […] every particular creature, being also in God's image, has an order and unity of its own which reflects in a degree or manner proportionate to its status the nature of its divine author" (*PO* 217). This idea already played a major role in *GA* as we saw in Chapter 3 §5. Allow me to observe that, for a philosopher, a nice thing about speaking about mediaeval culture is that one can introduce all kinds of theological concepts without

he warns his readers against "the danger of unduly idealizing the actual" (*PO* 206). Note that although Versfeld wants to get to the bottom of the metaphysics that he believes underlies this culture, his view is not simply epistemological, but rather cultural (i.e., concerning a form of life) or, in other words, practical.

This culture has its Greco-Roman roots, sure, but one would miss the central significance of its historical view on life and society if one bypasses the Hebrew source. This tapping from Jewish historical sensitivity is a precondition for spreading the doctrine of a historical incarnation of God. The doctrine of divine incarnation, in turn, instilled in "Europe a sense of the value and significance of flesh" (*PO* 207), and had concomitant effects on broader culture.

Far from a mere doctrine, the idea of God's incarnation results in "a transvaluation of all historical values, so that the things of time and the actions of men receive as it were an eternal dimension" (*PO* 207).[18] Versfeld's reference to Nietzsche is evident, but we are at the antipode of a devaluation of earthly life that Nietzsche liked to impute to Christianity.[19] Quite the contrary: "Catholicism [...] give[s] a profound significance to sensible and contingent things" (*PO* 208). Human life, in all its detail is contingent, mortal – "history [or time itself] is to be regarded as the procession of creatures to the vision of the face of God" (*PO* 208, 217 for the insertion).

This transvaluation of values imbues reality with a "sacramental sense", according to which historical events are "visible signs of invisible things" (*PO* 209). And he can support this with reference to Aquinas. Aesthetic creations are just a specific instantiation of a more general truth: "Works of art are reminders that the Universe itself is the work of art of a God who did not disdain the flesh of man as a medium for this own incarnation" (*PO* 215). Hence, everything has a "twofold reference": to God and to other creatures of the same unitary world. Accordingly, each being "reflects not only God but the order of the whole universe to the degree of which it is capable" (*PO* 218). From this follows not an oppressive totality, but a firm confirmation of "the infinite variety of creation" (*PO* 219). And from the prevalence of these ideas emerged "a civilisation which regarded the procession of creatures in its infinite but ordered diversity, as an analogue of the creativity of God" (*PO* 222).

---

having to justify them, since their historical occurrence serves as justification. Nevertheless, at a point the historian has to commit.

[18] This is not yet the "analogical spark" that I discussed in Chapters 3, §6.3 and Chapter 9, but we are getting close to it.

[19] That is, according to Versfeld, not Nietzsche – see again Chapter 4, where Paul van Tongeren discusses the tensions between these two philosophies.

These are salient aspects of what Versfeld calls "the perennial value of Incarnational Culture". One measures the importance of this claim by the fact that it is the only place in *The Perennial Order* where the word "perennial" is used.[20] This order may have its internal coherence and must be informed by real-life experience and scholarly work. Still one would have liked more elaboration on the tensions, contradictions, difficulties, unexamined assumptions that I suppose all cultures carry with them… But for present purposes, this is beside the point. I have highlighted these dimensions of the perennial order as reinterpreted and transmitted by mediaeval culture, according to Versfeld, with the aim of demonstrating how they could be identified in his later texts. But just before we get there, a last crucial point: these highlighted elements are integrated in a vast discussion covering aspects of the doctrine of the Mass, the Pope, the Church structure, St Mary, cathedral architecture, the completion of (human) nature by divine grace, papal views on art, scholastic education, mediaeval law, the saints, and so on. These form the natural habitat of the colourful birds I have thus far spotted in *The Perennial Order*.

Let us recapitulate this constellation of ideas with a string of key terms: God, history, the significance of the sensible and contingent, human contingency and mortality, creation as God's work of art, incarnation, the sacramental sense and a unitary world. And then, behold *Food for Thought*,[21] a booklet whose subtitle informs us that it is *A Philosopher's Cookbook*. This title is an insignia of Versfeld's "earthliness". On the back cover of my edition is a photo of the author, sitting on a log in a countryside environment with a half-loaf of bread beside him and a knife in his hand, presumably to prepare something for a pot that may be on a fire in front of him, beyond the frame. His mouth slightly open, the corner of his eye somewhat wrinkled as he concentrates on slicing – one has the impression that he is having a good time. And above the photo, the appreciative comment, not of any theologian, but of one André P. Brink: "*Food for Thought* […] is a cookbook as well as a book of profound wisdom and great delight […] [that] transcends our customary systems of thought to become an enquiry into human values". True, I

---

[20] I can recall only one other occurrence (*PO* 41), but there it clearly has a negative meaning: the term denotes the recurrent materialistic monism or spiritualistic monism, both of which Versfeld explicitly rejects on the same page.

[21] Again this book is chosen as an example – my argument could be expanded with a myriad of other texts. This is certainly not his only or first text on food: see *MP* 4–5; *KK* chapter 2; *PP* chapter 1; Marthinus Versfeld, "Wyn en wysheid," in *Wyn en wysheid. Vier sienings met foto's deur Chris Jansen*, edited by Marthinus Versfeld, Merwe Scholtz, and I.L. de Villiers (Cape Town: Tafelberg, 1978), 2–15, for instance.

do not know by which systems Brink was accustomed to think. But I wonder if he measured what was at work in the author's wise mind and delightful enquiries. Let us see, bearing our string of key terms in mind.

In a way, *God* is omnipresent in this book, but often Versfeld writes in such a way that those who do not believe in such a Being may well consider it "just a way of speaking". Nobody will think that Versfeld challenges contemporary astrophysics when he entitles chapter 2 "The Universe Is the Soup of God", hence one may also take the use of "God" as mere metaphor. Or if he exclaims, "For God's sake don't throw a commonwealth of meat and vegetables into the pot and clamp the lid on in order to have time to look over the agenda for the next meeting" (*FT* 95), God *seems* to be just an interjection. Or when he claims that "God did not, like Sartre, kotch over the orchids" (*FT* 90), one knows that his point is about Sartre's *La nausée* (cf. *FT* 89–90). When in other places "God" can be nobody else than the Lord of Christianity, the reader may pass it off as figurative talk. Versfeld also understands why many of his contemporaries prefer to dodge the literal meaning: "So far, I haven't had much to say about God. Indeed, he seems to be conspicuous by his absence, precisely because twentieth-century man feels himself to be so deeply in the soup" (*FT* 10). In short, starting with *God* is perhaps not the right entry to this book even if one cannot miss Him along the road.[22]

Reaching what Versfeld tries to get at is, it seems, as simple as opening one's eyes. He opens the lid of his cooking pot and observes how

> the bits and pieces in our soup pot are performing arabesques on the surface as the water boils. [...] Certainly there is an order there, an inscape, something like the beating of the sea on the rocks, or a swift eddy in a stream or the wind in the willows. These occurrences are asymmetrical and playful, each moment unique in its "suchness." By their very transience they are eternal [...] (*FT* 11)

The only thing that is eternal is transience itself, just like the only thing general is particularity itself.[23] In other words, "At very moment there is a new creation,

---

[22] Versfeld knew well that he could not – perhaps should not – take God's existence for granted. Cf. his own reference to the questions raised by Darwin's theory of evolution (*FT* 89).

[23] We may recall Versfeld's claim that "I want to speak as a South African [i.e. someone in particular – E.W.], because only thus have I anything to say of any general interest" (*MP* 3). See also *Persons* 15: "There is a Hassidic story which tells that when Rabbi Noah succeeded his father, Rabbi Mordechai, his disciples noted that he did not always do as his father had, and asked him about it. 'I act' he replied 'exactly as my father did. He never imitated others, and neither do I.'" Ruth Versfeld's biographical notes in Chapter 1 flesh out this point.

an indication of the surge of the Tao" (*FT* 11)[24] – but here the term "creation" floats ambiguously between phenomena observed in nature and human artistic creation. And the emergence of newness, of particularity as transience, can be accommodated by nothing other than a radically historically minded understanding of reality. Thus, by peering into a soup we are initiated into an aesthetics of the *sensible and contingent* – in nature, in art, in human life – and situated in a whole *history* of transient events.

But there is something terribly wrong with what I write: the blandness which neglects something essential, something like the enthusiasm and joy for what is there. My formal prose cannot do justice to this aesthetic sense Versfeld communicates, his joy and passion expressed in flowering forms of discourse (discussed in Chapter 2, §3). Be that as it may, it is in this passion for what is that Sartre and Versfeld part ways: "Sartre represents this godless universe as gooey and obscene, exuding a sort of nauseous plasma" (*FT* 90). To Versfeld this is simply descriptively implausible: how can one open the lid of the pot of soup, or look at a gladiolus, or study the people around you and become aware of nothing but increasingly boring instances of nauseous plasma ("hash" as he would say elsewhere)? And if natural phenomena are studied in such a way that they are simply reduced to functions of the system, how could one satisfactorily account for the amazement and wonder which sets such study in motion in the first place? Rather, Versfeld recommends that we simply recognise how touched we are by the beauty of things: "Things *are* superfluous: they overflow" (*FT* 90). Our aesthetic sensitivity invigorates our senses and prevents us from functionalistic reductions – "As for the orchids? Sheer fun and droll generosity – and pleasure in the unique" (*FT* 90). From this perspective "What is fundamental in reality is not self-preservation but generosity" (*FT* 92), and "the very universe is one great convivium blazing with joy" (*FT* 21).

Human *contingency and mortality* is nothing but a specific case of this superfluous abundance of uniqueness. People are "so utterly superfluous and

---

[24] And once absolute particularity has led us to generality, one could comment on history: "God is in history and orders things well because they are fluent and not repetitive" (*FT* 11). This transition to God can be made in different ways. In *MP*, long before *FT*, Versfeld allowed himself the following diversion: "Hash is a peculiar English monstrosity [...]. The blasphemy of hash consists in reducing to an anonymous goo what once had a character of its own. [...] Cooking is creation, and I do not believe that God made a hash of the world" (*MP* 4). Even so, we have to be careful in the conclusions we draw, because he could pursue: "[t]he first condemnation of hash with which I am acquainted is in the *Maitri Upanishad* (6.9) [...]" (*MP* 5 and see the whole passage that follows from this citation), evidently not requiring accreditation by the Christian God.

dispensable that [they are] lovable and will never be dispensed with" (*FT* 93). Thus, for both nature and people, the aesthetically accessible superfluity opens to an ethics of care for what is perishable.

This raises a question we need to remark upon in passing. Elsewhere I have already pointed out the regrettable fact that Versfeld did not have much to say about natural disasters – something his thought on natural beauty really calls for (a point already touched upon in Chapter 9). However, evil generated by humans did not evade his attention. Tyrants do not let things be (*FT* 12), they destroy the particular by dominating generality, they force society into planned order of utility: "We have heard totalitarian regimes praised for having created order – neat rows of soldiers, police with automatics, and gas ovens to tidy away the rubbish; strong governments that keep the pots of discontent from boiling over" (*FT* 11). In this way the disquiet about political reality is never far from the exuberance about the beauty of life; his aesthetics open to politics.

But back to the point. It would be a major mistake to think that these ideas limit us to the confines of the individual's mind or heart. That is another virtue of approaching this constellation of ideas from the point of cooking: one can hardly question that "partaking of food is the partaking of reality" (*FT* 18). In fact, Versfeld illustrates the interconnectedness of things by a little piece of autobiographical contextualisation:[25]

> Living as I do in Cape Town, I may be said to owe my origin and location to soup. The settlement of the Cape by the Dutch was prompted by the need for a station for victualling and refreshment on the long and scurvy voyage to the Spice Islands. Seamen landing in Table Bay would find themselves in a botanist's paradise, and the precursors of the great botanists of subsequent generations were the men gathering herbs and weeds to concoct, perhaps with a bit of salt pork or fish from a teeming coast, a healing soup against the ravages of scurvy. Cooking and medication were, in those days, very closely related [...]. (*FT* 9)

And we may continue with a passage from another book:

> That we shape the landscape with our teeth is something of which we can convince ourselves by going to any good viewpoint in an agricultural region like the Western Cape. The arable has been entirely worked over

---

[25] I remind the reader of the importance of (auto)biography – i.e. the narration of each particular, mysterious, human life as discussed in Chapter 2, §2.

to produce food. You will see great areas under vines, others covered by deciduous fruit-trees, and others under grains and pulses. You see numerous farmhouses and labourers' cottages, roads for the transport of produce, large factories and co-ops where the produce is converted into wines or tinned foods. Thus both the landscape and the cultural history of the Cape are tied up with the food-producing and food-consuming activities and habits of its inhabitants. (*PP* 6–7; similarly already in *KK* 29)

But for now, the point is that food and cooking help us understand the *unity* of things – or at least, this is Versfeld's claim. And the combination of the interconnectedness of things and his aesthetics of superfluity lead to radical conclusions: "Life is exuberant. And each of these lives is wonderful. [...] every life is a miracle" (*FT* 48). In short, "The secular is the miraculous" (*FT* 89). There cannot be something like *mere* food any more, hence the cook is "the priest of mutual arising" (*FT* 12). Where this is ignored, it should provoke our suspicion – Versfeld states in all seriousness that "[t]he possibility of living on American bread is not unrelated to the question of living with Americans" (*FT* 84).

Where this unity of the secular and the miraculous is fully recognised, it calls for our celebratory[26] participation: "Festivities, then, celebrate among other things the divinity of food" (*FT* 24). What prevents the reader from understanding that all food incarnates the Divine? Not Versfeld! He rather evokes

a Zen story of a man of Zen who was visited by a monk who said he came from the Monastery of Spiritual Light. The man of Zen replied: "In the day we have sunlight and at night lamplight. What is spiritual light?" When the monk could not answer, he said: "Sunlight, lamplight." That is the right point of view if you believe in the *Incarnation*. What is spiritual bread? The loaf in the oven. (*FT* 25, my emphasis; similarly *ACCG* 9–10)

In response to the generous world you may exclaim "Glory to God for dappled things" (*FT* 90) as Versfeld did, praising the Creator for his work of art in the

---

[26] Celebration does not mean disposing of lavish dishes, even though at some places in the book, Versfeld himself creates this impression. But his considered opinion is this: "Wherever you have celebrations in this spirit you have festivities. A festivity does not necessitate all sorts of gorgeous food. You can celebrate on bread and cheese if you hold them in your heart. It is far more essential for the heart to overflow than the dishes. Let that be your superfluity" (*FT* 25).

words of Hopkins.²⁷ But in the aesthetic view of the world he tries to open, words are redundant – "Prayer is cutting bread" (*ACCG* 9). Thus we have a *sacramental* sense of the world, albeit in pianissimo.

So we come to the end of this comparison: Versfeld's later aesthetics of a generous reality (exemplified in *Food for Thought*) corresponds on all the basic points with his early rendering of mediaeval theological metaphysics (exemplified by *The Perennial Order*). In all fairness, Versfeld explicitly rejected the idea of a return to the Middle Ages.²⁸ In the procession of all creatures there is no turning backwards. Also, it would be invalid to construe this overlap as Versfeld's assumption that he could simply confirm the Catholic convictions present among his readers (he knew very well that for many, perhaps most, he could not count on this). My point is neither a confirmation nor a questioning of Versfeld's constellation of ideas, but rather a demonstration of the repetition thereof in two apparently heterogeneous bodies of thought.²⁹ This repetition implies a relation of dependency of the latter texts on the former.

The unavoidable conclusion is that the assumed and even real proximity to the earth expressed in Versfeld's later work is built on top of a mediaeval metaphysics and theology. This begs the question whether the celebration of nature, food and art can stand on its own legs? Or, if the basis fell out, because people cannot be convinced of its validity, does it change anything? Or if this aesthetics does need some basis, what kind of performance could support it in a "post-metaphysical" context?³⁰ Perhaps a mobilisation of the army of rhetorical

---

27   But see *FT* 19: "The *Upanishad* ends with the line: 'Such is the mystic doctrine.' It is called a mystic doctrine because he who is established on food is one with ultimate reality, therefore is Brahman and hence no different from this manifold universe, the source of whose dynamic is the sustenance it receives from Brahman as the source of all growth, and nourishment, therefore, as Food."

   Besides, there are other ways to connect poetically with Versfeld's thought – as is exemplified by the poems of Van Niekerk and Krog in this volume.

28   "I do not attempt to defend the Middle Ages in this book. To me this expression is meaningless. I do not ask of anybody to return to the Middle Ages either. This is impossible in practice and in any case we live *out of* a tradition" (*RM* preface).

29   I do not see a sudden break – antecedents of the later thought abound in the earlier. For the sake of measuring the distance and proximity, I merely selected and contrasted the antipodes of his work.

30   A classical formulation of the problem is Jürgen Habermas's *Postmetaphysical Thinking: Philosophical Essays* (Cambridge, MA: MIT University Press, 1992). This is not to ignore the alternative view, defended by Versfeld, that metaphysics cannot be avoided. See Versfeld, "Talking Metaphysics. Also see Pierre Aubenque, *Faut-il déconstruire la métaphysique?* (Paris: PUF, 2009).

devices could do it. But then, are we sure that this is not what Versfeld had been doing all along – at least in parts of his later work? Finally, I think Versfeld may have retorted by pointing us in exactly the opposite direction. If all of these questions are valid, should this not rather motivate one to continue the very reappraisal of mediaeval thought he started in his early work: on the one hand to dismantle the persistent image of its lofty abstractness and on the other to reconsider the mediaeval argumentative practices?

In the next points I want to examine how one is to make oneself at home in a world of generosity.

5. Land in *Klip en klei* – You said, "the obvious"?

Versfeld gladly subscribed to Whitehead's claim that "it requires a great mind to take an interest in the obvious" (*PP* 1; likewise *PO* 92; *Persons* 17). On a certain level, this is indisputable: what has acquired the transparency of everyday familiarity can become stimulating food for thought; there is nothing too low for the philosophical mind. No phenomenologist would have differed. And yet, there is something irksome when one takes this adjective of the "obvious" into other contexts of Versfeld's thought, as he seems to invite us to do. I will do so with a second look at the book that arguably most contributed to his positive reception and reputation as a master of the small things, *Klip en klei* (*Stone and Clay*). To me this is his most ambiguous book.

Klip en klei covers a wide range of subjects, but one may consider them all focused on the question of the first chapter: how to make yourself at home in a generous world? My hesitation does not concern the ruminations about building, gardening, angling, furniture, the sea, hunting, carpentry, etc. that fill the pages of this book. Rather, I would like to raise two objections to the overall thrust of the book.

The first issue concerns the conditions for taking an interest in these obvious things. The experiences reflected upon in this book practices by which one could want to make oneself at home. Not a set of general prescriptions, but a spirit or a style. It is certainly viewed as Versfeld's response to nature's largesse. In this sense, it has the dimension of an ethics of permanent celebration. But this celebration is not overindulgence; it is rather an ethics of discretion. I do not object to this. I will come back to the virtues of such an ethics. For now, the question is what made this ethics, in the way Versfeld advocated it, possible?

The backdrop of his whole discourse is a milieu of farm and country life, of suburban homes and accessibility to the seas surrounding Cape Town. The cultural side of this milieu includes reference to rustic traditions,[31] popular practices, a quite paternalistic view of family life[32] and holiday activities outside of the city. And he remains critical of all sorts of dangers lurking in the celebration of this culture.[33] Indeed, one should not fail to notice that the book ends, in apparent breach of the preceding eight chapters, with a critical reflection on patriotism. But what I am trying to get at is his apparent ignorance of what had made all of his cherished experiences possible. Having some savings money available is part of it, but the core is: land ownership. Or at the very least, lawful access to land and the use of it.

I certainly do not reproach Versfeld for having made the best of what he had, especially if one bears in mind the modest conditions of his own childhood (cf. *KK* 49). The question is not if he knew how to be grateful (which is, by the way, a good synonym for taking an interest in the obvious). The question is if he included in his reflection on these things the fact that it was all but obvious that this particular individual would have ownership and access to those particular pieces of land.

This absence becomes conspicuous once one notices the number of references to the history of conquest and discriminatory land dispossession in his text. His uncle "was a captain of the burgers of Caledon in the Gcaleka war" (*KK* 66). Of Verdoemeniskloof he says that it was "one of the last strongholds of the old Bushmen" (*KK* 71). He evokes oral traces of previous inhabitants of the region ("Fingo's" and "Bushmen", *KK* 72). If this is the case, how is it possible that reflection on the violent history that deprived the majority of his South African contemporaries of land ownership and access to natural regions simply is not part of the book? Or was it that he took so much interest in the obvious, that he did not notice in this case, that such experiences were nothing but obvious to those people who could just lament the fact that as far as land is concerned "there is nothing rather than something"?

One has to be quite precise in formulating this issue. This is not a book by an ignorant or indifferent cultural conservative. Versfeld explicitly rejects both of the forms of political legitimation from which people – white people – drew

---

[31] Cf. for instance "boeretannies", "volksresepte", "voorslagriempies [...] sny", etc.
[32] See *KK* 31 for the father as head of the family.
[33] E.g., "Wat 'n volkshuis is, sal ons nie weet totdat ons uitvind wat 'n volk is nie en dit weet ons nie" (*KK* 14).

to justify land ownership: liberalism and nationalist romanticism.³⁴ He critiques Christians who miss the rightful place of the problem of nutrition in their own spiritual orientation (*KK* 29). He evokes in shorthand his decades-old critique of imperialism and adds to it his critique of slavery (*KK* 32). He mocks nationalist immigration and identity politics.³⁵ Racially structured labour hierarchies receive no mercy in his judgement (cf. *KK* 44–45). And he remains as explicit as ever in his condemnation of racism (*KK* 8, 114–115). In other words, the point of critique I raise is quite in the spirit of his own text; in fact, he even opens the way to such a critique when he exhorts his readers to mind the "washmaid" who is responsible for the clothing in which they carry out their daily activities (*KK* 122). Neglect her (and everyone else who make the life you know possible) and this will warp your view on reality. In the extension of this exhortation is the call to mind the historical conditions by which people have come in the position (and the laws by which they maintained a privileged access) to enjoy the sea, to hike the mountains or to gather rocks for building a cottage.³⁶ That is my first point.

This leads us to my second objection. A lot of the experiences on which Versfeld reflected in this book took place at the family holiday cottage he built on a piece of land in the Kouga, very far from their residence in Cape Town. For all the remarkable things Versfeld wrote about dwelling and homecoming, he is astonishingly silent about the fact that he owned two homes. Whether owning a second residence can be justified is simply not my question here; in principle, I wish that pleasure for all those who wish to enjoy it. My point is that Versfeld's philosophising about homes and homeliness essentially speaks about *one* home – the second one makes for a very strange intrusion in the coherence of what he says.

Take this citation as a first example: "Your home situates you in the world. It gives you an address, somewhere where people can address you" (*KK* 9). But what now with the second house, the one which is not his *domicilium citandi et*

---

34 He explicitly rejects nationalist racism as an illegitimate generalisation (*KK* 114). But for the same reason he was reluctant about liberalism (despite his early adherence to it): it is a "raceism" of the general human race and for that reason has difficulties with theorising human particularity. These views extend ideas developed in *MP* 102.
35 He asks ironically: "Why don't we encourage more Italian immigrants? They are so authentically Afrikaans, and so many Afrikaners are so inauthentic" (*KK* 36).
36 Again, from another text one can infer that Versfeld was not unaware of the issues I refer to: "It does not need much imagination to see that the phenomenology of spatial experience may make a valuable contribution to the study of politics, relevant to phenomena like colonisation, flight from one's country, forcible shifting of population, and the urge to explore outer space" (*Persons* 76). The Afrikaans original of this text (*Wat is kontemporêr?* 12) was published in 1966, two years before *Klip en klei*.

executandi? If the meaning of life consists in coming home,[37] if the gate to your home is the gate of heaven (*NA* 23), if it is sane to be all here rather than all there (*NA* 21), then the mere existence of a second residence becomes a strange thing and the celebration of it in serious conflict with the philosophy of the home. Whence could the family holiday cottage draw all its sung virtues, if the family had already made themselves at home in a suburb of the big city?

Furthermore, this second major objection may meet the first one. Versfeld claims, quite correctly to my mind, that one's home has an impact on the perspective one can adopt on the world (*KK* 9, cf. Chapter 5, §1 on looking for the truth from where we are; *Wat is kontemporêr?* 17 on this principle, and 18–19 on architecture and construction). And he even glosses: "If you own only an ax, then the world will be to you something that has to be felled" (*KK* 9). The relevant question is: how does the fact of owning not an axe, but a home and being at home in *two* homes – the first apparently not sufficing – impact the owner's perspective on reality? Would one not have expected of Versfeld to write somewhere in one of his autobiographical excursions that he was one of those people who owned both a suburban Cape Town home and a cottage in the countryside, *and* that this surely had to have an impact on the way he looked at the world? Nothing would have been more coherent for an author who teaches that "an author has to come to insight about his/her outlook and then give expression to this insight" (*KK* 25).

Allow me a few final comments. When it comes to ethics of discretion, Versfeld is superb. He is quite gifted for commenting on the material basis of his own wisdom, but he does so selectively. This strength and weakness have implications beyond personal ethics for the political side of social interaction. One thing is to assess these points retrospectively; another is to know how to deal with the same questions in contemporary society. One could capture the problem by paraphrasing Adorno: is it possible to live a life of justice in an unjust world? Here one has to reject both the Pollyanna-like voluntarism which ignores the limits of human action and the sceptic resignation on which the status quo thrives. Whatever needs to be done, I guess a good starting point is always an awareness of reality with which I have characterised Versfeld's thought, namely "gratitude".[38] And true recognition for what one has should prompt one to give recognition to others.

---

[37] Cf. again Hennie Rossouw, "Die kuns van die lewe is om tuis te kom".
[38] Not unrelated is his recounting of a hiking expedition in Lesotho, when he and his companion were caught in bad weather, and received two day's of hospitality from very poor locals (*KK* 85).

6. Ecology: The logos on our common home

> When St Francis talks about "brother sun", the fraternal attachment is a superior detachment because the sun properly focused is seen to be a creature of God, primarily God's because all creatures, the ten thousand things, are God's, given to us, and therefore ours because fundamentally they are not ours, so that we can at any moment give them back with open hands.
> (*OS* 2nd ed.)

There is a commonplace in the critique of modernity that holds that God's instruction in the Genesis narrative to Adam and Eve to rule over creation served as the religious licence to subjugate and destroy nature. You will find nothing of this in Versfeld.[39] His view of nature is indeed informed by a metaphysics of creation, but with a completely different perspective:

> [...] in the course of my reflections I have come to believe in what I may call the fundamental generosity of Being. This is a pretty universal belief, and in the Christian West it takes the form of a metaphysic of creation for which God is Being, Being identical with Goodness. Now the good is *diffusivum sui*, that is, it radiates itself because of a radical generosity. (*PP* 29)

We have seen this idea at work in Versfeld's aesthetics. But he also developed the implications of this view for ecology. Whatever one may think of his metaphysical perspective, there is no denying the extreme contemporary relevance of the conclusions he drew on the environment. Let us outline at least the basic points.

The correlate of Versfeld's view of nature as an overflowing generosity is his critique of the modernist view on nature. This is the vision of nature itself as a capitalist setup in which only the most ruthless entrepreneurs survive, always at the expense of others (*NA* 2nd ed. 80–81; *FT* 92). How far contemporary scientific work on the theory of evolution allows one to question this image is not clear to me. However, at the very least one may accept caution against viewing nature as a system of exploitation and domination (*PP* 6), and the justification of human imitation of this order that it may imply.

---

[39] See also his critique of Descartes's idea of humans as the masters and owners of nature in *Wat is kontemporêr?* 27, 30.

But Versfeld calls not only for a critical mindset. He also offers an alternative view on all reality – rocks, plants, animals, humans – as being gratuitous, before they are useful (cf. *PP* 24). Such a perspective on reality does not allow one to consider humans as owners of nature. Rather, humans are, as much as the natural environment, part of a generous radiance in which human ownership is only a recently emerged derivative. Ownership, with its correlates of use and consumption, remain therefore constructed on a basis from which its real meaning derives and which can be mobilised to critique excesses in the use of nature.

This is no moralistic precept. There are no owners, indeed, no humans at all, without an intricate web of relations by which nature allows them to be. The fact that nature is shaped by human intervention (after all, we live from farm produce, not from the trees of paradise) does not fundamentally change this fact. And since the human right to be is not primary, but preceded by nature on which we depend, one can understand Versfeld's radical question about where the right of humans to exist at all, derives from; indeed, he even asks where anything whatsoever derives that right from (*NA* 2nd ed. 51). Here, his point is of course first of all metaphysical, rather than political or legal. Before all else our reflection should be oriented by the inexplicable gratuitousness of being to which whomever wants to claim a right, owes his/her being. Versfeld's conviction is that if we miss this point, we miss the original source of value in reality, and violence, exploitation, abuse and destruction will follow. This is one of the reasons why the question "why is there something rather than nothing?" (cf. §3, above) has great importance beyond the confines of metaphysics.

But then there comes a point at which reflection on rights is quite appropriate. And not only rights of humans but also the rights of animals, plants and rocks.[40] This formulation is probably not devoid of provocation, but it does evoke a legitimate point, which is a reformulation of the old principle of justice: to each his or her due (*NA* 2nd ed. 56). But Versfeld appropriates this principle without exclusive restriction to humans. Other beings have their "rights" in this sense too, albeit relative rights (*PP* 21). Relative in two ways: different kinds of beings have rights that correspond to their kind of being (to plants less is due than to humans, but not nothing), and relative in the sense that reflection on rights has to consider each entity in its relation to others (what is due to each element can be established only through reflection on the whole environment in which it is situated). Relation is, then, a key idea, but one may also call it system,

---

[40] See e.g., the essay entitled "On the Rights of Man and the Rights of Rocks," *PP* 14–28.

environment or ecology. Two major consequences follow from this ecological understanding of value and ethics.

First, thinking about the rights of nature stands in relation to human reality, but is not a mere extension of human needs or values.[41] The "rights discourse" practised by Versfeld in this context does not take rights in the strict sense as fixed legal protections independent of context. The point is to sensitise his readers about what is really valuable, and hence the threat or exploitation of which is truly serious, no matter if it is human or nature. Besides, if I see correctly, such a view of rights does not exclude the possibility for rights in the strict legal sense applicable to interhuman exchanges – here they are conceivable as an acceptable "special case" based on the broader understanding of what is due to each.

Second, Versfeld confirms the mutual implication between human–human relations and human–nature relations.[42] One cannot think about the one without taking the other into consideration. Admittedly, one cannot evade the fact that our only way to think about all of this is in an anthropomorphic way. Versfeld is the first to grant this. As we saw in Chapter 5, we search for truth from where and what we are. Affirming the full implication of this point, Versfeld assumes that all other creatures see reality in their creaturomophic[43] way (*NA* 2nd ed. 23–24). This means that our anthropomorphic approach to reality is all right, provided we don't elevate this inevitability to anthropocentrism. Here, anthropocentrism entails that everything human is the sole domain of what is possibly valuable and non-human reality, having no such potential for value generation, has to be disposable for human usage.

The relations of mutual implication between human–human relations and human–nature relations go in two directions. On the one hand, what humans do to their environment has an impact on humans (*NA* 2nd ed. 22, 50). Exploitation of nature and exploitation of humans go hand in hand (*PP* 22). On the other hand, the ways we arrange our social relations will have impacts on the environment, both natural and human-made (*NA* 2nd ed. 24). Careful attention to these interrelations will quickly show that Versfeld's is no naive view on human reality and nature. His writings in this respect demonstrate an acute awareness of the "thirst" (*NA* 2nd ed. 23) of both nature and human life – that is, their fragility and need of care. One could draw the practical implications from these insights

---

[41] See for instance "The basis of nature conservation is a vision of nature as superfluous, and therefore generous because created in eternal generosity" (*FT* 92).
[42] This idea was already developed in *GA* 129 and 88.
[43] He uses the neologism "goggamorfies" (*NA* 2nd ed. 24), i.e., "buggomorphic" for the view insects have on reality.

on two levels. On the political level it calls for action in which the protection of the natural environment and of people is always planned and striven for together. This is completely in sync with what is nowadays called environmental justice, but the vision is much broader. On a more personal, ethical level, one may point out that the "ethics of discretion" present in *Klip en klei* and *Die buitelewe* gains a lot of credibility as responses to this call for care.

We have come quite far from the original metaphysical assumptions. Here we have an outline of a social and political ecology. Even this brief outline suffices to claim that this is a very living part of Versfeld's philosophy.

7. On subtle critique

In Chapter 2 (§6) I characterised Versfeld's thought as politically sensitive, as infused with political concerns, without containing substantial political theorising or commentary. He engaged with an array of political issues of his time, but more often than not in the form of fragments integrated into larger social-critical or generally philosophical studies. Sometimes his critique is quite subtle and I wish to demonstrate why it could be worthwhile to examine at least one such instance more closely.

Versfeld's coordination of large-scale critique of Western civilisation and detail of apartheid discrimination is nowhere better illustrated than in an apparent passing remark in *Rondom die Middeleeue*. It is 1962 and Versfeld writes to introduce the Afrikaans reader to the "Mediaeval spirit" (*RM* preface). Why should they take an interest in the Middle Ages at all? Because this is the era when the West's "intellectual character traits" (*RM* 1) developed. If the West has something worth transmitting to the present, a study of this period will help to appreciate what it is. But how to access this huge period? Significantly, Versfeld proposes, that the primary entry to the Western intellectual heritage is not through the Greeks, or Jesus of Nazareth, or the politico-religious compromise of Constantine, but through Augustine. *He* combined Athens and Jerusalem, *he* gave the authoritative formulation of the Christian faith for the early mediaeval period, *his Confessions* represent the discovery of "personality" (*RM* 3) and of autobiography, *his* conversion therefore stands for the conversion of the ancient (Western) world (cf. *RM* 4). It is hard to assign a more crucial role to one person than Versfeld does with Augustine in the development of Western civilisation.

You, inheritor of Western culture, you want to call yourself civilised? Well, you fool yourself if you bypass Augustine! Versfeld's argument is more complex, but that is at least the schema of it. And then Versfeld simply adds: "For us, South Africans, it is inspiring to remember that Augustine stems from Africa and it is a healthy fact to ponder that, due to his complexion, it would not even have been possible to converse with him in a train wagon".[44] Versfeld does not elaborate this any further. However, from that point, one cannot stop the dominos from falling: such was the political setup in South Africa that it could stand by Augustine only at the expense of pure hypocrisy. Or otherwise, those who followed the logic of racial separation of train wagons in a consistent way (that means of apartheid legislation in general) would have to discard Augustine and in doing so reveal themselves as lacking the civilisation they boasted to represent. More generally, by banning blackness from Afrikanerdom, the "torchbearers of civilisation" to the "dark continent" deprived themselves of the very flame they claimed to carry.

One could say that, for Versfeld, there was indeed something dark in Africa. Not the *a priori* darkness that many of his contemporaries attributed to African cultures. Rather, the darkness of the abyss of human nature in every human being (*RM* 3). But exploration of this "dark continent" can help one to make precious – if uncomfortable – discoveries, among which, that of one's own complicity in injustice.

For our understanding of Versfeld, it is certainly no trivial matter to recall here the importance of Augustine for his own thought. Augustine's idea of the *abyssus humanae naturae* is at the core of Versfeld's anthropology: the South African drew ample inspiration from the *City of God* in his political analysis and a good number of his studies are devoted to Augustine. In this sense, it is entirely reasonable to place Versfeld's work under the symbol of an ever-deepening conversation with a black man on a train.

But even if all of this is granted, one may want to object: is this argument not simply too delicate to have any punch? Most likely. And if this is so, one has to question the value of such subtle critique. Nevertheless, it is worthwhile standing still at the dilemma Versfeld faced. One should not forget that by 1962 Versfeld had already his uncompromising and vocal critique of exploitation, violence and racism in *Oor gode en afgode* behind him (see Chapter 3, §3.3). Having tried that, would it not have helped (Versfeld could ask) to try another strategy of aiming at

---

[44] "Vir ons Suid-Afrikaners is dit besielend om te onthou dat Augustinus ook uit Afrika stam, en dis 'n gesonde feit om te bepeins dat ons weens sy gelaatskleur nie eens saam in 'n treinwa sou kon gesels nie" (*RM* 4). Here Versfeld refers to the racial separations in force in public transport in South Africa at that time.

a more specific target? Assuming that this was Versfeld's strategy, one could argue that the more indirect approach did not dilute his point: the subtlety thereof is *part* of the point. For is Versfeld not calling on his compatriots to reconsider their tradition? Is he not challenging the cultural supremacists with reference to the very object of their presumed superiority, namely the intellectual tradition at the heart of which lies the art of *subtilitas legendi*? Hence, for those of his intellectual contemporaries for whom such subtlety carried no weight, one has to acknowledge that they had already extinguished part of the flame of civilisation that they claimed to bear. After all – and one may well suspect an irony here – "it is proper to the civilised person to come to selfconsciousness and not to disregard the tradition out of which s/he lives" (*RM* 93).

But one can derive another point of contemporary value by ruminating on Versfeld's reading of Augustine. Let us be clear about what Augustine-as-African represents for him. Augustine combined his knowledge of Platonism, his love for Virgil and his Christian convictions. In this sense, he does not represent traditional African thought. But neither does he simply represent Western thought and culture, because the synthesis with which he is synonymous was partly created by him. Versfeld's point is not that Augustine takes the central place in Western civilisation because he was already Western, or because he was an African. Neither is his centrality due to his incarnating human being in general. He became the figure of excellence he was by making the best of the contingent historical situation in which he lived. Augustine was a human being, a particular one. This is not a point about the African roots of European civilisation, as epitomised in the work of Cheikh Anta Diop. It is by another strategy that Versfeld, evoking Augustine's "race" at the crucial junction of Western history, strives to undermine the "clash of institutionalised forms of ignorance".[45] Surely the continuous concern of purifying one's tradition from racist bias is an essential part of opening up to the wisdom of other intellectual traditions, and of promoting their sociopolitical recognition? This openness is also a condition of the dialogue and invention by which one may live *out of* one's own traditions.

---

[45] Mohammed Arkoun, "Clarifier le passé pour construire le futur," *Confluences. Méditerranée* 16 (1995–1996): 17–30, here 19.

8. Ambiguities of anthropology

The least one can say is that anthropology has become a difficult and precarious enterprise. This holds no less for the more philosophical version than for anthropology in the stricter disciplinary sense. For more than half a century scholarly discourse about humans – in their generality or particularity – has been subjected to severe and certainly necessary critique. Time and time again the same problems are brought to light: what is presented as insight into universal anthropological traits turn out be paternalistic, sexist or ethnocentric prejudice; what claims to be understanding of anthropological diversity is unmasked as essentialising, ahistorical deformations. In both cases, the knowledge, power and economic interests of such discourses arouse suspicion and indignation. One cannot avoid the question of how to deal with this problem in an author for whom anthropology was "first philosophy".[46]

True enough, Versfeld's count among the more sophisticated approaches: first, he takes as central the mystery of human existence (rather than his own scientific confidence); second, his claim to have anything of universal value to say passes through the explicit recognition of his own particularity (cf. *MP* 3) and that of others;[47] third, although limited (as argued above), there is a sustained and serious attempt to expose himself to insights from the cultural other. If this suffices to warrant a careful reading of his anthropology, it certainly does not exempt him from critical scrutiny.

While acknowledging the shameful history and problematic present of (philosophical) anthropology, I cannot see how one can simply avoid it. And this for at least three reasons. First, there are human beings. As long as this is the case and as long as we bother to think, this fact imposes itself with tenacity to our reflection. Second, those academics who do not simply assume the flawless authority of their own cultural tradition, or of their personal religious faith, have a hard time in ethics. Personally, I have not yet been able to figure out how a relativist aestheticisation of matters ethical will lead us to nihilism-overcoming insights. And with these alternatives discredited, we are running out of options of justification for our ethical claims. One remaining option is to consider history as a project whereby people set themselves objectives that they have to realise through

---

[46] See Chapter 2, § 2 and Chapter 5, § 2.
[47] Cf. "Human nature is the same in the thirteenth and the twentieth century, in Peking and in Cape Town. But no two persons are the same" (*Persons* 17).

a long process of cultural learning. The critiques of modernity confront this option with substantial resistance. The only other option is by way of reflection on what flourishing human life may entail. A hugely problematic enterprise, as I have stated. But I cannot see how one can simply abolish it. Third, at the same time, all critique of anthropology, even the most subtle and sophisticated, is a performative act which presupposes the ability of understanding and even mobilisation in response to it.[48] This is not a weakness; it is simply unavoidable. This means that even the harshest critique depends in its practice on anthropological assumptions of compatibility, mutual understanding, the possibility of creating "third spaces"[49] of commonality. If our belief in this point is abolished, we remain face to face with others like animals of different species, bleating and barking at each other in incomprehensible noises.[50]

Even this short plea in favour of anthropological study (in Versfeld's line or not) does not absolve us from prudence in anthropological claims. As far as I am concerned, we can simply continue to advance our best possible ideas. But then always with the understanding that they remain provisional – the best we can do until the other corrects us. Uncertainty is not necessarily an intellectual weakness.

---

[48] Cf. Martin Saar, "Genealogische Kritik," in *Was ist Kritik?*, ed. Rahel Jaeggi and Tilo Wesche (Frankfurt-am-Main: Suhrkamp, 2009), 221–246.
[49] Cf. Bernhard Waldenfels, *Grundmotive einer Phänomenologie des Fremden* (Frankfurt-am-Main: Suhrkamp, 2010), 110–111.
[50] Cf. Ernst Wolff, "Adam Small's Shade of Black Consciousness," in *Philosophy on the Border. Decoloniality and the Shudder of the Origin*, ed. Leonard Praeg (Pietermaritzburg: UKZN Press, 2019), 112–147, here 125–126 and Ernst Wolff, *Between Daily Routine and Violent Protest* (Berlin: De Gruyter, 2021), chapter 6, §§ 6.1 and 7.

9. The end

> His contribution is mainly based on the fact that he was mentally gifted and I have to acknowledge that it is a bit presumptuous to want to write about him.
> (*RM* 1, Versfeld on Augustine)

Perhaps it has even been self-flattering to liken myself to a vulture in the subtitle of this chapter. Maybe I have rather been more of a blowfly (*brommer*), like Versfeld said of some reviewers, since "they live from what they have not created themselves" (*KK* 26). Still, blowflies are no different from philosophers, insofar as they look at their world from where and what they are. As much as I strove for precision and fairness, this "conclusion" documents only what Versfeld looks like when studied with my composite eyes. That this contains many of my own ideas and convictions is inevitable. In writing about what is living and what is dead in Versfeld, my end was not to draw up the definitive assessment as if to make up other readers' minds for them. Rather by dialoguing with Versfeld, I am dialoguing with his readers and mine.

BIBLIOGRAPHY

A list of majors works by Martin Versfeld can be found at beginning of the book.

Jonathan Allen, "A Competing Discourse on Empire," in *South Africa, Greece and Rome: Classical Confrontations*, ed. Grant Parker (Cambridge: Cambridge University Press, 2017), 235–261.

Thomas Aquinas, *De Natura Materiae*, http://www.documentacatholicaomnia.eu/03d/1225-1274,_Thomas_Aquinas,_De_Natura_Materiae_et_Dimensionibus_Interminatis,_LT.pdf [last access 8 August 2020].

Hannah Arendt, *Men in dark times* (San Diego: Harcourt Brace Jovanovich, 1968).

Mohammed Arkoun, "Clarifier le passé pour construire le futur," *Confluences. Méditerranée* 16 (1995–1996): 17–30.

Pierre Aubenque, *Faut-il déconstruire la métaphysique?* (Paris: PUF, 2009).

Rudolf Bernet, "La réduction phénoménologique et la double vie du sujet," in *La vie du sujet. Recherches sur l'interprétation de Husserl dans la phénoménologie* (Paris: PUF, 1994).

Archibald Bowman, *The Absurdity of Christianity and Other Essays* (New York: The Liberal Arts Press, 1958).

Breyten Breytenbach, *Dog Heart. A Memoir* (London: Faber & Faber, 1999).

André Brink, "In Praise of All that Is Fleeting and Eternal," introduction to Marthinus Versfeld, *Pots and Poetry and other Essays* (2nd edition) (Pretoria: Protea, 2009), 7–16.

Jane Carruthers, "Men in my (historical) life," *Historia* 52, vol. 2 (2007): 269–272.

F. Edward Cranz, "Reviewed Work(s): *A Guide to the City of God* by Marthinus Versfeld," *Speculum* 34, vol. 4 (1959): 696–697.

Benedetto Croce, *What Is Living and What is Dead of the Philosophy of Hegel*, trans. Douglas Ainslie (London: Macmillan, 1915).

Jeremy Cronin, "Interview with Helena Sheehan," recorded on 17 April 2001 at the University of Cape Town. http://helenasheehan.ie/interview-with-jeremy-cronin/ [last access 12 February 2020].

W.A. de Klerk "Marthinus Versfeld: die man en sy denke," *Tydskrif vir Letterkunde* 4 (1966): 62–72.

W.A. de Klerk, "Marthinus Versfeld: mens en denker," *Tydskrif vir Geesteswetenskappe* 23, no. 3 (1983): 178–186.

Alain De Libera, "Où va la philosophie médiévale? *Leçon inaugurale prononcée le jeudi 13 février 2014*" (Paris: Collège de France, 2014), https://books.openedition.org/cdf/3634 [last access 20 May 2020].

Pieter Duvenage, *Afrikaanse filosofie* (Bloemfontein: SUN Press, 2016).

Jürgen Habermas, *Postmetaphysical Thinking: Philosophical Essays* (Cambridge: MIT Press, 1992).

Keith Hart and Vishnu Padayachee, "A history of South African capitalism in national and global perspective," *Transformation: Critical Perspectives on Southern Africa* 81/82 (2013): 55–85.

Christoph Horn, "Augustinus, De Civitate Dei (ca. 413–427)," in *Geschichte des politischen Denkens. Ein Handbuch*, ed. Manfred Brocker (4th edition) (Frankfurt-am-Main: Suhrkamp, 2012), 62–77.

Ansfried Hulsbosch, *God's Creation: Creation, Sin and Redemption in an Evolving World*, trans. Martin Versfeld (London and Melbourne: Sheed and Ward, [1963] 1965).

Dirk Kaesler, "Religiös unmusikalisch. Anmerkungen zum Verhältnis von Jürgen Habermas zu Max Weber," *literaturkritik.de* 6 (June 2009), https://literaturkritik.de/id/13142 [last access 20 May 2020].

Sybille Krämer, *Medium, Messenger, Transmission. An Approach to Media Philosophy* (Amsterdam: Amsterdam University Press, 2015), 87–96.

Antjie Krog, "Sunday lunch", "the founding principle of generosity", "to feed someone" and "convivium", in *Synapse*, trans. Karen Press (Cape Town: Human & Rousseau, 2014), 26, 43, 44, 80–82.

Hans Küng, "Augustine: The Father of All Western Latin Theology," in *Great Christian Thinkers* (London: SCM Press, 1994), 69–98.

Gottfried Wilhelm Leibniz, "Principles of Nature and Grace, Based on Reason" (1714), in *Philosophical Essays*, ed. and trans. Roger Ariew and Daniel Garber (Indianapolis and Cambridge: Hackett Publishing Company, 1989), 206–213.

Johann Lodewyk Marais, "Marthinus Versfeld (3)," http://versindaba.co.za/tag/marthinus-versfeld/ [last access 3 March 2020].

A.H. Murray, "Die Afrikaanse se wysgerige denke," in *Kultuurgeskiedenis van die Afrikaner*, ed. P. de V. Pienaar (Cape Town: Nationale Boekhandel, [1947] 1968), 183–189.

Cléophas Nketo Lumba, *La faim sans fin en Afrique* (Paris: L'Harmattan, 2015).

Mahmood Mamdani, "Between the public intellectual and the scholar: Decolonization and some post-independence initiatives in African higher education," *Inter-Asia Cultural Studies* 17, no. 1 (2016): 68–83.

Gabriel Marcel, *Journal Métaphysique* (Paris: Gallimard, 1927).

V.Y. Mudimbe, *The Invention of Africa. Gnosis, Philosophy and the Order of Knowledge* (Bloomington: Indianapolis University Press, 1988).

Andrew Nash, "Marxism and dialectic, from Sharpeville to the negotiated settlement," in *The dialectical tradition in South Africa* (London and New York: Routledge, 2009), 159–184.

Friedrich Nietzsche, *Beyond Good and Evil*, trans. W. Kaufmann (New York: Vintage, 1966).

Friedrich Nietzsche, *On the Genealogy of Morals*, trans. W. Kaufmann and R. Hollingdale (New York: Vintage, 1969).

Friedrich Nietzsche, *The Gay Science*, trans. W. Kaufmann (New York: Vintage, 1974).

Friedrich Nietzsche, *Thus Spoke Zarathustra*, in *The Portable Nietzsche*, trans. W. Kaufmann (New York: Penguin, 1976).

Friedrich Nietzsche, *Sämtliche Werke*. Kritische Studienausgabe in 15 Bänden, eds. G. Colli and M. Montinari (Munich and Berlin: DTV and De Gruyter, 1980).

Friedrich Nietzsche, *Human, All Too Human. A Book for Free Spirits*, trans. R. Hollingdale (Cambridge: Cambridge University Press, 1986).
Friedrich Nietzsche, *Twilight of the Idols*, trans. R. Hollingdale (London: Penguin, 1990).
Friedrich Nietzsche, "On the Utility and Liability of History for Life," in *Unfashionable Observations*, trans. R.T. Gray (San Francisco: Stanford University Press, 1995).
Tshiamalenga Ntumba, "Die Philosophie in der aktuellen Situation Afrikas," *Zeitschrift für Philosophische Forschung* 33, no. 3 (1979): 428–433.
Deborah Posel, "The apartheid project, 1948–1970," in Robert Ross, Anne Kelk Mager, and Bill Nasson (eds.), *The Cambridge history of South Africa. Volume 2: 1885–1994* (Cambridge: Cambridge University Press, 2011), 319–368.
Hennie Rossouw, "Versfeld – filosoof met eie boodskap" in *Die Burger*, 12 July 1979.
Hennie Rossouw, "Die kuns van die lewe is om tuis te kom. Gedagtes oor die filosofie van Martin Versfeld," *Tydskrif vir Geesteswetenskappe* 36, no. 1 (1996): 11–20.
Martin Saar, "Genealogische Kritik," in *Was ist Kritik?*, ed. Rahel Jaeggi and Tilo Wesche (Frankfurt-am-Main: Suhrkamp, 2009), 221–246.
Michel Serres, *La légende des anges* (Paris: Flammarion, 1993).
Harriet Swain, "Students want their curriculums decolonised. Are universities listening?" *The Guardian*, 30 January 2019, https://www.theguardian.com/education/2019/jan/30/students-want-their-curriculums-decolonised-are-universities-listening [last access 6 February 2020].
Leonard Thompson, *A history of South Africa*, ed. Lynn Berat (revised 4th edition) (New Haven and London: Yale University Press, 2014).
Ernst Tugendhat, "Anthropologie als 'erste Philosophie'," in *Anthropologie statt Metaphysik*. (München: Beck, 2007), 34–54.
Marlene van Niekerk, "Martin Versfeld. Anargis van die liefde" ["Martin Versfeld. Anarchist of Love"], *Die Suid-Afrikaan* (April/May, 1992): 70 and 77.
Marlene van Niekerk, "Die etende Afrikaner. Aantekeninge vir 'n klein tipologie," in *Van Volksmoeder tot Fokofpolisiekar. Kritiese opstelle oor Afrikaanse herinneringsplekke*, ed. A.M. Grundlingh and S. Huigen (Stellenbosch: SUN Press, 2008), 75–92
Paul van Tongeren, *Reinterpreting Modern Culture. An Introduction to Friedrich Nietzsche's Philosophy* (West Lafayette: Purdue University Press, 2000).
Paul van Tongeren, "Nietzsche's Naturalism," in *Nietzsche and the German Tradition*, ed. Nicholas Martin (Bern: Peter Lang, 2003), 205–215.
Paul van Tongeren, *Friedrich Nietzsche and European Nihilism* (Newcastle upon Tyne: Cambridge Scholars Publishing, 2018).
Martin Versfeld, "On justice and human rights," *Acta juridica* 1 (1960): 1–10.
Martin Versfeld, "Reflections on Evolutionary Knowledge," *International Philosophical Quarterly* 5, no. 2 (May 1965): 221–247.
Martin Versfeld, "St Thomas, Newman and the Existence of God," *New Scholasticism* 41, no. 1 (Winter 1967): 3 – 30.
Martin Versfeld, "Die pampoen" ["The Pumpkin"], in *Borde borde boordevol. Verhale en essays oor kos*, ed. Hennie Aucamp (Cape Town: Tafelberg, 1998), 157–159.
Martin Versfeld, "Die pampoen" ["The Pumpkin"], in *Vertellers 2: Die tweede groot verhaalboek*, ed. M. Scholtz (Cape Town: Tafelberg, 1991), 404–406.
Martin Versfeld, "Oor huise" ["On Homes"], in *Vertellers: die groot Afrikaanse verhaalboek*, ed. M. Scholz (Cape Town: Tafelberg, 1990), 23–41.

Neil Viljoen, "Shakespeare's *The Tempest* and Martin Versfeld's 'Comments on the Rapist Society,'" *English Academy Review* 5, no. 5 (1988): 116–137.

Remona Voges, "Antjie Krog, gemeenskaplikheid en die behoefte aan interverbondenheid in Mede-wete (2014)," *LitNet Akademies* 16, no. 1 (2019), https://www.litnet.co.za/wp-content/uploads/2019/06/LitNet_Akademies_16-1_Voges_145-165.pdf [last access 12 February 2020].

Bernhard Waldenfels, *Grundmotive einer Phänomenologie des Fremden* (Frankfurt-am-Main: Suhrkamp, 2010), 110–111.

Dennis Walder, *Athol Fugard* (London: Macmillan, 1984).

Ernst Wolff, "Sanctus Marthinus laudator philosophicus," *Fragmente* 4, (1999): 87–101 [cf. Chapter 3].

Ernst Wolff, "Anatomie van 'n teologiese ideologie. Die Hervormde Kerk se steun aan die Apartheid ideologie" [Anatomy of a theological ideology. The Reformed Church's support of the apartheid ideology], *Historia* 51, no. 1 (May 2006): 141–162.

Ernst Wolff, "Die neukery met verval en herstel in Versfeld se storie van die appelboom," *Koers* 74, no. 3 (2009): 539–542 [inserted into Chapter 7].

Ernst Wolff, "Grasping the truth from where we are," introduction to the re-edition of Martin Versfeld, *Our Selves* (Pretoria: Protea, 2010), 7–39 [cf. Chapter 5].

Ernst Wolff, "*Poiesis*. Oor maaksels en hul wêreld na aanleiding van Versfeld se *Pots and Poetry*," *Tydskrif vir Letterkunde* 48, no. 1 (2011): 206–215 [cf. Chapter 7].

Ernst Wolff, "Selfkennis en verstandigheid in 'n tyd van politieke raserny," introduction to the re-edition of Martin Versfeld, *Oor gode en afgode* (Pretoria: Protea, 2010), 7–40 and an extended version, "Selfkennis, verstandigheid en inkarnasie. 'n Interpretasie van Versfeld se *Oor gode en afgode*," *LitNet* 7, no. 2 (2010): 257–279 [cf. Chapter 3].

Ernst Wolff, "Four questions on curriculum development in contemporary South Africa," *South African Journal of Philosophy* 35, no. 4 (2016): 444–459.

Ernst Wolff, "Decolonizing Philosophy. On the protests in South African universities," *Books and Ideas*, published 15 May 2017 (original French version published 28 October 2016), http://www.booksandideas.net/Decolonizing-Philosophy.html [last access 3 March 2020].

Ernst Wolff, "Adam Small's Shade of Black Consciousness," in *Philosophy on the Border. Decoloniality and the Shudder of the Origin*, ed. Leonard Praeg (Pietermaritzburg: UKZN Press, 2019), 112–147.

Ernst Wolff, *Mongameli Mabona. His life and work* (Leuven: Leuven University Press, 2020).

Ernst Wolff, *Between Daily Routine and Violent Protest* (Berlin: De Gruyter, 2021).

Material from the Martin Versfeld Archive at the University of Cape Town
By Martin Versfeld

Letter to Revd Conradie, UCT Archive, file 102 (30 August 1938).

Letter to the editor of *Die Burger*, UCT Archive, file 102 (13 January 1939).

Letter to the editor of *Die Spantou*, UCT Archive, file 19 (August 1940).

"A Moral Philosopher Looks at His World," typescript, UCT Archive, file 19 (probably written early 1940s).

Radio presentation "Die mens as sosiale wese" ["The Human Being as a Social Being"], UCT Archive, file 107 (12 March 1944).

"Rationalism and Politics," manuscript, UCT Archive, file 18 (probably written during the early part of World War II).
"War against superstition," UCT Archive, file 107 (broadcast on 18 March 1945).
"Morals and Machines", UCT Archive, file 23 (1949 or earlier).
Text on Rousseau, UCT Archive, file 34.
Lecture series on Nietzsche, UCT Archive, file 60 (before 1951).
"The Human Vision," typescript essay, UCT Archive, file 59 (probably late 1950s).
"Waarom ek Katoliek geword het …" ["Why I Became a Catholic …"], UCT Archive, file 59.
A Saraband of the Sons of God, typescript of an unpublished collection of essays, UCT Archive, files 155, 156 and 157 (compiled circa 1971).
"*Toynbee het gesoek na die betekenis van die geskiedenis*" ["Toynbee searched for the meaning of history"], *Die Burger*, 27 October 1975, in UCT Archive, file 195.
"The Yin and the Yang in Christian Culture," earlier draft of *OS* chapter 5, UCT Archive, file 135.

By others

"Germany – New Holy Land. 'ABC of the Heathen' Published," *Cape Times*, 11 February 1935 (UCT Archive, file 195).
Radio talk by Tjaart Büning on *GA*, UCT Archive, file 205 (broadcast from Johannesburg on 17 March 1949).
H.G. Stoker, review of *GA*, in *Koers*, February 1949, UCT Archive, file 205.
"Mirror of Enlightenment'," anonymous review of *Our Selves*, in *The Cape Times*, 12 May 1979.
Daniel Sabia, Review of *Our Selves,* in *African Book Publishing Record* VI, no. 3/4, 1980.

Lightning Source UK Ltd.
Milton Keynes UK
UKHW022055300921
391375UK00008B/175